AMERICAN INDIANS, TIME, AND THE LAW

American Indians, Time, and the Law

*Native Societies in a
Modern Constitutional Democracy*

CHARLES F. WILKINSON

Yale University Press
New Haven and London

Designed by James J. Johnson
and set in Caledonia Roman.
Printed in the United States of America by
Murray Printing Company, Westford, Mass.

Library of Congress Cataloging-in-Publication Data

Wilkinson, Charles F., 1941–
    American Indians, time, and the law.

    Bibliography: p.
    Includes index.
    1. Indians of North America—Legal status, laws,
etc.—History.   2. United States. Supreme Court—
History.   I. Title.
KF8205.W53 1986   342.73'0872   86–9164
ISBNs: 0–300–03589–6 (cloth) 347.302872
        0–300–04136–5 (pbk.)

10   9   8   7   6   5   4

To
the people,
past, present, and future,
of the Native American Rights Fund

Contents

Preface

I have been working and reworking these pages for some four years, but the real conception of this book goes back a decade and a half, when I entered the practice of Indian law. Like many others, I was frustrated from the outset by the lack of consistent doctrine in the field. Indian law is complex but the problem is broader than that. The classic categories—federal, state, and tribal powers; tribal sovereignty; the trust relationship; criminal and civil jurisdiction; Indian property rights; hunting, fishing, and water rights—do not fully envelop all of the stresses in the field. I sensed early on that those avenues of rules must be traveled but that they skirt the center of Indian law.

Four great occurrences dominate Indian law, history, and policy, and they are better understood in terms of time periods than doctrines. They are the existence of aboriginal culture and sovereignty during pre-Columbian times; the location of separate Indian societies on reservations; the imposition of assimilationist policies, including the opening of most reservations to settlement by non-Indians; and the efforts of Indians during the last quarter century to reverse the press of assimilation by reestablishing viable, separate sovereignties in Indian country. In turn, each of these periods needs to be reconciled with the egalitarian and libertarian laws and traditions of the majority society. I attempt here to search out an understanding of these zones of time, of the relationship of each to the other, and of their relationship to the larger constitutional democracy. Indian law encompasses not only Indians and law but also time.

This has been a consummately enriching project. During the seven years that I served as managing editor of the recent revision of Felix S. Cohen's treatise on federal Indian law, I benefited from electric discussions with my fellow members of the board of editors, Rennard Strickland, Reid Chambers, Bob Clinton, Rick Collins, David Getches, Carole Goldberg-Ambrose, Ralph Johnson, and Monroe Price. I thank each of them, for their ideas are embedded here. I have a special debt to the knowledge, creativity, and incisiveness of Sam Deloria, who took the time to talk through many of the most difficult issues; this includes the long and memorable night that we shared a bottle of champagne into the early morning hours of March 3, 1982, to celebrate the 150th anniversary of Chief Justice John Marshall's opinion in *Worcester v. Georgia*.

The future of Indian law is sure to be influenced by the growing interest of scholars from other fields, especially constitutional law. I appreciate the observations and perspectives of Bob Nagel, Milner Ball, Peter Westen, Lee Bollinger, Ad Hoebel, James O'Fallon, Phil Frickey, Chuck O'Kelley, Steve Williams, and Peter Stern. Carol Hamilton made invaluable contributions by testing my views and conducting necessary research in law, history, political science, and anthropology.

Sandy Hansen acted as a one-woman law review staff and contributed many substantive suggestions. Jerilyn DeCoteau and Tod Smith prepared excellent papers on difficult topics. Melody McCoy capably took on research responsibilities, as did Liz McCoy and Mike Larson. The book was improved by the care and good judgment of my editors at Yale, Marian Neal Ash, Lawrence Kenney, and Ruth Kummer. My deans at Oregon, Chapin Clark, Derrick Bell, and Fred Merrill, supported this project in every possible way. During my stay as a visitor at the University of Colorado School of Law, Dean Betsy Levin was inordinately generous in providing needed research assistants and secretarial support. The manuscript was conscientiously prepared by Marilyn Martin, Sandy Bigtree, Marilyn White, Marcia Murphy, and Marcea Metzler.

This is also a fine place to thank my longtime colleague, friend, and secretary, Mary Jo Guy, for her contributions here and many other places.

Finally, I wish to pay brief tribute to the tribal leaders and lawyers who have labored during modern times to revive the old promises. It has become trite to ask minorities to work within the system. But there has been nothing trite about the professional, determined way in which Indians and their representatives have used the judicial and legislative processes to reclaim land, natural resources, and political power. However abstract the rule of law may often seem to be, my guess is that most observers will find the concept to be considerably sharper after observing how contemporary American Indians have reached back in time to find old and seemingly outmoded laws that, more often than not, have proved to be enforceable. But if legal institutions deserve some measure of credit, the events chronicled here stand even more clearly as testament to the larger truth that ultimately law is passive: the old promises would have lain dormant but for the vision and dedication of those people who enforced them.

Introduction

On January 12, 1959, the Supreme Court decided *Williams v. Lee*[1] and, in so doing, opened the modern era of federal Indian law. The Justices, the few government and private attorneys who practiced in the field, and the small community of working scholars could have perceived only dimly the dimensions of the judicial process that *Williams* would set in motion.

Williams involved a non-Indian's suit in the Apache County, Arizona, Superior Court to enforce a debt entered into by Indians on the Navajo Reservation. An action on a contract is normally a transitory cause of action that can be brought to suit in a forum other than the one in which the contract was executed. Thus a contract made in another state, or even in a foreign country, would be within the subject matter jurisdiction of the Apache County Superior Court. The rule in *Williams*, however, requires that the case be heard exclusively within the tribal system in order to promote and protect tribal self-government.[2]

The rendering of the *Williams* decision can fairly be set as a watershed for several reasons. For decades before, Indian law decisions had been rendered fitfully by the Supreme Court. The tribes and the federal government instituted few cases to establish or expand tribal powers. Most of the litigation to reach the Court during the twentieth century before 1959 arose out of disputes involving individual Indians or even non-Indians; as a result, the decisions lacked the public law overtones of either the modern era or the nineteenth century.[3] Most of those cases that did involve tribes as plaintiffs were brought to recover money damages for tribal lands that had been taken by the United States.[4] After *Williams* the pace of decisions began to accelerate, with the result that the Court has become more active in Indian law than in fields such as securities, bankruptcy, pollution control, and international law. Twelve Indian law cases were handed down during the 1960s, and the extraordinary number of thirty-five Indian law decisions were reported by the Supreme Court during the 1970s, easily the most active decade in Indian law in the Court's history. Thirty-two decisions in the field have already been rendered during the first seven terms of the 1980s.*

Further, the magnitude of the controversies and affected interests has grown. For, as the Court haltingly legitimized relatively minor exercises of tribal power early in the modern era, the tribes enlarged their legislative and judicial operations and took actions that raised the ante to stakes not imagined when *Williams* was decided. A routine collection case implicating one of the few Indian courts operating on the reservations moved to the emotionally charged issue of tribal criminal jurisdiction over non-Indians and then to major personal injury cases.[5] The fishing rights cases first involved a remote county in Wisconsin, then the Puyallup River; today Puget Sound, the Columbia River, and the Great Lakes are front and center.[6] Tribal civil regulation of non-Indians evolved from the licensing of the Blue Bull Tavern near Lander, Wyoming, to the taxation of major oil, gas, and coal fields.[7]

Williams is also a fair dividing line simply because of its importance. The case continues to be widely cited.[8] Its paradigm of exclusive tribal judicial jurisdiction is a leading example of the special rules that the Court has recognized during the modern era in order to protect tribal government in Indian country.

But ultimately *Williams* holds a special significance in defining eras in the field because for the first time the Court was presented with Indian issues in a modern context. During most of the quarter century since *Williams*, the dominant issues in Indian country have focused on the steadily increasing exertions of authority by tribal

---

* The opinions of the modern era are collected and described in summary fashion in the Appendix.

governments and, concomitantly, on tribal resistance to state jurisdiction. The same dynamic was at work until the mid–nineteenth
century but by the late 1800s tribal governments had been over-
come, first by federal military might, then by the opening of many
reservations to non-Indian settlement, and finally by a stifling federal bureaucracy. The tribes began a revival as a result of the Indian Reorganization Act of 1934 and related movements, but
organized tribal activity was delayed by World War II, by the termination program of the 1950s, which disbanded one hundred
tribes, and by the transcendent difficulty of recharging governments that had lain so long dormant. Until the 1960s, tribes simply did not govern much and certainly had little impact except on
their own members.[9]

Williams presaged and may in part have spurred the recent
resurgence of tribal activity. Technically the case involved state
court jurisdiction over a contract claim arising on the reservation,
but the real question was whether Indian tribal courts had exclusive
jurisdiction over such cases. In finding exclusive tribal judicial
power, the Court recognized a broad tribal jurisdiction and a con-
tracted state jurisdiction and unknowingly began a continuing search
to sharpen those broad concepts.

This book is an attempt to assess the Indian law cases of the
modern era. It is not a restatement or survey of doctrine. Rather,
I seek to explore the central ideas—the undercurrents of doctrine—
that explain and justify the elaborate structure the Supreme Court
has built in this field during the last quarter of a century. In doing
this, I have been drawn primarily to the holdings and results of the
cases, not just to the Court's stated reasons. This means that I
sometimes identify concepts and employ terms not found in the
opinions. Nonetheless, I am convinced that my approach accurately
describes what in fact has occurred and that it plants a principled
and comprehensive set of justifications for the field of Indian law.

Federal Indian law presents uniquely formidable obstacles to
the development of consistent and unitary legal doctrine. There are
a number of scattering forces that push Indian law away from any
center. Taken together, these splintering influences have the potential of creating a body of law almost without precedent, of re-
ducing each dispute to the particular complex of circumstances at
issue—the tribe, its treaty or enabling statute, the races of the

parties, the tract-book location of the land where the case arose, the narrow tribal or state power involved, and other factors. Further, the task of rendering coherent judicial decisions in Indian law is profoundly complicated by the passage of time. In most cases a crucial issue—seldom mentioned in the opinions but implicitly a weighty presence to the parties and judges—is how an old treaty, statute, or court decision should be applied in times bearing little resemblance to the era in which the words of law were originally written.

Leading scholars have been sharply critical of the Court's performance during the modern era. They have attacked both the lack of coherent doctrine and the substance of doctrine.[10] Many of their criticisms are well founded. Opinions commonly have been cursory and conclusory or, at the other extreme, so tediously fact-bound as to be of little assistance as precedent. Others seem to be born of an ethnocentric reluctance to allow tribal control, however limited, over non-Indians. The three 1983 decisions involving water disputes in the arid West accept uncritically the premise of western water interests that all water cases, even those involving federally protected tribal rights, must be heard in state courts.

Yet, on balance, I drew a somewhat different set of conclusions. Purely on the basis of ordering a complex field of law, the Court has made important strides; during this work of more than two decades, the Justices have laid down a large number of clearly stated rules that have resolved conceptual issues of great significance to Indian law and policy.[11] In some instances, especially in the crucial area of tribal–state relations, the final specific shape of doctrine has yet to be formed. Even there, however, the Court has resolved important questions and set out general models to resolve others.[12] To be sure, the decisions hardly have been rendered efficiently— the job could have been accomplished in many fewer decisions— but much of the task has been completed.

Further, in my view the decisions generally have been principled, even courageous. The recurring theme during the modern era—presented in numerous variations—is whether and to what extent old promises should be honored today. The essential promise, made to tribes primarily in nineteenth-century treaties and treaty substitutes, is that the tribes would be guaranteed a measured separatism on their reservation homelands, free to rule their internal affairs outside of state compulsion but subject to an overriding federal power and duty of protection. The promise of a measured separatism, however, appears on one level to have been eviscerated by the passage of time. Numerous later federal laws suggest, although they do not so state, that the old promises have been eliminated or modified. Similar suggestions flow from deep societal changes, both within the tribes and within the larger society, that have not hardened into positive statutory law but that cannot be ignored.

The Court, presented repeatedly with the option of honoring the old laws or of respecting the force of the changed circumstances, mostly has chosen to enforce the promises. Granted, it is the substance of the promises, not all of their potential dimensions, that has been enforced. Nevertheless, to do that, the Court has cut directly against the normal inclinations of Anglo-American judicial decision making by enforcing laws of another age in the face of compelling, pragmatic arguments that tribalism is anachronistic, antiegalitarian, and unworkable in the context of contemporary American society. In part, then, this book is a study of the effects of time on law, of how old and inconvenient laws are eroded, of how they can resist those influences and remain unchanged, and of how, in some instances, they can actually gain force.

The Indian law decisions rendered by the United States Supreme Court during the last quarter of a century also are of considerable interest to aboriginal people in other nations. This is a time when native people worldwide are asserting claims to land and sovereignty. As Justice Thomas R. Berger wrote in 1982, "[t]he issue of aboriginal rights is the oldest question of human rights in Canada. At the same time it is also the most recent, for it is only in the last decade that it has entered our consciousness and our political bloodstream."[13] Similar statements can be made of Australia, China, India, Latin America, and other countries.[14]

Federal Indian law is not what American Indians would choose. Their rights to land and political power are diluted, not pure. Nevertheless, for all of its many flaws, the policy of the United States toward its native people is one of the most progressive of any nation.[15] This is particularly true of judge-made law. As a result, the doctrines developed here can be instructive—and in some cases can be rallying cries—elsewhere.

Chapter 1 of this book sets the complex milieu in which Indian legal issues must be resolved by examining the stress imposed by the passing years and by other factors peculiar to the field of Indian law. The remaining chapters examine the decisions of the modern era. Chapters 2 and 3 evaluate concepts, explicit or implicit, that have allowed tribes both to be shielded from some of the negative ramifications of the passage of time and, on the other hand, to benefit from the advances of the modern era. Finally, chapter 4 explores the territorial law of the reservation system—the collection of several hundred enclaves that constitute more than 2 1/2 percent of all land in the United States. My analysis includes an attempt to articulate the constitutional status of tribalism, both as to the institutional place of tribal governments within the federal system and as to the implications of equal protection and due process principles for Indian tribes. Chapter 4 concludes with a discussion of an ultimate question, one that suggests as well as any the profound manner in which time has become enmeshed in the field of Indian law: even if separate lands were promised to tribal control more than a century ago, how can the United States, consistent with its democratic ideals, allow race-based Indian tribes to govern the non-Indians who have lawfully entered those lands to live and to do business over the course of ensuing generations?

1

The Challenge of the Modern Era

THE FIELD OF INDIAN LAW: BARRIERS TO UNITARY DOCTRINE

The Scattering Forces

Indian tribes are the basic unit in Indian law. Each has its own internal laws and virtually every one is the subject of one or more federal treaties or statutes that deal with it in individualized terms. The sheer number of tribes—well over 500 by any count—invites chaos. There are 306 tribes in the lower forty-eight states and 197 entities in Alaska now recognized by the federal government; others never have been recognized, and still others were once recognized but have since had that relationship terminated.[1]

The organic powers of tribes are manifested in different ways. About half of the tribes in the lower forty-eight states have constitutions approved by the Bureau of Indian Affairs (BIA) pursuant to the Indian Reorganization Act and related legislation; other tribes operate under constitutions not related to that act; still others, including such large landholding tribes as the Yakima and the Navajo, have no written constitutions at all. This diversity among the tribes is a leading factor that presses the field toward case-by-case dispute resolution.

There are many other such forces. Over the course of two hundred years the United States has used various procedural devices to recognize tribes and, thus, to establish reservations. Although some 389 treaties were negotiated, treaty making is not as dominant as it is often thought to be. Of the 52 million acres of trust land now held by tribes and individual Indians, only about 20 million were originally recognized by treaty.[2] The majority of Indian land was set aside in reservation status by procedures that amount to treaty substitutes. Reservations were confirmed by bilateral agreements enacted after 1871, when the United States renounced formal treaty making with tribes; these agreements were negotiated in the field between federal and tribal representatives and then approved through the normal legislative process involving both houses rather than through the procedure for treaties, which involved only the Senate's advice and consent.[3] Indian reservations have also been established by unilateral congressional statutes and by the Interior Department acting pursuant to delegated authority from Congress.[4] The largest amount of trust land, 23 million acres, was established by yet another means, the promulgation of executive orders between 1855 and 1919. In turn, more than 90 percent of that executive order land was later confirmed by statute.[5] In several cases, individual reservations contain some or all of these various kinds of land.

Leaving aside the manner in which Indian reservations were initially recognized, one finds that the landscape of Indian law is variegated in another respect. The treaties and treaty substitutes usually established title in the tribes so that nearly all acres were under single ownership at the time of the treaties and treaty substitutes. Some tribes still hold most lands within reservation boundaries in blocks, but subsequent federal policies have altered land title to the majority of the reservations. The primary force at work here was the General Allotment Act of 1887, sometimes referred to as the Dawes Act. Proceeding on the notion that "[i]t is doubtful whether any high degree of civilization is possible without individual ownership of land," the federal government passed legislation providing for allotment of tribal lands in severalty to individual Indians and sale of the surplus lands to white homesteaders. Before this federal "civilization" program was ultimately halted, Indian landholdings were reduced from 138 million to 52 million acres.[6] As a result of these and other factors, Indian country today contains in addition to tribal land, allotted trust land held by individual Indians, fee land held by individual Indians, fee land held by non-Indians, federal public land, and state and county land. In some areas the surface estate is owned by an individual and the subsurface estate is owned by the tribe, the United States, or a private entity.[7]

This so-called checkerboard pattern (a more accurate description would be a patchwork) is not as efficient as a body of land held by one owner, such as the tribe, and creates a variety of problems related to economic development. The checkerboard pattern also has serious ramifications for purposes of jurisdiction. Checkerboard jurisdiction is clumsy and, without consolidating doctrine, leads to various possibilities of tribal, federal, and state jurisdiction dependent upon continual recourse to state and federal land office records.[8]

When combined, these complexities threaten to mount a set of permutations that builds the specter of repetitious litigation sure to drain the resources of tribes and individual Indians, the parties who must litigate against them, and the federal, state, and tribal courts that must hear the cases. Lack of a reasonably well defined matrix of doctrine also undercuts one of the most encouraging developments in Indian country—the increasing willingness of tribes and states to settle their differences extrajudicially.[9] This growing atmosphere of cooperation is inevitably premised upon the existence of doctrinal benchmarks to guide parties at the bargaining table.

There is urgency of a considerably grand scale to this need to channel the scattering forces and build predictable doctrine. Indian hunting and fishing litigation, affecting an array of commercial and sports interests, threatens to make the courts "fishmasters."[10] Indian water rights cases are typically as complex as major antitrust actions. Most of the great rivers of the arid West have major Indian holdings within their drainages and, while extensive litigation is inevitable, the scope of the cases can be narrowed by reasoned precedent. There is urgency, too, on a less grand scale. To put a poignant dynamic in cold legal terms, the question of whether a two-year-old Pueblo child will be allowed to retain her culture and traditions or be assimilated into the majority society can become moot during the pendency of an average civil adoption case that is taken to the appellate courts. The same is true of the asserted right of an eighty-year-old medicine man to convey his sacred beliefs through the use of peyote or eagle feathers.

The Form of Statutory Law

Many of the scattering forces just discussed are implicit in Indian law—tribes are separate ethnological units with individual needs, so that some degree of particularized treatment is both inevitable and desirable. At the same time, as the preceding material shows, the need for uniformity is real. Congress has virtually unfettered power over Indian policy and, as I will discuss, has adopted statutes dealing comprehensively with some aspects of Indian policy. Major issues, however, have not been addressed by Congress. The result is that the task of crafting Indian law has been left in significant measure to the courts.

Congressional action in the field of Indian law can be viewed as existing on three levels. First, a myriad of treaties and statutes deal with the affairs of individual tribes. This category includes the vaguely worded treaties and treaty substitutes that initially recognized tribes and established, piece by piece, the reservation system.[11] This first category also includes literally thousands of laws that have been enacted since federal recognition to deal with individualized issues that have arisen on specific reservations.[12] In spite of the great number of laws involving particular tribes, few expressly set out the organic law for any tribe—they provide no explicit guide to the nature of a tribal government's rights and obligations with respect to the United States, the state or county within which it is located, or even its own members.[13]

While many Indian statutes have dealt with individual tribes, a second kind of legislation is far more general. Congressional actions have often set broad Indian policy but have left implementation to subsequent legislation or administrative action. Examples are the Northwest Ordinance of 1787, promising "perfect good faith toward the Indian";[14] the General Allotment Act of 1887, prescribing the transmutation of tribal real property into individual property but leaving action in regard to each tribe to later statutes or departmental action;[15] the Indian Reorganization Act of 1934, allowing tribes to establish tribal governments and corporations according to the provisions of the law;[16] House Concurrent Resolution 108 in 1953, calling for termination of the federal–tribal relationship as a matter of policy but contemplating implementation in later statutes;[17] Public Law 280, also in 1953, transferring judicial jurisdiction over specified reservations to the states but leaving treatment of all other tribes to future action by states;[18] and the Indian Self-Determination and Education Assistance Act of 1975, invoking the program of tribal "self-determination" and delegating administration of the program to the BIA.[19] Sweeping though all of these initiatives would be if fully carried out, they have amounted only to policy statements, not positive law, except as to those tribes affected by the implementing actions that, in some instances, followed.

A third classification of federal legislative activity regarding Indians is substantive, self-implementing legislation that deals with a specific subject area within Indian law and applies across the board to all tribes. Laws that fall within this classification are thus comprehensive in the sense that they cover all, or nearly all, tribes, become effective immediately because they do not depend upon implementing legislation or administrative action, and deal exhaustively with the covered subject matter.[20] Leading examples are the Trade and Intercourse Acts of 1790 through 1834, which federalized many Indian land and commercial dealings and which remain in effect today;[21] the various statutes dealing with criminal jurisdiction throughout Indian country;[22] the Indian Claims Commission Act of 1946, allowing money damage claims against the United States for federal takings of Indian land;[23] the Indian Civil Rights Act of 1968, imposing on tribal governments some of the provisions of the Bill of Rights and other procedural limitations;[24] and the Indian Child Welfare Act of 1978, delineating rules for adoption and child custody cases involving Indian children.[25]

To be sure, these laws set a number of rules, often crucial ones, but many important areas have been left untouched. There has been no legislative resolution of essential questions: What are the limits of federal powers? What is the scope of tribal regulatory powers? What is the civil jurisdiction of tribal courts? What are state regulatory powers within Indian country? What is the taxing authority of states? What are tribal resource rights? Indian law has no Uniform Commercial Code, no National Labor Relations Act, no Securities and Exchange Act.

Thus in the many cases where Congress has not provided explicit guidance, the courts have been left to fashion rules built on a collage of factors. One primary line of inquiry, which I will discuss below, is to draw meaning from the negotiations, understandings, and legislative history underlying the treaties and treaty substitutes. In addition, American judges have been able to build upon the work of European jurists, who have struggled since the sixteenth century with questions of aboriginal property, sovereignty, and humanity in the New World.[26] The Indian Commerce Clause—authorizing Congress "to regulate Commerce . . . with the Indian Tribes"—mandates in very general terms federal primacy over state authority in Indian affairs.[27] The courts, too, have looked to nonlegal historical and anthropological sources to elucidate the law.[28]

This is not, strictly speaking, the development of "federal common law." In nearly all cases, judges are construing federal laws in order to determine congressional intent or, in the case of bilateral agreements such as treaties and agreements, the shared intent, such as it may have been, of tribal and federal negotiators. But the federal laws often hold out so little guidance that the courts have been forced to look to such diverse sources of authority that they might as well be making common law.[29]

The most crucial documents, the treaties and treaty substitutes, are exceedingly general. In modern times, the Court has been required to allocate Pacific salmon and steelhead worth millions of dollars annually based mainly on the treaty provision that tribes would be guaranteed the right to fish "in common with the citizens of the territory." In the Great Lakes, a similar allocation was made based on no explicit treaty language at all. The right of the states of Arizona, New Mexico, and Utah to impose taxes on the 15-million-acre Navajo Reservation was adjudicated primarily on treaty words saying that Navajo lands would be set aside "for the use and occupation of the Navajo tribe of Indians." The bitterly contested issue of tribes' right to try non-Indians for criminal offenses had to be resolved on the basis of no express treaty reference to criminal jurisdiction. Five tribes were awarded nearly one-tenth of the annual flow of the Colorado River, the only significant watercourse in the parched region comprising 14 percent of the contiguous United States, on the basis of executive orders.[30] The orders read as follows in their entirety, except for the technical legal description of the reservation lands:[31]

> It is hereby ordered that [legal description of lands composing the reservation] are hereby withdrawn and set apart for the use and occupancy of the Cocopah Indians, subject to any valid prior existing

rights of any person or persons thereto, and preserving a right of way thereon for ditches or canals constructed by the United States.

WOODROW WILSON
The White House, 27 September, 1917

The Legacy of Time

Superimposed on these structural complexities is the legacy of time. Indian policy is one of the few threads of federal activity that is continuous from the founding of the Republic, when Indian relations was one of the most pressing federal issues. During its initial five weeks of existence, the First Congress enacted four laws dealing with Indian affairs.[32] Treaty making with Indian tribes was a principal aspect of the Senate's early business.[33] Most of the old laws remain on the statute books in some fashion and, of course, have been multiplied many times over by the steady enactment of Indian statutes since.

Inevitably, Indian policy has been cyclic. This is due in part to the sheer length of time during which it has been made. Even more fundamentally, federal Indian policy has always been the product of the tension between two conflicting forces—separatism and assimilation—and Congress has never made a final choice as to which of the two it will pursue. Thus the laws are not only numerous; they are also conflicting, born of the explicit regimen and implicit tone of the eras in which they were enacted.

As a consequence, Indian law, more than any body of law that regularly comes before the Supreme Court, is a time-warped field. Although there has been ample legislative activity in Indian affairs during the twentieth century, many of the basic rights of Indian tribes depend upon constructions of treaties, statutes, and executive orders promulgated during the nineteenth century or even the eighteenth century. Leaving aside interpretations of the Constitution itself, a large segment of the Court's recent rulings on laws enacted early in the Republic has occurred in the field of Indian law. From 1970 through 1981, for example, the Court directly construed 22 laws enacted before 1800, and 8 of those constructions involved Indian law. Of the 29 recent interpretations of statutes and treaties enacted between 1800 and 1850, 14 were of Indian laws. During the same period (1970 through 1981), the Court ruled on 182 laws passed between 1850 and 1875, 32 of which involved Indian law. In other words, from 1970 to 1981 Indian laws constituted close to one-fourth of the Court's interpretations of laws enacted during the nation's first century. Further, except for the Reconstruction era civil rights statutes, Indian law has been the vehicle for the modern analysis of laws enacted during the nation's first century of existence more frequently than any other body of law.[34] This continual process of drawing meaning from statutes of another age creates much of the distinctiveness of the field.

SETTING RIGHTS WITHIN THE RESERVATIONS: THE LAWS OF THE NINETEENTH CENTURY

The old laws that most often dominate modern cases in Indian law are the treaties and treaty substitutes that established Indian reservations.[35] These laws are unique in our jurisprudence, for they set aside territory within the United States for self-government, subject to federal supervision, by sovereigns that are both preconstitutional and extraconstitutional.[36] Much of this book, and of the field of Indian law, is an attempt to determine the meaning and ramifications of the treaties and treaty substitutes and of modifications to them.[37]

The Promise of a Measured Separatism

A central thrust of the old laws, shared both by the tribes and by the United States, was to create a measured separatism. That is, the reservation system was intended to establish homelands for the tribes, islands of tribalism largely free from interference by non-Indians or future state governments. This separatism is measured, rather than absolute, because it contemplates supervision and support by the United States. As I will discuss shortly, the measured separatism was subsequently modified by federal legislation, especially the allotment program of the late nineteenth century that opened most reservations for settlement. In turn, the opening of the reservations created equities in non-Indian settlers and businesspeople, considerations that are properly part of modern decision making. But the necessary foundation is an understanding of the treaties and treaty substitutes.

These documents, and the discussions leading up to them, have an opaque quality that evidences the obstacles facing federal and tribal representatives in the field. The difficulties far outstripped the fact that the negotiations usually were required to be conducted through interpreters. Well beyond that, these negotiators were people with radically different world views. They had fundamentally divergent ways of conceptualizing the very things that had forced them together: land, religion, trade, political power, family, and natural resources. Each side must have experienced a torturing mixture of pride and fear, earnestness and contempt, hope and impatience.[38] In the largest sense, there was a gulf that no document could bridge. Still, perhaps because such transcendent matters were at issue and because the parties had little choice but to resolve them in some fashion, the existence and meaning of certain first principles can fairly be gleaned from the talks at these frontier transactions and from the papers that memorialized them.

The core concept of a measured separatism is strongly suggested by the structure and words of the treaties, spare though these documents are. In virtually every treaty the tribes, who possessed both governmental authority over[39] and an ownership interest in[40] their aboriginal lands before the treaty negotiations, ceded away their real property interest in most of the lands, often in Article I of the treaties. Another article then described the tribal retained land; the phraseology differed, but Indian possession was often described as "permanent" or as reserving to them the right of "use and occupancy."[41]

The United States typically agreed to extend its "protection" to these reservations and to provide various services and goods, often in considerable detail. The provisions included such matters as farming tools, grist- and sawmills, cattle, and clothing. The later treaties usually promised educational opportunities in the form of teachers, schoolhouses, or funding. The 1852 Treaty of Santa Fe with the Apaches provided that the federal government would grant "such donations, presents, and implements, and adopt such other liberal and humane measures as such government may deem meet and proper."[42] The fulfillment of these treaty provisions evolved into the system of service programs now provided to Indians by the United States.[43]

Significantly, isolation of Indian societies on the reservations was a common policy goal of both the tribal and federal negotiators. The tribes wanted to be left to themselves, and the United States wanted to avoid violence between the Indians and future settlers. Several treaties provided that the tribes would be guaranteed "absolute and undisturbed use and occupation" or that "no persons except those herein so authorized to do . . . shall ever be permitted to pass over, settle upon, or reside in, the territory described in this article."[44] The Omaha and Menominee treaties, among others, described the tribal reservation as a "home."[45] Justice Powell accurately summarized the situation:

> The primary purpose of the six treaties negotiated by Governor Stevens was to resolve growing disputes between the settlers claiming title to land in the Washington Territory . . . and the Indians who had occupied the land for generations. Under the bargain struck in the treaties, the Indians ceded their claims to vast tracts of land, retaining only certain specified areas as reservations, where they would have exclusive rights of possession and use. In exchange, the Indian tribes were given substantial sums of money and were promised various forms of aid. By thus separating the Indians from the settlers it was hoped that friction could be minimized.[46]

As a result, the idea that Indian treaties guaranteed a substantial separatism as well as federal protection and provision of services has been embodied in the case law from the beginning.[47]

The conclusion that both sets of negotiators intended a measured separatism is sharpened by a review of the minutes of the treaty negotiations.[48] For their part, government negotiators waxed eloquent with promises of tribal homelands "of promise and of peace" where Indian societies would be "perpetuated and preserved" as nations.[49] Clearly, this oratory was inspired more by expediency than by beneficence. The growing demands for Indian lands by a white population increasingly animated by conviction in a manifest destiny created inexorable pressure on government officials to locate the tribes in remote areas.[50]

The idea of removing the Eastern Indians to the trans-Mississippi territories had been considered by presidents as a solution to the so-called "Indian problem" since the formation of the Republic.[51] However, not until the 1830s did Andrew Jackson, a fervent believer in state sovereignty, set federal Indian policy steadfastly on a course

of removing tribes to federal territory west of any states.[52] The same
dynamic occurred later, as tribes were moved to isolated tracts of
land in various regions in the West.[53] Interestingly, while Jackson
opposed dealing with the tribes through the treaty process, even
he seems to have found nothing anomalous about recognizing and
protecting tribal self-government in the new homelands. Thus he
said that the Indians were to have "governments of their own choice,
subject to no other control from the United States than such as may
be necessary to preserve peace on the frontier and between the
several tribes."[54]

But whatever the motives and whenever the era, presidents,
commissioners, and Indian agents repeatedly reassured treaty tribes
that the Great Father in Washington would secure the Indian people
in their newly demarcated lands against the rising tide of white
civilization. For example, the Chippewas, Ottawas, and Potawatamies were told that "the Great Spirit has ordained that your Great
Father and Congress should be to the Red Man, as Guardians and
Fathers. . . . [S]oon . . . you shall be at a permanent home from which
there will be no danger of your moving again, you will receive their
full benefit."[55] A treaty commissioner made the following promise
to the Nez Perce concerning their reservation in what would later
be Idaho: "The land on which you live will be your own and when
you die it will be your children's. . . . [Your] homes [will] be secured
by the paper [you] receive and by other laws, besides the Treaty."[56]
President Jackson made this entreaty to the Choctaws:

> Brothers, listen. . . . Your Great Father will give [this land] to you
> forever that it may belong to you and your children while you shall
> exist as a nation far from all interruptions. . . . Peace invites you thus,
> annoyances will be left behind. Within your limits no state or territorial
> authority will be permitted. Intruders, traders, and above all ardent
> spirits so destructive to health and morals will be kept from among
> you only as the law and ordinances of your nation may sanction their
> admissions.[57]

Tribal acquiescence to being located on comparatively small
reservations, often in regions that were removed from their aboriginal territory, was predictable simply because there was no real
choice. After the end of the War of 1812, the United States owned
a military advantage over the tribes.[58] In a few cases tribal leaders
seemed genuinely interested in the cultural and material fruits of

white society. As a Chippewa chief put it, "I would like my children
to be dressed like you white people, and to live like you do. What
I mean is I want a person, a priest or a missionary to come and
teach us."[59] Much more common, however, was a desire to continue
the traditional ways: "We cannot get our living like the whites, we
cannot live and work as they do—and we must not be crowded."[60]
Even to the extent that tribes were willing to adopt some of white
society's habits and customs, they most likely were motivated by a
desire to preserve tribal integrity:

> The reason we wish to go to Washington is to change our situation
> and benefit our children—and adopt the customs and habits of the
> Whites. We think by so doing the Whites would not molest nor in-
> terfere with our rights as Indians.[61]

Implicit in all the talk was not only the expectation that each
tribe would remain a people, but also the perception that a homeland, separate and distinct from the surrounding white culture, was
a requisite element of that survival.[62] For people with close physical
and spiritual relationships with the earth, preserving these new
reservation land bases was seen as essential to preserving tribal
cultures. A Quapaw chief implored, "We want to continue . . . any
where, even in the swamps where the whites will never settle. If
our Great Father will grant our request, he may keep our money,
we will give it all to him."[63] In the end, tribes sacrificed most of
their ancestral lands for assurances that they would be protected in
their new homelands by the "strong fences" and "long arms" of the
Great Father in Washington:

> We were glad to hear you say that you had come here to build a strong
> fence and that if any strange animal gets over it your arms are long
> and strong enough to pull it back. We expect that . . . you will put
> down this interference in our business. . . .
> Our people have depended on the promise of the Great Father
> that the Whites should not intrude upon [our] land and hope it will
> not be forgotten.[64]

The essence of these laws, then, as viewed both by Indian tribes
and by the United States, was to limit tribes to significantly smaller
domains but also to preserve substantially intact a set of societal
conditions and tribal prerogatives that existed then. The larger society and the Indian cultures that exist within it have since undergone profound changes. Most of the old laws, however, have not

been expressly repealed or amended. Those promises are the point
of departure for modern federal Indian law and policy.

The Promise Modified: Opening the Reservations

Isolation of Indians on reservations remained federal policy until
late in the nineteenth century, when assimilationist policy became
dominant. As is usually the case with fixing historical eras, the line
of transition cannot be set with certainty. Allotment of tribal land
to individual members, a primary element of late-nineteenth-century assimilation, has ancient roots in Indian affairs, was employed
in some treaties in the early nineteenth century, and was regularly
pressed upon tribes beginning with the administration of Commissioner Manypenny in 1853.[65] Congress's decision in 1871 to bring
treaty making with tribes to an end signaled a downgrading in the
political status of tribes. The accelerated use of education as an
assimilationist device to erase the traditions of Indian children was
marked by the opening of BIA boarding schools during the 1870s
and early 1880s.[66]

But by most lights the passage of the General Allotment, or
Dawes, Act of 1887[67] was the dominant force in this era that Father
Prucha has called "the most critical period in the whole history of
Indian–White relations in the United States."[68] Allotment and the
other assimilationist programs that complemented it devastated the
Indian land base, weakened Indian culture, sapped the vitality of
tribal legislative and judicial processes, and opened most Indian
reservations for settlement by non-Indians. Ultimately, it compro-
mised the guarantee of measured separatism by dashing any remaining hopes that traditional Indian societies might remain truly
separate. As Theodore Roosevelt put it, "The General Allotment
Act is a mighty pulverizing engine to break up the tribal mass. It
acts directly upon the family and the individual."[69]

The General Allotment Act initially delegated to the BIA authority to allot 160 acres of tribal land to each head of household
and 40 acres to each minor and was soon amended to provide for
allotments of 80 acres of agricultural land, or 160 acres of grazing
land, to each tribal member. Allotments were originally to remain
in trust for twenty-five years, but the Burke Act of 1906 allowed
the transfer of a fee patent to "competent" Indians. Competency

commissions were promptly established to decide which Indians were eligible to receive their allotments free of trust restrictions against sale, encumbrances, and tax obligations. In addition to allowing for allotments, the 1887 act made provisions for opening so-called surplus lands for homesteading by non-Indians.[70]

An enormous loss of Indian land followed, with total Indian landholdings falling from 138 million acres in 1887 to 52 million acres in 1934. More than 26 million acres of allotted land was transferred out of Indian hands after it passed out of trust. Some of this individual allotted land was sold by arms-length transactions and some of it was lost by fraud, sharp dealing, mortgage foreclosures, and tax sales.[71] Debo summarizes the flow of Indian allotments to non-Indian opportunists in Oklahoma:

> It was immediately apparent that even these advanced Indians, who had supported themselves thriftily and governed themselves well, had no concept of the written instruments—deeds, mortgages, leases, powers of attorney—that regulated the white man's land transactions. Theoretically, as United States citizens they had access to the courts, but the entire legal system of eastern Oklahoma was warped to strip them of their property. The term *grafter* was universally applied to dealers in Indian land and was frankly accepted by them.[72]

In addition, great chunks were carved out of many reservations when surplus lands were opened for homesteading. Sixty million of the 86 million acres lost to Indians by the allotment regime were due to the surplus lands facet of the 1887 act.[73]

The opening of the reservations in this fashion had many ramifications other than the sheer loss of land. Much of the remaining Indian land estate was crippled. As any large rancher, miner, or timber executive can attest, effective resource management can best be achieved on a large, contiguous block of land in single ownership. The allotment program deprived most tribes of that opportunity. The tribal land ownership pattern became checkerboarded, with individual Indian, non-Indian, and corporate ownership interspersed. On allotted lands, scores, even hundreds, of heirs succeeded to the original allottee's ownership as generations passed, creating the fractionated heirship problem. Further, much tribal and allotted land was leased to non-Indians when it became clear that Indians would not move quickly to the agricultural society envisioned by the reformers of the allotment era.[74]

Just as the proprietary side of tribes was hamstrung by allotment, so too was the governmental capacity of tribes. Traditional governance came naturally in reasonably tight-knit, cohesive societies. Evolution into more elaborate forms of government would have occurred most smoothly on reservations composed solely of tribal Indians and tribal land. When the reservations were opened, true traditional governments were essentially doomed in most tribes, and the authority of any form of tribal rule was undermined.

With the land base slashed back once again and with strange new faces within most reservations, tribal councils and courts went dormant. The BIA moved in as the real government. This was the heyday of the Christian missionaries, who were able on many reservations to drive out traditional religions or at least force them underground. The 1880s marked the beginning of a half century of twilight operations by the tribes, a time when the essence of the measured separatism—tribal self-rule—was debilitated nearly to the ultimate degree. Washburn described the era in these terms:

> No longer did many tribal Indians feel pride in the tribal possession of hundreds of square miles of territory which they could use as a member of the tribe. Now they were forced to limit their life and their vision to an incomprehensible individual plot of 160 or so acres in a checkerboard of neighbors, hostile and friendly, rich and poor, white and red.
> The blow was less economic than psychological and even spiritual. A way of life had been smashed; a value system destroyed. Indian poverty, ignorance, and ill health were the results. The admired order and the sense of community often observed in early Indian communities were replaced by the easily caricatured features of rootless, shiftless, drunken outcasts, so familiar to the reader of early twentieth-century newspapers.[75]

American Indian tribes have made a historic recovery from those sterile years. The reforms of the Indian Reorganization Act of 1934 [IRA] and related policies allowed the beginnings of a revival of tribalism. Tribal councils and courts reorganized or began operating formally for the first time.[76] Tribal progress was stilled by the interlude of the termination era during the 1950s,[77] but by the 1960s tribes were in a position to capitalize on the opportunity of self-rule held out both by the treaties and the IRA. Tribes have reasserted their inherent powers during the modern era and seek to fulfill their prerogative of self-rule almost as though the opening of the reservations had never occurred.

The opening, however, has occurred, and that fact complicates

all of Indian law and policy. The promise of a measured separatism—
of a comprehensive tribal sovereignty within reservation boundaries—can fairly be called into question simply because the demog-
raphy of Indian country is so changed from what it was when the
promises were made. Non-Indians outnumber Indians on some reservations. Towns, chartered under state authority, commonly are
located within Indian country. Retail businesses often operate within
reservations, not to trade just with tribal members, but to deal with
a mixed clientele or one made up predominantly of non-Indians.
Mineral development firms have established substantial operations.
Further, state and federal highways cross most reservations, so that
numerous non-Indians pass through Indian country destined for
other locations.

As a result of these and other factors, state and county governments perform a variety of functions within Indian country. State
services, often of considerable importance and benefit to Indian
people, include the provision of schools, police and fire protection,
sanitation services, voter registration, the maintenance of roads, and
the distribution of welfare and other social benefits.[78] To be sure,
many Indian tribal governments fulfill most of these functions themselves, and on those reservations the state presence is comparatively
minimal. A prime example is the Navajo Nation, by far the largest
Indian tribe both in terms of membership and land holdings, which
has an extensive governmental structure that offers a comprehensive
range of social and economic services on the reservation. Comparisons between the Navajo Nation and the small states (certainly
western states at the time of their statehood) are entirely appropriate
in many respects. Scores of other tribes—the Warm Springs of
Oregon, the Hopi of Arizona, and the Menominee of Wisconsin, to
name a few—provide a range of services generally comparable to
those provided by rural counties. But the existence of such situations
should not obscure the fact that the structuring of broad principles
in the field of Indian law must also account for those reservations
where the presence of non-Indian citizens and state governmental
apparatus is strong, even dominant.

The case of non-Indian residents of reservations deserves special attention. Their land titles usually are the end product of the
federal allotment policy, which has been widely and justly criticized.
Non-Indians often obtained Indian land through fraud or sharp deal-

ing.[79] Yet the fact remains that the United States invited its citizens to homestead Indian land and that non-Indians accordingly built homes and livelihoods within reservation boundaries. If many entered by means of illicit if not illegal transactions born of avarice, many others came simply in pursuit of honest dreams opened up by the homestead policy.[80] Many tribes were dormant as governments, under the yoke of federal suppression at its tightest, and prospective residents saw them as not much more than miscellaneous bumps on the horizon.[81] Doubtless there are cases where homesteaders were altogether oblivious of the fact that their new homes were within Indian reservations. These settlers came as families to open new land, not to do business with Indians.

These expectations cannot harden automatically into a right to be free of all tribal laws. The tribes had expectations, too, and they were merged into treaties and treaty substitutes that protected historic tribal governmental prerogatives within reservation boundaries. Yet neither can the expectations of the non-Indian residents, themselves premised upon open invitations tracing to federal law, fairly be ignored. The recurrent, essential task for the judiciary in Indian law has been to construct a reconciliation of the laws to which the two sets of expectations trace.

INDIAN LAW AT THE BEGINNING OF THE MODERN ERA

Most of the recent Indian cases have presented in stark terms the tension between the old laws and the seemingly inexorable pressure of societal change. Indian law is in large part the law of time: results repeatedly turn on the tension between maintaining integrity and stability in the law and affording the flexibility that law must maintain in order to meet the demands of changing circumstances. It is elucidating to examine Indian law as it existed in the late 1950s, when the modern era began, in order fully to appreciate the challenge that the Court faced as it began the task of reconciling nineteenth century laws with twentieth century society.

The Classic Formulations

Supreme Court opinions in Indian law had been rendered sporadically during the first half of the twentieth century, reflecting the decline of tribal governmental activity during that period. As the modern era began, the construct of Indian law ultimately rested on two separate braces of opinions. The first line began with the Marshall Trilogy, handed down between 1823 and 1832 and consisting of *Johnson v. McIntosh,*[82] *Cherokee Nation v. Georgia,*[83] and, especially, *Worcester v. Georgia.*[84] In the Marshall Trilogy, Chief Justice John Marshall conceived a model that can be described broadly as calling for largely autonomous tribal governments subject to an overriding federal authority but essentially free of state control. Later opinions in the same vein include *Ex parte Crow Dog*[85] and *Talton v. Mayes,*[86] which recognized tribes as independent sovereigns free of constitutional constraints and of general federal laws unless Congress had expressly limited tribal powers. *Crow Dog,* an 1883 decision involving the murder of an Indian by an Indian, denied federal court jurisdiction and deferred to punishment by the tribe because Congress had never asserted federal jurisdiction. *Talton,* rendered in 1896, ruled that Indian tribes were not constitutionally required to provide a Fifth Amendment grand jury proceeding because tribal powers preexisted the Constitution and were not affected by the passage of the Fifth Amendment. This first set of opinions can be called the *Worcester–Crow Dog–Talton* line.

The second line of opinions comprises late-nineteenth- and early-twentieth-century cases such as *United States v. Kagama,*[87] *McBratney v. United States,*[88] and *Lone Wolf v. Hitchcock*[89] in which the Court recognized a seemingly unlimited federal power to alter tribal property and jurisdictional prerogatives contemplated by the treaties and treaty substitutes. *Kagama* upheld congressional power to enact the Major Crimes Act and thus infringe upon internal tribal resolution of disputes. *McBratney* allowed state court jurisdiction over a murder of a non-Indian by a non-Indian within Indian country even though there was no congressional grant of authority to the states. *Lone Wolf* announced the unilateral power of Congress to abrogate Indian treaties and to transmute tribal property rights into individual allotments. The *Kagama–McBratney–Lone Wolf* line implicitly conceptualized tribes as lost societies without power, as minions of the federal government. Since the tribes were presumptively unable to wield an acceptable level of governmental authority, the Court looked to federal or state authority to fill the void. In the words of the *Kagama* Court,

These Indian tribes *are* the wards of the nation. They are communities *dependent* on the United States. Dependent largely for their daily food. Dependent for their political rights. They owe no allegiance to the States, and receive from them no protection. Because of the local ill feeling, the people of the States where they are found are often their deadliest enemies. From their very weakness and helplessness, so largely due to the course of dealing of the Federal Government with them and the treaties in which it has been promised, there arises the duty of protection, and with it the power. This has always been recognized by the Executive and by Congress, and by this court, whenever the question has arisen.[90]

The *Worcester–Crow Dog–Talton* line set out doctrine justifying extensive tribal power with considerable clarity, but such clarity has had the ironic effect of complicating modern adjudication. Because societal conditions have changed so much since, adopting that earlier strain of authority squarely poses the dilemma of transposing ancient tribal traditions—wilderness principles to most white Americans—into a technological age. Excruciating pressures have been brought to bear upon the old doctrines that accord a special status to tribal rights. The Marshall Trilogy was rendered at a time when Indian affairs occupied a central position in federal policy. Most Indian tribes had not yet been included within state boundaries. In terms of both military power and population, Indian tribes were a significant factor. Today Indian affairs are only an eddy within national policy.[91] Indian tribes have no military capability and Indians are outnumbered by non-Indians nearly 200 to 1. Nor is Indian country always remote, as it once was. All Indian reservations are within state boundaries and some reservations are close to, or even within, population centers. Indian reservations are located, for example, near Santa Fe, Tucson, Phoenix, Pendleton, Oregon, Seattle, and Miami. They are located within Reno, Palm Springs, and Tacoma.

The *Kagama–McBratney–Lone Wolf* line produced pressures of another kind in post-*Brown* America: the specter of maintaining a sort of federally sanctioned serfdom in the face of a broad based expansion of civil rights.[92] Any movement away from either model not only had profound and wide-ranging implications for vested property rights and civil liberties of both Indians and non-Indians, but also was charged with jurisprudential consequences of the first order: What of the rule of law, of the toughness of law that must exist for an ordered society to resolve its disputes in a principled manner?

The Work of the Lower Courts at Midcentury

The range of options available to the Supreme Court as the modern era began in the 1960s was explicated in a divergent mass of contemporary lower court opinions that had wrestled with these tensions between the old laws and the modern society. One group of opinions viewed tribes as organizations with minimal powers and considered reservations as places where state authority was paramount. The opinions in this mold typically worked from the notion that broad-based tribal powers, if they had ever existed, had eroded over time. There were several theories available to support this conclusion. The admission of states to the Union on an equal footing with the original states could be viewed as extending state and local police power to those reservations that were established before statehood.[93] Courts suggested that major alterations in the special status of Indians had been made by the 1871 act bringing an end to treaty making with Indian tribes[94] and by the 1924 act granting citizenship to Indians.[95] Another approach, based on Justice McLean's concurring opinion in *Worcester v. Georgia*,[96] would require judges to assess the circumstances in each case and allow state jurisdiction when Indians on a particular reservation had become assimilated into the main society.[97] Some courts viewed tribal authority as being restricted to those powers expressly delegated by Congress, thus obliterating the inherent tribal sovereignty aptly described by one commentator as a "cornucopia" of governmental authority.[98]

Other opinions worked off a seemingly hypertechnical, but in fact pivotal, premise. These courts recognized that state authority could be ousted by a superior federal power over Indian affairs but concluded that some explicit federal action was required. In the absence of an express federal prohibition of the particular state power being asserted, state police power extended to Indian country as it did elsewhere within the state.[99] Because the language of Indian treaties is so general and because Indian treaties usually predated statehood, treaties rarely referred to state law; therefore, a rule requiring an express federal ouster of state law would allow broad state jurisdiction in Indian country.[100] A few courts went further, ruling that even explicit congressional language might not suffice because of a presumed narrow scope of federal power that could override state prerogatives only in limited circumstances.[101]

Yet another approach was to deny independent tribal powers by merging tribes with the federal government.[102] Other judges, with pungent language but no clear explication of their reasoning, simply declared tribal sovereignty to be a myth and proclaimed that state power would fill the announced void. The issue was joined in the following manner by the Montana Supreme Court as late as 1974:

> The myth of Indian sovereignty has pervaded judicial attempts by state courts to deal with contemporary Indian problems. Such rationale must yield to the realities of modern life, both on and off the reservation. . . . Only by throwing off the strictures of Indian sovereignty can state courts enter the arena and meet the problems of the modern Indian. If Congress and the federal appellate courts have a better solution, let them come forward.[103]

The view that tribalism was a thing of the past in the United States was also well represented in the academic literature. One scholar concluded in 1959 that Indian tribal sovereignty "has been pure legal fiction for decades."[104] Another suggested that courts could void Indian treaties by invoking the international law doctrine of *rebus sic stantibus,* the rule that treaty provisions cease to be binding when the original circumstances have been completely altered: "Circumstances [have] changed so radically that the treaty agreement with the Indians, in the minds of most Americans—expecially those in policy-making positions—became meaningless. The historical–social phenomenon of the submersion of the tribal political entities into the national entity of the United States is an undeniable fact."[105]

All of these approaches were consistent with the *Kagama–McBratney–Lone Wolf* notion that tribes were fading entities moving toward extinction. That perception, carried to various extremes, would fairly call for state laws and institutions to fill the perceived vacuum.

Other opinions leading into the modern era conceptualized tribes with dramatically more dignity than the foregoing cases. They traced their reasoning to the *Worcester–Crow Dog–Talton* model of tribes as independent sovereigns retaining all powers not expressly ceded away by the tribes or extinguished by Congress. A leading example is *Iron Crow v. Ogallala Sioux Tribe*,[106] in which a federal district judge in South Dakota analyzed the nature of tribal sovereignty at considerable length. In denying the plaintiffs' argument that the Sioux tribal court was a recent creation, the district court portrayed a long, historic tradition of tribal self-rule that antedated contact with Europeans:

> From time immemorial the members of the Ogallala Sioux tribe have exercised powers of local self-government, regulating domestic problems and conducting foreign affairs *including in later years* the negotiation of treaties and agreements with the United States.[107]

The Eighth Circuit affirmed in 1958, cataloging a series of broad tribal powers tracing to the "original precept of tribal sovereignty."[108] Later in the same year, the Eighth Circuit relied on the *Iron Crow* formulation of inherent tribal sovereignty and upheld a tribal tax on non-Indians.[109]

Other opinions also recognized a strand of governmental authority, the only one in the nation, that traces to a source other than the Constitution or the American Revolution—governments, if you will, that in an industrialized society link their legitimacy to Stone Age times. The Tenth Circuit, in adhering to the nineteenth-century ruling in *Talton v. Mayes* that neither the Bill of Rights nor the Fourteenth Amendment limits the power of Indian tribes, went so far as to say that Indian tribes "have a status higher than that of states. . . . No provision in the Constitution makes the First Amendment applicable to Indian nations nor is there any law of Congress doing so."[110] The Arizona Supreme Court held that an Indian tribe possesses sovereign immunity, even for a tort committed off the reservation, and that there had been no waiver of the immunity; the court made it clear that it was fully cognizant of just how remarkable the ruling was:

> This case demonstrates the unique legal status enjoyed by the Indian tribes. If the alleged tort-feasor under an identical state of facts had been a state or municipal government, the federal government, or a foreign nation, it would have been amenable to suit in either state or federal court.[111]

The Dilemma for Contemporary Judges

The divergent formulations found in the lower court opinions leading up to the modern era amount to two separate bodies of jurisprudence. They are irreconcilable because they base their foundations on different zones of time. The first, which denies tribes most powers and which traces to the *Kagama–McBratney–Lone Wolf* line, is premised on modern realities. Those courts proceeded as courts intuitively do, by drawing from the lifeblood of the common law, by setting the case in contemporary social and economic conditions. "Change is not only the law of life; it is the life of the law."[112]

This method is pragmatic and logical, and it has served this nation's jurisprudence well. Relevant current conditions, the reasoning goes, are undeniable: Indian tribes are small and powerless; state governments are well equipped to exercise a police power that serves the day-to-day needs of state citizens. Further, state governments are egalitarian, because citizens of all races can vote and participate in government, while citizenship in Indian tribes is defined by blood. The regulation through state law of most issues relating to families, business transactions, crimes, and taxes, and the resort to state courts to resolve disputes in these areas and countless others, are thoroughly ingrained and comprehensive; our society instinctively keens toward state law to control these subject areas.[113] Whatever may have been appropriate during territorial days, well-tested, almost universally accepted premises leave little or no room today for the exercise of modern governmental powers by primitive societies. Judges rendering the first line of opinions accepted these precepts.

The lower court judges writing the other body of opinions looked to the *Worcester–Crow Dog–Talton* line, which in turn led those courts out of contemporary society back to pre-Columbian times. That process, so jolting to a judiciary that prides itself on being forward-looking and progressive, brought focus to bear on traditional tribal justice systems. By definition they held complete power before contact with European nations—there were no competitors save other tribes. If that original status is legitimized and is accepted as continuing until adjusted by the United States—and *Worcester* clearly accorded it that legitimacy[114]—then the courts must turn away from modern realities as a setting and toward an almost mechanical, linear analysis of whether relevant aspects of pre-Columbian status have been abridged by the United States. If not, the pre-Columbian status continues. Damn the anomaly, damn the illogic of seating a nearly "foreign" government in rural Minnesota, South Dakota, or, for that matter, downtown Tacoma, Washington.

In the courts' deliberations these pressures have repeatedly distilled down to the question of the continued vitality of *Worcester v. Georgia. Worcester*, although written in 1832, remained the dominant opinion as the modern era began. In it, the third opinion in the Marshall Trilogy, Marshall clarified and expanded concepts that had been formulated in *Johnson v. McIntosh, Cherokee Nation v. Georgia*, and other cases. It is a lengthy and truly comprehensive opinion: there is little in Indian law that the Chief Justice did not touch.[115] Although aspects of the opinion can be interpreted in various ways,[116] the thrust of *Worcester* cannot be disputed. Tribes are sovereign nations with broad inherent powers that, almost without exception, exist by dint of inherent right, not by delegation.[117] Tribes are substantially independent of state law—Marshall went so far as to say that they are "extraterritorial" to the states.[118] These conclusions were buttressed by analyses of international law,[119] the Constitution,[120] federal statutes,[121] history,[122] and morality.[123]

Written by another judge, in another way, or under different extrajudicial circumstances, these—yes, "platonic"[124]—rules might have proved ephemeral. But factors of personality, history, pragmatism, and philosophy have locked together to make *Worcester* an enduring artifice, almost a physical presence. The case is continually cited in the modern Indian law decisions.[125] Indeed, regardless of subject matter, *Worcester* is one of the Supreme Court's most lasting statements; modern federal and state courts rely upon it more than upon nearly any other pre–Civil War opinion in any field.[126] *Worcester* epitomizes the struggle between the old laws and the modern society.

In the remainder of this book I shall analyze the Court's performance in reconciling the diverse forces discussed in this chapter. How should the passage of time be treated—as an eroding or cementing force? How should tribalism be conceptualized? To what extent should territoriality operate to set Indian reservations off as islands apart from the states and local governments? How should courts deal with the civil rights of non-Indians in Indian country when tribes seek to exert power over them? In each of these areas, the Court has arrived at a substantial reaffirmation of the measured separatism and of *Worcester v. Georgia,* a recognition of Indian tribes as permanent, separate sovereigns, a third level of government in this constitutional democracy.

2

Insulation Against Time

In the modern litigation the tribes continually have sought to prevent the use of time against them. States may have legislated or enforced laws in Indian country to fill vacuums formed during the long years when tribal governments were in atrophy. Non-Indian landowners may have resided in good faith for generations on lands to which a tribe now claims title. In spite of such settled and reasonable expectations, the tribes have taken the position that tribal prerogatives were set when the reservations were established and cannot be diminished over time.

The modern cases reflect the premise that tribes should be insulated against the passage of time. Inevitably, there are some exceptions, but the mainstream of opinions has built a number of rules that prevent state powers and private rights from expanding to encroach upon tribal prerogatives except by express congressional permission.

PROTECTION AGAINST DE FACTO TERMINATION

A fundamental issue in modern Indian law is how courts should treat those tribes that have become largely assimilated since their reservations were established in the nineteenth century. The question is a recurring one because so many reservations were opened to settlement through the allotment policy of the late nineteenth century. On those reservations, non-Indian land often predominates over Indian land, and Indian residents carry on regular commercial and social dealings with non-Indians. The tightness of tribal society has loosened, often dramatically. Should the courts acknowledge these societal conditions and decree that state law extends de facto to those tribes that have been heavily assimilated?

At the beginning of the modern era respectable authority supported a case-by-case analysis that would allow for state law to apply on reservations where assimilation had cut deeply and tribal members had accommodated themselves to non-Indians and their way of life. The theoretical basis for the judicial extension of state law to assimilated tribes was first expostulated by Justice McLean in his concurrence in *Worcester v. Georgia.*[1] Justice McLean acknowledged that the Cherokee Nation remained separate and that no basis for the extension of state law existed in the case at bar. He also expressed doubts as to whether the application of state law was an appropriate "judicial question" in the absence of Congressional attention to the issue. Nevertheless, in dictum Justice McLean set out an argument for de facto termination based on assimilation:

> If a tribe of Indians shall become so degraded or reduced in numbers, as to lose the power of self-government, the protection of the local law, of necessity, must be extended over them.
>
> * * *
>
> The exercise of the power of self-government by the Indians within a State, is undoubtedly contemplated to be temporary. This is shown by the settled policy of the government in the extinguishment of their title, and especially by the compact with the State of Georgia. It is a question, not of abstract right, but of public policy. I do not mean to say that the same moral rule which should regulate the affairs of private life, should not be regarded by communities or nations. But, a sound national policy does require that the Indian tribes within our states should exchange their territories, upon equitable principles, or eventually consent to become amalgamated in our political communities.
>
> At best they can enjoy a very limited independence within the boundaries of a state, and such a residence must always subject them to encroachments from the settlements around them; and their existence within a state as a separate and independent community, may seriously embarrass or obstruct the operation of the state laws. If, therefore, it would be inconsistent with the political welfare of the states, and the social advance of their citizens, that an independent and permanent power should exist within their limits, this power must

give way to the greater power which surrounds it, or seek its exercise beyond the sphere of state authority.[2]

Justice McLean soon resolved any doubts about the judiciary's power to decree de facto termination. In 1835, while riding circuit in Ohio, he rendered the opinion in *United States v. Cisna*,[3] in which his dictum in the *Worcester* concurrence ripened into a holding. In *Cisna*, Justice McLean ruled that a non-Indian was subject to state criminal prosecution for an alleged theft of a horse from an Indian on the Wyandott Reservation. The conflict between federal and state statutory schemes was similar to the issues in *Worcester v. Georgia;* the Trade and Intercourse Act of 1802 provided that the offense was subject to federal law but Ohio had recently asserted its jurisdiction over criminal offenses by non-Indians on the Wyandott Reservation.[4] McLean, however, found the facts at Wyandott in Ohio "wholly dissimilar" to the situation of the Cherokees in Georgia, apparently because the Wyandotts were "surrounded by a dense white population, which have daily intercourse with the Indians. . . . They own property of almost every kind, and enjoy the comforts of life in as high a degree as many of their white neighbors."[5] Because of this "force of circumstances," Justice McLean found that Congress's power under the Indian Commerce Clause no longer existed. Alternatively, he found that the degree of assimilation since the 1802 act was so great that its provisions had been repealed by implication as to the Wyandotts.[6]

Justice McLean's theory was treated in various fashions by later courts. *Cisna* was argued to the Supreme Court but the reasoning was rejected in the important mid-nineteenth-century tax case *The Kansas Indians*,[7] in which the Court struck down a state property tax on tribal lands. The tax exemption implied in the treaty was not vitiated even though "some of [the tribe's] customs have been abandoned, owing to the proximity of their white neighbors." Rather, the Court found, state tax laws do not affect tribal trust lands until Congress so provides or until there is "a voluntary abandonment of their tribal organization." *Cisna* was applied more consistently with Justice McLean's views in another leading nineteenth-century case, *McBratney v. United States*,[8] one of the first opinions allowing state law in Indian country. State jurisdiction over the murder of one non-Indian by another was upheld in spite of a federal statute that facially seems to deny state power.[9] The 1882 opinion cited *Cisna*,

and, while the Court did not find that the reservation in question
was terminated for all purposes, *McBratney* is an important example
of judicial acceptance of a gradual breakdown of reservation boundaries at a time when assimilationist sentiments were building in
Congress and increasing numbers of non-Indians were beginning to
enter Indian country.

McLean's view that de facto termination should be recognized
by the courts was squarely adopted in state supreme court opinions
of the late nineteenth century. The foremost example is *In re Narragansett Indians*,[10] in which the Supreme Court of Rhode Island
relied upon *Cisna* and Justice McLean's concurring opinion in
Worcester. The court upheld broad-based state laws that purported
to terminate the existence of the tribe. A principal supporting argument was that "a time must come when, from the necessities of
the case, the action of the States over Indians must be more and
more exercised."

The notion that tribal existence could be terminated because
of the passage of time, without congressional action, continued to
be reflected in numerous federal and state cases during the twentieth
century.[11] The issue was pressed by Arizona in *McClanahan v.
Arizona State Tax Comm'n*[12] in 1973, but the Court rejected the
argument, in the context of the Navajo Reservation, in a footnote.
The Navajo Reservation, in any event, was precisely the wrong place
for the states to argue for de facto termination. The Navajos, the
largest tribe in both population and reservation acreage, have man-
aged to keep their land base and their culture intact to a degree far
exceeding most tribes. Three years later the issue was squarely
joined over the Flathead Reservation in Montana, where assimilation has taken a much greater toll.

The *Moe v. Confederated Salish & Kootenai Tribes*[13] litigation
involved Montana's attempt to assess several of its taxes within the
Flathead Reservation. Ultimately the Court upheld a state cigarette
tax on sales by Indians to non-Indians and struck down all state
taxes sought to be imposed on tribal members. The specific issues
of taxation in *Moe* have proven to be of significance,[14] but its enduring value is more likely to be its rejection of the de facto termination theory.

Moe's facts were tailor-made for Justice McLean's reasoning.
The Treaty of Hell Gate of 1855 reserved a land area of some 1.25

million acres in northwestern Montana to the Salish and Kootenai Tribes. The reservation is one of the glory places of the American West, encompassing much of the Flathead River drainage and Flathead Lake. The region's beauty and natural resources proved to be the undoing of the Salish and Kootenai, for non-Indian settlers soon exerted intense pressures to open the Mission Valley for settlement. This was accomplished through the allotment program and other means. Today more than one-half of the land within the reservation is owned by non-Indians; 81 percent of the reservation's residents are non-Indians. Large irrigation projects water non-Indian farms and ranches, and several towns, incorporated under state law, are within the limits of the Flathead Reservation.[15]

The case for de facto termination was set out forcefully by District Judge Russell E. Smith, who disagreed with his colleagues on the three-judge court.[16] Judge Smith recognized that the legal issues were similar to those in *McClanahan v. Arizona State Tax Comm'n* but argued that "the underlying principles on which the Navajo decisions are based do not fit the situation of the Flathead Indians." Rather, Judge Smith concluded, courts should structure their rulings to reflect the actual demographic, cultural, and economic conditions at issue:

> The Flathead Reservation and the Navajo Reservation are not now the same and do not have the same history. Different facts justify different results, even where the subject matter is Indians or Indian reservations. Allotments in severalty were not made on the Navajo Reservation and the provisions of the General Allotment Act never applied to the Indians on that reservation. There are no non-Indian ownerships within the exterior boundaries of the Navajo Reservation. The Navajos live to themselves—largely apart from the non-Indian community. The non-Indians on the reservation, such as Indian traders and government officials, are the invitees of the tribe or the federal government.[17]

The Supreme Court rejected Judge Smith's reasoning. Employing the *Kansas Indians* test, Justice Rehnquist concluded in *Moe* that the Confederated Salish and Kootenai Tribes, "like the Navajo had not abandoned its tribal organization."[18] Therefore, in spite of the clearly documented and extreme differences between the Flathead and Navajo reservations, "there is no basis for distinguishing *McClanahan* on this ground."[19]

The Court was correct not to take the path of judicially decreed termination on selected reservations. Attempts to assess the degree of assimilation would run counter to the prudential role that the Court has played, and should play, in Indian law.[20] Congress has authority to assess the effects of assimilation and to mandate the partial or total application of state law to selected reservations.[21] Further, whatever the substantive merits might be in cases like *Moe* and *McClanahan*, the Court has properly rejected the kind of case-by-case litigation implicit in the de facto termination doctrine; any other course would breed multiplicitous litigation on a tribe-by-tribe basis. As a matter of process, adjudication of tribal status in a unitary fashion, based on congressional recognition of tribes, is preferable. The Court, therefore, has fixed the line between judicial and legislative prerogatives at the proper meridian by insisting that Congress is the proper body to determine when reservation status should be brought to an end in order to meet the realities of assimilation or other factors.[22]

PROTECTION AGAINST ENCROACHMENT DUE TO NONUSER

Indian tribes are peculiarly vulnerable to arguments based on waiver, laches, forfeiture, statutes of limitation, adverse possession, and other doctrines premised on dilatory conduct. Tribal governmental powers existing at the time of federal recognition have often gone dormant, especially during the apparent twilight of tribalism from the 1880s to the 1960s. Tribal land claims based on the Nonintercourse Act involve vast acreage that the tribes seemingly surrendered in the nineteenth century or earlier.[23] These patterns of nonuser create powerful equities in those governments and private landowners who have ruled or occupied lands in the stead of the tribes. Those kinds of equities normally harden into deeply ingrained legal rules, reflected in doctrines such as those just mentioned, that are highly protective of the holders of settled expectations.[24]

Striking down individual Indian rights on the basis of nonuser would not amount to as broad-based an assault on tribes as would wholesale de facto termination. The argument for nonuser works only against those specific powers and prerogatives that have not been exercised. Thus, for example, a particular tribe might continue to exist for legal purposes but it might be barred by laches from asserting a land claim or might be prohibited by the doctrine of estoppel from taxing or regulating a non-Indian within reservation boundaries because such authority had never previously been exercised by the tribe. Nevertheless, the elimination of tribal powers on this basis would cause a marked erosion of tribalism by steadily depleting the store of powers that resides in Indian tribes in the first instance as a result of the inherent sovereignty doctrine.

In the main the Court has refused to find that the tribes are prejudiced by their nonuser and by the consequent encroachment of states to fill the vacuum created by a lack of tribal activity. In *Fisher v. District Court*,[25] the state had exercised jurisdiction over adoptions of Indian children on the Northern Cheyenne reservations until 1935, when the tribe established a tribal court. The respondent argued that the latter-day assertion of jurisdiction by the tribe could not divest the state of authority. The Court held that the historical failure of the tribe to execute its powers did not bar a modern tribal assumption of jurisdiction.[26] *Kennerly v. District Court*,[27] involving state court jurisdiction over an action on a debt by a non-Indian against an Indian, presented an even stronger case for waiver of tribal powers. The Blackfeet Tribal Council had affirmatively passed a resolution purporting to grant concurrent jurisdiction to state courts. The Montana Supreme Court upheld state court jurisdiction but the Supreme Court reversed, concluding that Congress had set statutory procedures for the transfer of tribal jurisdiction to a state, that the process had not been followed on the Blackfeet Reservation, and that even voluntary relinquishment by the tribal council was insufficient to divest the tribe of its exclusive jurisdiction.[28]

There are many other examples of a judicial refusal to deny Indian rights based on acquiescence to state jurisdiction. State taxes on reservation Indians have been struck down in spite of a pattern of acquiescence in the form of voluntary payments.[29] Tribes have failed to exercise reserved water rights, but the rights were later validated. The long-standing use of water by non-Indians under state law did not control: unexercised tribal water rights within a particular state "are to be charged against that state's apportionment" when development occurs.[30] Similarly, Indian fishers had taken less than 10 precent of the salmon catch since the turn of the century, and a large non-Indian commercial and sports fishery had become dependent on the allocation accorded to them by state regulation. In spite of this reliance, the Court upheld an allocation of approximately one-half of the harvestable run to Indian commercial fishers.[31]

A recent major ruling on tribal nonuser is *Merrion v. Jicarilla Apache Tribe*,[32] decided in 1982. Beginning in 1953, the tribe entered into oil and gas leases with mineral development companies. The leases, which provided for royalties to the tribe, made no mention of tribal taxation, and the tribal constitution in force did not delegate taxing authority to the tribal council. In 1969 the tribe amended its constitution, and in 1976 enacted a tax ordinance in order to impose a severance tax on the companies. Rejecting the arguments of three dissenting justices who contended that the tax unfairly ran counter to the reasonable expectations of the lessees, the majority held that the tribe could both receive royalties in its capacity as a property owner and also exact further revenues in its newly formulated status as a taxing sovereign: "sovereign power, even when unexercised, is an enduring presence that governs all contracts subject to the sovereign's jurisdiction, and will remain intact unless surrendered in unmistakable terms."

The protection against nonuser was carried to its most prominent extension in the modern Indian land title cases, involving tribal claims in the eastern states. In the first decision in the Marshall Trilogy, the 1823 opinion in *Johnson v. McIntosh*,[33] the Court ruled that Indian tribes continued to possess a right of occupancy (variously called Indian title, aboriginal title, and original title) in their aboriginal lands after discovery by European nations. This right of occupancy, a unique real property interest previously recognized in the New World by Great Britain and tracing to the writings of sixteenth-century philosophers, is a compromise between tribal rights and prerogatives of the discovering nations. The Indian right of occupancy is well short of complete fee ownership—it can, for example, be extinguished by the United States without compensation. On the other hand, original Indian title is a valid interest in land under American real property law, good against all but the federal government, allowing the tribes to reside on their lands and to exclude outsiders. Under both British law and the federal Nonintercourse Acts, first enacted in 1790, a transfer of the tribal right of possession is void unless sanctioned by the United States. Since the first year of the Republic, these statutes, currently found at 25 U.S.C. § 177, have provided protection to Indians against an unfamiliar system and those who would abuse it and brought order to the potential chaos of frontier land transactions.[34]

Original Indian title must be extinguished with the approval of the United States, in other words, before settlers can legally occupy aboriginal Indian lands. Federal treaties and, after 1871, the treaty substitutes, were the methods used to aquire lands held as original Indian title for settlement by non-Indians. In several instances in the East, however, the states negotiated directly with the tribes for tribal land. Many of these treaties or deeds were never approved by the federal government. Tribal members, resentful of transactions they believed to be unfair, kept alive over the generations the idea that tribal title continued. Meanwhile, the eastern states long ago had transferred the land to businesses and homeowners; almost without exception, their modern-day successors had no clue that the cloud of Indian title hung over the land.

In the early 1970s, tribes began to bring lawsuits to enforce the rule of the Nonintercourse Acts and *Johnson v. McIntosh* that the tribal right of possession continues in force because the old transactions with the states were illegal in that they lacked the sanction of the United States. Two cases in the 1970s dealt with the issue in a preliminary way. The first *Oneida* opinion, issued in 1974, held that the tribe could sue in federal court because Indian real property matters are "inherently federal."[35] The Court remanded the case and did not decide whether the transactions with the state were void, but the language seemed to foreshadow that ultimate question:

> It very early became accepted doctrine in this Court that although fee title to the lands occupied by Indians when the colonists arrived became vested in the sovereign—first the discovering European nation and later the original States and the United States—a right of occupancy in the Indian tribes was nevertheless recognized. That right, sometimes called Indian title and good against all but the sovereign, could be terminated only by sovereign act. Once the United States was organized and the Constitution adopted, these tribal rights to Indian lands became the exclusive province of the federal law. Indian title, recognized to be only a right of occupancy, was extinguishable only by the United States. . . . This has remained the policy of the United States to this day. See 25 U.S.C. § 177.[36]

In 1979, the Court reiterated that Indian title "was recognized and extinguishable only by agreement with the tribe with the consent of the United States."[37] In the lower courts, decisions unanimously found that tribal land claims are not barred by defenses based on state statutes of limitations, laches, and adverse possession.[38] Their reasoning was that tribal title was federally protected and that state law defenses based on dilatory conduct were inapplicable.

In 1985, the Supreme Court resolved the matter in *County of Oneida v. Oneida Indian Nation.*[39] At issue was a 1795 agreement with the State of New York in which the Oneida Nation purported to transfer away some 100,000 acres. Suit was not filed until 1970. As Justice Stevens commented in dissent, "it is worthy of emphasis that this claim arose when George Washington was President of the United States." Nevertheless, the Court held the 175-year-old transaction invalid because it had not gained the requisite federal approval. The Oneida Nation had the right to sue on a common law cause of action for unlawful possession and was not time-barred by any statute of limitation or abatement. The tribe had an " 'unquestioned right' . . . to the exclusive possession of their lands. . . . [T]he Indian's right of occupancy is 'as sacred as the fee simple of the whites. . . . ' [T]he possessory right claimed [by the Oneidas] is a *federal* right to the lands at issue in this case.' "[40]

This remarkable litigation, which epitomizes the play of time in modern Indian law, asked the judiciary to cast aside some of the fundamental precepts of Anglo-American jurisprudence. In doctrine after doctrine and statute after statute, our legal system hews toward stability and the continuation of settled expectations, such as those of the longtime, non-Indian landowners in upstate New York. Perhaps no moment has more embodied contemporary Indian law and policy than when Arlinda Locklear, a brilliant oral advocate and the first Indian woman to argue before the Supreme Court, stood alone at the Bar and marshaled a congeries of law, history, and morality in her struggle to counteract the equities accumulated during the course of 175 years. The tension in the capably written majority and dissenting opinions makes the case seem somehow closer even than a 5–4 count would suggest. But, by the reed of one vote, the tribal position was accepted and the 1985 *Oneida* decision stands tall as a fit monument of the tribes' continuing efforts to enforce solemn promises of another age.

In two significant instances the Court has departed from this pattern of providing protection against nonuser and expressly approved the incursion of state jurisdiction as a factor in striking down tribal authority. *Rosebud Sioux Tribe v. Kneip*[41] involved a determination of the exterior boundaries of the Rosebud Sioux Reservation. After the reservation had been established by treaty, a series of acts passed in 1904, 1907, and 1910 opened much of the reservation for homesteading. The question was whether the later statutes resulted in disestablishment of the reservation so that four South Dakota counties, now mostly in the hands of non-Indians, were no longer Indian country. In holding that the reservation had been disestablished, the Court found that the clear congressional intent in passing the statutes was to exclude the four counties from the reservation.[42] To buttress that conclusion, the Court also looked to the "unquestioned actual assumption of state jurisdiction over the unallotted lands" in the area since the passage of the legislation: "[t]he longstanding assumption of jurisdiction by the State over an area that is over 90% non-Indian, both in population and land use, not only demonstrates the parties' understanding of the meaning of the Act, but has created justifiable expectations which should not be upset by so strained a reading of the Acts of Congress as petitioner urges."[43]

The second example of the Court's allowing encroachment by nonuser is the specialized situation presented by *Nevada v. United States*[44] and *Arizona v. California II*,[45] two 1983 cases involving the final adjudication of tribal water rights. In *Nevada*, the Pyramid Lake Paiute Tribe of Indians alleged that it possessed extensive reserved rights for fisheries' purposes as a result of the 1874 executive order establishing the reservation. A formal adjudication of the tribe's rights and those of other users on the Truckee River system, however, was made final in 1944. The decree awarded only minimal water rights to the tribe, all for irrigation purposes. In spite of compelling reasons explaining why the fisheries' right had never been raised (including a conflict of interest on behalf of the tribe's government attorney),[46] the Court held that the earlier decree was entitled to res judicata effect. *Nevada* presented reliance-based equities of non-Indians—in his concurring opinion, Justice Brennan noted that a result of the res judicata holding was that "thousands of small farmers in northwestern Nevada can rely on specific promises made to their forebears two and three generations ago"—but the determinative factor surely was the decree itself, not the equities standing alone. In *Arizona v. California II*, the Court refused to reopen its 1964 decree as to the amount of irrigable acreage, ruling that reopening was barred by finality. By way of emphasizing the strong policy supporting the finality of judicial decrees, the Court said:

> In no context is this more true than with respect to rights in real property. Abraham Lincoln once described with scorn those who sat in the basements of courthouses combing property records to upset established titles. Our reports are replete with reaffirmations that questions affecting title to land, once decided, should no longer be considered open. Certainty of rights is particularly important with respect to water rights in the Western United States.[47]

Tribal nonuser may have influenced two other major decisions. In *Montana v. United States*,[48] the opinion referred in a footnote to the traditional exercise of "near exclusive" state regulation of non-Indian hunting and fishing in upholding state authority, but it is not clear whether the Court placed substantial weight on that factor in reaching the result.[49] Developed expectations may have been an extrajudicial consideration in *Oliphant v. Suquamish Indian Tribe*,[50] denying tribal criminal jurisdiction over non-Indians, but it is far more likely that the Court's holding was based on Congress's perceived concern with the civil liberties of United States citizens, and, one can surmise, on the Justices' own visceral reaction to the issue. The result in *Oliphant*, in other words, would likely have been reached by this Court or an earlier one even if the tribes historically had sought to impose criminal authority over non-Indians.[51]

Cases involving established expectations based on the tribes' failure to exercise their powers present an especially vivid example of how the preservation of tribal prerogatives is pitted against contrary and highly pragmatic factors. In *Rosebud Sioux*, the Court bowed to practicality. The decision can be explained in part as an exceptionally difficult case for tribal powers: it is anomalous in the extreme to uphold tribal self-government over a vast region of non-Indian land overwhelmingly populated by non-Indians. Further, the reliance on settled expectations in *Rosebud Sioux* was employed as supporting reasoning for the principal analysis, which was that Congress had demonstrated its intent to disestablish the area when

the legislation was initially enacted. The case, and the body of law
in general, however, can best be understood by recognizing that in
extreme situations good faith reliance by non-Indians may be considered in a determination as to whether tribal rights can be exercised after having lain dormant for generations.

But the existence of *Rosebud Sioux*, the two water cases, and,
to a much lesser extent, *Montana v. United States* and *Oliphant v.
Suquamish Indian Tribe*, should not obscure the Court's extreme
reluctance to allow settled expectations, even over lengthy periods
of time, to deny tribal prerogatives. Other fact situations have presented pragmatic concerns at least as compelling as those in *Rosebud
Sioux*, but tribal nonuser has been rejected as a bar to the recognition
of newly asserted Indian claims. The highly structured systems of
state water law, and the large water users that depend on them,
were disrupted by the decision on the Colorado River.[52] The non-
Indian commercial fishing industry suffered widespread dislocation
as a result of the decisions on Indian fishing rights.[53] The ruling in
Merrion will alter the economics of mineral development in Indian
lands.[54] The eastern land claims cases threaten to disturb presumptively settled land titles. The clear tendency in the Supreme Court
decisions, then, has been to rule on newly asserted tribal powers
without reference to contrary expectations that may have developed
over time.

There are several justifications for this judicial protection
against the tribes' nonuser. The tribes have their own equities based
on modern pragmatic concerns: the exercise of long-dormant governmental and economic powers is their best hope for breaking the
cycle of a gripping poverty that has debilitated Indians since the
reservation system was established.[55] Purely legal justifications exist
also. State law has been inapplicable to possession of Indian lands
since the early days of the Republic because Congress necessarily
developed a uniform federal system to regulate Indian land transactions.[56] The comprehensive congressional plan to bring order to
the transfer of tens of millions of acres of land by federalizing Indian
land issues was a matter of considerable national urgency at the
time.[57] If latter-day Indian claims seriously jeopardize good faith
settlers, then Congress retains authority to reach legislative solutions based on the particularized needs and equities, as it did in

resolving tribal claims to large areas in New Mexico, Alaska, and Maine.[58]

The status of tribes as governments is also essential to understanding the Court's refusal to base results on tribal nonuser. Governments do not lose land title by adverse possession or general statutes of limitation, and legislative powers are not diminished because a government chooses not to exercise them.[59] The latter point was expressly made by the Supreme Court in *Merrion v. Jicarilla Apache Tribe*,[60] in which the Court invoked the protection against the tribe's nonuser of its taxing authority in the face of claims by mineral development companies that they had relied on the tribe's failure to exercise taxing authority:

> No claim is asserted in this litigation, nor could one be, that petitioners' leases contain the clear and unmistakable surrender of taxing power required for its extinction. We could find a waiver of the Tribe's taxing power only if we inferred it from silence in the leases. To presume that a sovereign forever waives the right to exercise one of its sovereign powers unless it expressly reserves the right to exercise that power in a commercial agreement turns the concept of sovereignty on its head, and we do not adopt this analysis.[61]

Even broader concerns lend perspective to the protections against encroachment due to nonuser. During the nineteenth century the tribes placed themselves under the protection of the United States, both in law and in fact. They were told, and believed, that their reservation lands would remain islands within the greater society, free from the advance of non-Indians. Congress, of course, chose to exert its overriding military and legal authority and departed from that promise, forcing many tribes to accept successive treaties and agreements. The allotment process opened many reservations to settlement by outsiders, while tribal governments were stifled by BIA policies. In spite of the hard work done in Washington and on the reservations during the administration of the Indian Reorganization Act in the 1930s and 1940s, most tribes did not begin serious revivals until recent times.

We are well past the point where it is fruitful to assess fault over the course of Indian affairs in this country, and reference to history is not made here for that purpose.[62] What we learn from history in this context is that the tribes, too, have been disadvan-

taged by reliance—a necessary reliance on an immensely more powerful society—and that the consequent failure to exercise
governmental powers should be understood as having occurred in
that context. In analyzing the nonuser of a tribe's regulatory authority over non-Indian hunting and fishing, Judge Monroe G.
McKay of the Tenth Circuit Court of Appeals set out the ultimate
philosophical basis for the protection against nonuser due to
encroachment:

> The State questions the existence of any inherent tribal powers in this
> case. It argues that the Tribe could not have exclusive rights in any
> traditional territory because, in effect, there is no traditional territory:
> "the Mescaleros were being swept from their lands by a tide of white
> settlers." If we were to accept the State's argument, we would be
> enshrining the rather perverse notion that traditional rights are not
> to be protected in precisely those instances when protection is essen-
> tial, i.e., when a dominant group has succeeded in temporarily frus-
> trating exercise of those rights. We prefer a view more compatible
> with the theory of this nation's founding: rights do not cease to exist
> because a government fails to secure them. See The Declaration of
> Independence (1776).[63]

PROTECTION AGAINST MODERN STATUTES

Questions of implied repeal arise disproportionately often in Indian
law. This is due in part to the comparatively ancient recognition of
tribal prerogatives in the treaties and treaty substitutes. Congress
has had generations to pass general laws on related subjects. Further, tribal prerogatives established in the old laws cover a wide
range of subject areas, including hunting and fishing rights, tax
exemptions, rights to land tenure, and tribal self-government. The
last-named category deserves special mention, for the promise of a
measured separatism allows tribes a broad-based power to regulate
internal affairs on the reservations; when Congress exercises its
regulatory authority without mentioning tribes, a question almost
inevitably arises whether some facet of the tribes' own power to
regulate has been overridden by implication. Thus the age and scope
of many Indian laws make them especially likely to come within the
facial coverage of general regulatory laws that do not explicitly refer
to Indians. This has bred controversy over implied repeals on numerous issues, including federal taxation, civil rights, the environment, wildlife, public works, and regulatory law generally.[64]

One encouraging development is that Congress has alleviated the problem, at least as to those laws enacted during roughly the last decade. Several recent statutes have expressly resolved tribal rights in the text of the general legislation because Congress has become increasingly aware of the possibility of an impact on Indians from legislation dealing with seemingly unrelated subjects.[65] Thus the chance of a statute's having an inadvertent impact on Indian rights is considerably less in recent legislation. Nevertheless, a continuing business of the Court in Indian law is to determine whether Indian rights have been impliedly abrogated by general statutes that appear on their face to collide with Indian rights under the old laws.

Our law has long recognized sound reasons for requiring courts to be solicitous of Indian rights when federal enactments must be interpreted. The rules that treaties and agreements should be construed as the Indians would have understood them and that ambiguities should be read in their favor follow logically from the fact that the United States drew up the documents in its own language. The federal government, possessing the advantage of having drafted the papers, should not be allowed to benefit if there are unclear passages. Similar ideas are applied in favor of consumers who sign adhesion contracts—insurance policies, bank loans, and the like. But the Indian law rules just discussed, as well as the overarching principle that all Indian laws should be read liberally in favor of the Indians, can be traced to an even deeper quick—the need for the United States, as trustee, to deal openly and fairly with the aboriginal peoples toward whom it has assumed special obligations. Thus the Court correctly identified the ultimate reason for the protections against modern statutes when it stated in 1985 that "the canons of construction applicable in Indian law are rooted in the unique trust relationship between the United States and the Indians."[66]

The modern decisions, reflecting these policies, have been highly protective of tribal prerogatives established under the old laws when arguments of implied repeal have been made. This can be measured both by what the Court has said and by what it has done.

To begin with what the Court has said. The law of abrogation of Indian rights has had a long and sometimes inconsistent history. Various tests have been employed, and the tests are sufficiently different in substance that varying results flowed.[67] Doctrine coalesced in 1968, when *Menominee Tribe of Indians v. United States*[68] announced that an Indian treaty right could not be abrogated in a "backhanded way"; normally an express legislative statement is required or the right continues. Other cases followed,[69] and the controlling test was articulated in simple language in the 1979 Northwest fishing cases,[70] in which the Court refused to find that Indian fishing rights had been abrogated by a later treaty between the United States and Canada:

> "Absent explicit statutory language, we have been extremely reluctant to find Congressional abrogation of treaty rights."[71]

Let me turn to what the Court has done. In *Menominee Tribe of Indians v. United States,* still the most influential case on implied repeal, the question was whether the hunting laws of Wisconsin applied to the members of the Menominee Tribe after the tribe was terminated. The Termination Act provided that henceforth "the laws of the several States shall apply to the Tribe and its members in the same manner as they apply to other citizens or persons within their jurisdiction." The Court held that hunting rights had not been abrogated because "the intention to abrogate or modify a treaty is not to be lightly imputed to the Congress." Because compensation would be required if the hunting rights were abrogated, the Court found it "difficult to believe that Congress, without explicit statement, would subject the United States to a claim for compensation." But one should not allow the Court's statement of the rules to obscure the extraordinary protection accorded to Indian hunting rights in *Menominee Tribe:* after all, *the issue in the case was whether the wildlife laws of Wisconsin applied to the tribe and its members in the same manner as they applied to other citizens or persons within the state's jurisdiction,* virtually the precise language of the Termination Act.[72]

Of the several other cases in which rules against implied repeal were applied in a manner highly favorable to Indians,[73] five deserve particular mention. *Morton v. Mancari,*[74] decided in 1974, upheld a 1934 hiring preference for Indians for employment in the BIA as against an asserted implied repeal based on the provisions of the 1972 Equal Employment Opportunity Act requiring equal treatment in federal employment. The Court approved the Indian preference, as an exception to the general rule against preferences based on race, in spite of the fact that affirmative action was at that moment a highly controversial and difficult issue facing the Supreme Court.[75] In *Santa Clara Pueblo v. Martinez,* [76] the Court ruled that a claim of sex discrimination by a female tribal member could not be brought against the tribe in federal court because the provisions of the Indian Civil Rights Act of 1968 did not expressly abrogate tribal sovereign immunity by subjecting the tribe to civil suits in federal court.[77] This 1978 ruling was made in spite of the express extension of the equal protection guarantee to Indian tribes in the Indian Civil Rights Act and in spite of the provision of 28 U.S.C. § 1343(4) granting federal district courts jurisdiction over suits brought "under any Act of Congress providing for the protection of civil rights."[78] The important interests sought to be vindicated by the plaintiffs in *Santa Clara* did not, the majority found, justify a departure from the rule that incursion on tribal sovereignty will be upheld only when there is an "unequivocal expression" of congressional intent.

The third decision is *Bryan v. Itasca County,*[79] a 1976 opinion that sharply limited the effect of Public Law 280, a termination-era statute long criticized by Indian people.[80] The case involved the application of a state tax on personal property within the borders of the Leech Lake Reservation in Minnesota, which was covered by Public Law 280. Public Law 280 provides that, on reservations subject to the act, "those civil laws of such State . . . that are of general application to private persons or private property shall have the same force and effect within such Indian country as they have elsewhere within the State." In spite of this seemingly explicit language, the Court found that the statute must be construed in favor of tribal prerogatives and constricted the coverage of Public Law 280 by holding that Congress intended to extend only state court jurisdiction over private causes of action, not state tax or regulatory jurisdiction, into Indian country by means of Public Law 280: "[I]f congress in enacting Pub. L. 280 had intended to confer upon the States general civil regulatory powers, including taxation, over reservation Indians, it would have expressly said so." The Court was also rigorous in applying the Indian law rules of interpretation in the 1985 *Oneida Nation* opinion.[81] The non-Indian parties recognized that the 1795 conveyance of tribal land to the State of New York had not been separately ratified by Congress in accordance with the Nonintercourse Act, but they argued that ratification of the 1795 transaction should be found through federal approval of a 1798 treaty referring to "the last purchase" and an 1802 treaty referring to "other lands heretofore ceded." The Court, invoking the strict approach of *Menominee Tribe* and the Northwest fishing cases, held that there was no plain and unambiguous federal ratification.

The final example that highlights the Court's adherence to the doctrines of construction favoring Indian rights in difficult cases is the 1985 decision in *Montana v. Blackfeet Tribe of Indians.*[82] Montana sought to tax the tribe's royalties from oil and gas production. The first Indian mineral leasing statute, enacted in 1891, was amended in 1924 to provide expressly for state taxation. Congress enacted comprehensive mineral leasing legislation in 1938. The 1938 act did not refer to state taxation but neither did it repeal the 1924 act. In spite of the fact that the express authorization to tax contained in the 1924 act remained on the books, the Court, finding no taxing authority in the 1938 act, held that the rule of construction in favor of the tribes required that the states be barred from collecting taxes on leases executed after 1938.

The Court has, of course, at times drawn lines in the dirt. In *DeCoteau v. District County Court,*[83] the Supreme Court found that the Lake Traverse Reservation in South Dakota, an area heavy in both non-Indian people and land, had been disestablished. The Court recognized the rules requiring construction of statutes in favor of Indians but stated—properly—that "a canon of construction is not a license to disregard clear expressions of tribal and congressional intent." In two important water cases[84] the Court held that the sovereign immunity of the United States, as trustee for Indian water rights, was impliedly waived by the McCarran Amendment of 1952.[85] *United States v. Dion*[86] found that the treaty right to hunt eagles was abrogated by the Eagle Protection Act. An especially bitter setback for Indian tribes was *Montana v. United States,*[87] in which the bed of the Big Horn River, which is located within the boundaries of the Crow Tribe's reservation established by treaty, was found to have passed by implication to the State of Montana when Montana subsequently became a state.

These cases demonstrate the kinds of limits that are inherent in the canons of construction favoring Indians. *DeCoteau* presented an enormously hard fact situation: although logic could support the conclusion that the area was Indian country, it strains the sense of equities of many to accord Indian country status to an area with 780,000 acres of non-Indian land where Indian residents are outnumbered ten to one. The McCarran Amendment cases are an example of an instance in which the legislative history fairly supports the conclusion that Congress may have clearly intended to include Indian water rights within the waiver contemplated by the McCarran Amendment.[88] Similarly, the legislative deliberations at issue in *Dion* show that Congress considered the question of Indian eagle hunting in a specific way. *Montana v. United States* presents another facet of the statutory construction issue. In *Montana*, the Court was forced to counterpoise the special Indian rules against another special rule, the principle that lands under navigable watercourses normally pass to new states at statehood.[89] Importantly, like the Indian cases, the navigable watercourse doctrine is framed in terms of a trust duty to the states. *Montana* thus raises the rare instance when the Indian rules, which are premised upon a trust relationship, are neutralized by a competing body of law also based on trust principles.

All of the cases just discussed involve balancing tests that can lead to different results under facts more favorable to the tribe in question. Thus, tribes have prevailed in Indian country disestablishment cases since *DeCoteau;* have remained in federal court in water adjudications in spite of the McCarran Amendment cases; and have prevailed in cases involving ownership of the beds of navigable watercourses since *Montana.*[90]

The force of the Indian implied repeal cases during the modern era also can be appreciated by noting the several instances in which the special Indian rules prevailed over opposing special bodies of law. *In Morton v. Mancari,*[91] the Indian hiring preference was upheld even though it involved affirmative action directly based on race. *Santa Clara Pueblo v. Martinez*[92] denied federal court jurisdiction in a case alleging discrimination based on sex. In *Bryan v. Itasca County,*[93] the Court upheld an Indian tax exemption as against the rule that tax exemptions are narrowly construed.[94] Thus, even when the Indian canons have collided with other special rules, the Indian rules have prevailed more often than not.

The furthest that the Court can go in protecting Indian rights procedurally against implied repeals by modern statutes is to require that the repeal be expressed on the face of the statute, a position I have advocated and continue to hold.[95] The Court has balked at going that far and it may well continue to do so. Although the rule of express legislative action has many advantages, especially in the context of Indian statutes, it has the signal disadvantage of inflexibility. The Court seems inclined to keep open an exception for extraordinary circumstances where the congressional desire to abrogate tribal prerogatives is not set out explicitly; as the Justices said in *Dion,* although "explicit statement by Congress is preferable for the purpose of ensuring legislative accountability for the abrogation of treaty rights," that preference is not "a *per se* rule."[96] But the modern cases have generally hewed to the standard of express language as a benchmark and have rarely dispensed with the requirement.[97]

Rules of construction are notoriously slippery. Judge Goldberg was not far from the mark when he compared statutory construction to leapfrog: "the most basic principle of statutory interpretation, (not to mention leap-frog itself)... is that the last leap wins."[98] Nevertheless, although the last leap cannot always be charted with certitude, the Supreme Court has put all who deal with Indian laws—whether they be state or federal judges, administrators, or lawyers—on notice that this is a special field and that words may not mean what they appear to mean. If Indians are involved, you should infuse all federal laws, old and new, with the policy of the special Indian trust relationship and read those laws with a heavy bias in favor of Indian and tribal prerogatives. If the first reading does not produce a result in favor of the Indians, you should read the document again. And once again—with an inventive mind.

Yes, almost anyone who has worked in this field will acknowledge that some leapfrogging is involved in this. But by any reasonable standard, the modern Court has canted sharply toward principled constructions of statutes in favor of Indians. Taken as a whole, the statutory construction cases are a central reason why the old rights have endured over the course of a century of congressional legislation that has had the clear potential of limiting or destroying many of those basic Indian rights.

3

The Elevation of Tribalism

The tribes, then, have sought and obtained a substantial measure of insulation from many of the negative effects of the passage of time. Concurrently, however, they have attempted to make time work in their favor by seeking to establish a vigorous, modern tribal sovereignty with actual powers far beyond those exercised at the time of the treaties and treaty substitutes.

The modern Court moved slowly before employing the word *sovereignty*—so loaded is it with implications from international law and policy—to describe the status of Indian tribal governments. Indian tribal sovereignty, however, is now regularly acknowledged by the Court and it constitutes the fiber of modern Indian law, implicating much of the field in ways both subtle and dramatic. Indian tribes possess a right to change and to grow: they are not frozen in time. Indian tribes are permanent entities in the American political system.

To be sure, tribes are subject to the overriding power of Congress. The ultimate and sweeping superiority of the national legislature has been hedged only marginally by the modern Court, and that nearly plenary power surely will continue in force. But tribes have come to understand the workings of Congress. The result is that these sovereign Indian governments generally have been successful not only in fending off legislative proposals aimed at limiting special tribal rights but also in persuading Congress to exercise its broad power in a manner beneficial to Indians. Ultimately, during the modern era the tribes have used their sovereign status in numerous pragmatic ways to rise from the termination era and gain a place, new though it may now be, in the community of governments in the United States.

THE NOMENCLATURE OF SOVEREIGNTY

The "desperate maze"[1] of sovereignty has generated centuries of debate as a term of art in political science and international affairs. Jean Bodin used the concept of sovereignty as a recipe for political stability at a time when sixteenth-century France was passing out of the last stages of feudalism into a centralized state. Bodin's concept was absolutist, as it vested undivided and unlimited power in the Crown by divine right. Other philosophers differed on where sovereign authority resides and how it is justified, but most agreed that sovereignty is absolute, indivisible, and unlimited.[2]

Post-Revolutionary political theorists in America were challenged to develop a theoretical foundation for sovereignty in a federal system where power by definition was diffuse.[3] Thus with federalism came the notion of dual, or divided, sovereignty, and the assertion, as Thomas Jefferson put it, that sovereignty in its absolutist sense was "an idea belonging to the other side of the Atlantic."[4] To explain and justify the concept of divided sovereignty, nineteenth-century legal theorists began to distinguish between legal sovereignty, which was vested in the various concrete organs and agents of government, and political sovereignty, which ultimately rested with the people. In this scheme, the governments of neither the states nor the United States had absolute power. Further, absolute sovereignty does not exist in modern nations even as to external relations, for individual nations are accountable in the international community, either in the form of military force or world opinion. Theorists commonly argue that the doctrine has so little application to today's world that it should be discarded entirely.[5]

Nevertheless, the term *sovereignty* continues to be employed, even though its meaning has little connection with its absolutist origins. While sovereignty now, as then, presupposes a culturally distinct people within defined territorial limits, it connotes legal competence rather than absolute power. It is used in the narrow sense of the power of a people to make governmental arrangements to protect and limit personal liberty by social control. Thus sovereignty, among other things, is utilized as a means of distinguishing the formation of a government from the creation of a business entity or a social organization.[6]

The application of the notion of sovereignty to Indian tribes has been controversial in its own right. During the modern era the existence of tribal sovereignty, and what it means, has been the subject of heated and extensive scholarly debate.[7] As I shall discuss, the question of whether tribes initially possessed sovereignty in pre-Columbian times and whether tribes today possess sovereignty (that is, governmental authority) has substantive content—much more than a choice of words is involved. Further, the concept of sovereignty carries with it an aura that transcends technical considerations of political science and law. Designation as a sovereign, however imprecise the term may be, implies a kind of dignity and respectability beyond its literal meaning. The struggle over the doctrine of tribal sovereignty is well worth tracing.

Chief Justice Marshall's opinions made it clear that Indian tribes were sovereign before contact with Europeans and that some, but not all, sovereign powers continued in existence after relations with Europeans and the United States were established. In *Johnson v. McIntosh*,[8] the Court ruled that the tribes' "rights to complete sovereignty, as independent nations, were necessarily diminished." The tribal right held to be diminished in *Johnson* was the ability to transfer land. Indian real property could be alienated only to the European nations, and later the United States, which obtained title through the doctrine of discovery.[9] *Cherokee Nation v. Georgia*[10] held that tribes are not foreign nations and that "[t]hey may, more correctly, perhaps, be denominated domestic dependent nations." As they were not foreign nations, one sovereign power impliedly relinquished by the tribes as they came under the dominion of the United States was the power to ally with any other nation.

The third case in the Marshall Trilogy, *Worcester v. Georgia*,[11] dealt with tribal powers both before and after contact with European nations. Before contact, "America, separated from Europe by a wide ocean, was inhabited by a distinct people, divided into separate nations, independent of each other and of the rest of the world, having institutions of their own, and governing themselves by their own laws." Much of that original sovereignty survived contact: "The Indian nations had always been considered as distinct, independent political communities retaining their original natural rights, as the undisputed possessors of the soil, from time immemorial, with the single exception of that imposed by irresistible power." This kind of sovereignty was, Marshall found, consistent with principles of international law that allow "[a] weak state . . . [to] place itself under the protection of one more powerful, without stripping itself of the right of government, and ceasing to be a state." In other words, the original rights of the tribes continued, exept those abridged by the United States. In Marshall's conception, tribes in aboriginal times possessed a sovereignty as complete as that of any European nation. After forming political alliances with the United States, they surrendered their external sovereignty but remained sovereigns in the sense that the term has generally been used since the early nineteenth century.

For nearly a century and a half after *Worcester* tribal sovereignty was treated by the Court in a manner that was, at best, checkered. Two leading late-nineteenth-century cases, *Ex parte Crow Dog*[12] and *Talton v. Mayes*,[13] gave content to inherent tribal sovereignty, though neither expressly used the term. *Crow Dog* held that tribes retained jurisdiction, to the exclusion of federal courts, over a murder of one Indian by another in Indian country, a result that was promptly negated by Congress two years later.[14] *Talton* held that the "powers of local self-government enjoyed by the Cherokee Nation existed prior to the Constitution" and that therefore the Fifth Amendment's requirement of a grand jury in federal criminal actions did not apply to tribal prosecutions.[15] Like *Crow Dog*, *Talton* was partially overturned by Congress: the tribal courts of the Cherokee and the other Five Civilized Tribes were abolished three years later by the Curtis Act of 1898.[16]

Other decisions were ambiguous about tribal sovereignty.[17] Sovereign immunity of tribes was the basis of the 1940 ruling in *United States v. United States Fidelity & Guaranty Co.*,[18] but the opinion suggests that this element of sovereignty existed in the tribe only before dealings with the United States and that the immunity is now held by the United States: "These Indian Nations are exempt from suit without Congressional authorization. It is as though the immunity which was theirs as sovereigns passed to the United States for their benefit, as their tribal properties did."

The dominant theme in the time between Chief Justice Marshall and the modern era, however, was sounded in 1886 in *United States v. Kagama.*[19] The opinion upheld sweeping congressional power over tribes in the form of the Major Crimes Act, which extended federal criminal jurisdiction over specified crimes to Indian country.[20] The Court could have justified the federal legislation simply by invoking the notion that Congress possesses broad power over Indian affairs and that it can legislate over the tribes, as dependent sovereignties, a concept already thoroughly formulated in the Marshall Trilogy. Instead, the *Kagama* Court recognized the superior sovereignty of both the United States and the states, reference to the latter being unnecessary since the act in question did not involve state jurisdiction, and flatly denied the existence of tribal sovereignty: "Indians are within the geographical limits of the United States. The soil and the people within these limits are under the political control of the Government of the United States, or of the States of the Union. There exist within the broad domain of sovereignty but these two."[21] The Court made other findings derogatory of tribal sovereignty during the late nineteenth and early twentieth centuries. In *Cherokee Nation v. Southern Kansas Ry. Co.*,[22] it stated that "[t]he proposition that the Cherokee Nation is a sovereign in the sense that the United States is sovereign, or in the sense that the states are sovereign, . . . finds no support." In *Montoya v. United States*,[23] it concluded that "[t]he North American Indians do not and never have constituted 'nations'. . . . In short, the word 'nation' as applied to the uncivilized Indians is so much of a misnomer as to be little more than a compliment."

With the case law in such disarray, the scholarship of Felix Cohen during the 1940s played a cardinal role in preserving the doctrine of tribal sovereignty for modern courts. Looking to the Marshall Trilogy, Cohen expostulated upon tribal sovereignty, calling it "perhaps the most basic principle of all Indian law."[24] The old cases, although they applied the term *sovereignty* to tribes just once,[25] were firmly in support of Cohen's thesis. But the more recent opinions were not. Cohen refused to acknowledge that the law could change so dramatically, even in light of the demonstrably dramatic change in the social and legal structure governing Indians, and set out his (and John Marshall's) essential paradigm: tribes initially possessed complete sovereignty, they lost some of those powers to a more powerful nation, and they retain all powers not lost. Cohen, whose pen was at once scalpel and sledgehammer, said,

> Perhaps the most basic principle of all Indian law, supported by a host of decisions hereinafter analyzed, is the principle that *those powers which are lawfully vested in an Indian tribe are not, in general, delegated powers granted by express acts of Congress, but rather inherent powers of a limited sovereignty which has never been extinguished.* Each Indian tribe begins its relationship with the Federal Government as a sovereign power, recognized as such in treaty and legislation. The powers of sovereignty have been limited from time to time by special treaties and laws designed to take from the Indian tribes control of matters which, in the judgment of Congress, these tribes could no longer be safely permitted to handle. The statutes of Congress, then, must be examined to determine the limitations of tribal sovereignty rather than to determine its sources or its positive content. What is not expressly limited remains within the domain of tribal sovereignty.
>
> * * *
>
> The whole course of judicial decision on the nature of Indian tribal powers is marked by adherence to three fundamental principles: (1) An Indian tribe possesses, in the first instance, all the powers of any sovereign state. (2) Conquest renders the tribe subject to the legislative power of the United States and, in substance, terminates the external powers of sovereignty of the tribe, e.g., its power to enter into treaties with foreign nations, but does not by itself affect the internal sovereignty of the tribe, i.e., its powers of local self-government. (3) These powers are subject to qualification by treaties and by express legislation of Congress, but, save as thus expressly qualified, full powers of internal sovereignty are vested in the Indian tribes and in their duly constituted organs of governments.[26]

Cohen's view—the Marshall–Cohen formulation—effectively stemmed the tide of opinions that threatened to bury the doctrine of tribal sovereignty in the name of changed circumstances. Cohen's position, set out in 1942, was cited repeatedly by the courts and attained something of the weight of a Supreme Court opinion.[27] Cohen's forceful writing style and his reputation help account for the significance his views attained. Further, his prodigious scholarship—including dozens of articles and respected books such as *The Legal Conscience* and *Ethical Systems and Legal Ideas*—went far beyond Indian law, encompassing an array of subjects within the fields of jurisprudence, ethics, and international law.[28] He was a leader in the legal realism movement.[29] But Cohen's thinking was also available to the modern Court for use as precedent simply because his work was the only comprehensive scholarship available, a factor that must have counted for much as courts researched a complex field that most judges viewed as being of tangential importance at most. And surely—although Cohen in fact was a committed advocate for Indians[30]—a mantle of objectivity was cast on his work because it was published under the name of the Department of the Interior. Surely this government-commissioned work must be definitive; surely it would not overstate the powers of nonfederal entities as against the United States. It was on the back of such disparate and miscellaneous circumstances that the Marshall–Cohen view of tribal sovereignty was available, in a serious way, for affirmation by the modern Court, in spite of a pronounced dearth of support in the judicial opinions during the first sixty years of this century.

Given the ambiguous status of the tribal sovereignty doctrine, it is not surprising that the Court proceeded gingerly early in the modern era. Justice Black's majority opinion in *Williams v. Lee*[31] in 1959 discussed *Worcester* at some length and concluded that "this Court has modified these principles in cases where essential tribal relations were not involved and where the rights of Indians would not be jeopardized." But the *Williams* opinion also characterized *Worcester* as "one of [Chief Justice Marshall's] most courageous and eloquent opinions" and found that "the basic policy of *Worcester* has remained" and that "the broad principles of that decision came to be accepted as law." Having adopted the thrust of *Worcester's* protective stance toward tribal self-government, the Court handed down its holding that exclusive jurisdiction over a contract case involving a non-Indian and an Indian lay with the Navajo court.

After two cases limited state jurisdiction partly because of the importance of tribal self-government,[32] the Court explicitly discussed tribal sovereignty for the first time in more than thirty years—and for only the second time in the century—in 1973 in *McClanahan v. Arizona State Tax Comm'n.*[33] The results of this major opinion were mixed. The holding, which struck down an Arizona state personal income tax on an Indian in Indian country,

supported tribal self-government and so did much of the language
in the opinion.[34] The Court, however, concluded that the doctrine
of tribal sovereignty has "undergone considerable evolution" since
Worcester and that the state tax law was excluded by federal preemption, not by tribal sovereignty:

> [T]he trend has been away from the idea of inherent tribal sovereignty
> as a bar to state jurisdiction and toward reliance on federal preemption.
> The modern cases thus tend to avoid reliance on platonic notions of
> Indian sovereignty and to look instead to the applicable treaties and
> statutes which define the limits of state power. The Indian sovereignty
> doctrine is relevant, then, not because it provides a definitive reso-
> lution of the issues in this suit, but because it provides a backdrop
> against which the applicable treaties and federal statutes must be
> read.[35]

In spite of *McClanahan's* brightly drawn line protecting the
reservations (the state income tax was struck down even though it
did not directly touch the tribe or a tribal employee), the opinion
was viewed by a good many as signaling the demise of tribal sovereignty, now a "platonic notion" and a "backdrop." With federal
preemption being invoked for the first time in Indian law, *Mc-
Clanahan* seemed to suggest that in the future tribal powers
would be defined in the first instance by Congress, not by original
sovereignty.[36]

The next case to deal with these issues was *United States v.
Mazurie.*[37] The question was whether the Wind River Tribes in
Wyoming could license a tavern operated by a non-Indian on non-
Indian land within the reservation. The Court upheld tribal licensing
authority because regulatory power over liquor issues had been
expressly delegated to tribes by Congress. Could inherent tribal
sovereignty support the regulation without the federal delegation?
The Court gave no answer, saying only that tribes possess "attributes
of sovereignty" and "a certain degree of independent authority over
matters that affect the internal and social relations of tribal life."
Mazurie highlighted the importance of tribal sovereignty as an independent source of authority. If sovereignty could not support
regulatory power over non-Indians, then tribal authority over non-
Indians would be limited to liquor and hunting and fishing issues,
areas where Congress had delegated regulatory powers to tribes by
statute.[38]

The 1978 decision in *Oliphant v. Suquamish Indian Tribe*[39] appeared to take several major strides down a road now seeming to lead inexorably toward a doctrine that would base tribal powers on federal delegation. In denying inherent tribal criminal jurisdiction over non-Indians, the Court added a third "inherent limitation" on tribal powers.[40] The doctrine of implied limitations on tribal powers, which had not been invoked by the Court since *Cherokee Nation v. Georgia* in 1831, was phrased in broad terms. Justice Rehnquist's majority opinion in *Oliphant* found that tribes inherently lack all powers *"inconsistent with their status"* and resurrected a statement in an 1810 concurring opinion by Justice Johnson to the effect that the implied limits on tribal sovereignty prohibit tribes from *"governing every person within their limits except themselves."*[41] The *Oliphant* opinion, which conceded little more than that "Indian tribes do retain elements of 'quasi-sovereign' authority after ceding their lands to the United States and announcing their dependence on the Federal Government," marked the historic low ebb of the doctrine of tribal sovereignty and of the Marshall–Cohen view of the field.

Somewhat astonishingly, just sixteen days after deciding *Oliphant* the Court rendered an endorsement of the tribal sovereignty doctrine in such ringing terms that the existence of the doctrine, so uncertain just a few days before, now seemed irrevocably to be established as part of the nation's constitutional and political system. *United States v. Wheeler*[42] can fairly be characterized in such broad terms because Justice Stewart's opinion, holding that successive prosecutions of Indians in tribal and federal courts are not barred by the double jeopardy provision of the Fifth Amendment, set out at considerable and unequivocal length the special governmental status of Indian tribes. Relying upon key passages from both *Worcester* and Cohen, the Court traced tribal powers to an inherent tribal sovereignty that has never been relinquished. Distinguishing Indian tribes from both cities and federal territories, which derive their power from the states and the federal government, respectively, the Court found that Indian tribes possess a third source of sovereignty in the United States.[43] *Wheeler*, the first Supreme Court holding since *Talton v. Mayes*[44] in 1896 based explicitly upon inherent tribal sovereignty, resolved a major ambiguity in the field by making it clear that tribal powers trace to inherent sovereignty, not to grants from the United States. Tribal powers are both pre-constitutional and extraconstitutional.

Wheeler dealt only with the source of tribal powers, not with difficult questions relating to their scope.[45] Six later opinions have recognized, for example, that inherent sovereignty includes tribal civil jurisdiction over non-Indians.[46] But Wheeler played the crucial role of reviving the tribal sovereignty doctrine and analyzing it at sufficient length to lay the doctrinal foundation for the opinions that followed.

Cohen's conclusion that inherent tribal sovereignty is "perhaps the most basic principle of all Indian law" is right. The acceptance of the doctrine, and the renunciation of the concept that tribal powers are delegated from the United States, lays the conceptual outlines for the field. Although not all ramifications of the following issues are resolved by the tribal sovereignty doctrine, the Marshall–Cohen view, as accepted in modern times by Wheeler and later cases, decides or directly implicates each of the following central issues. First, tribal powers are defined initially by looking to the entire store of authority possessed by any nation, not by searching for federal statutes establishing tribal prerogatives.[47] Second, Indian tribes possess sovereign immunity.[48] Third, tribes can exert regulatory authority over landowners within tribal territory because tribes are governments, not just proprietors.[49] Fourth, limits on the powers of states and the United States in the Constitution do not restrict Indian tribes.[50] Fifth, tribal existence depends on the tribes' own will, not on recognition by the United States.[51] Sixth, since tribes are separate sovereigns, general grants of federal jurisdiction do not allow for judicial review of tribal actions.[52] Seventh, tribes possess the inherent authority to adopt regulatory laws without the approval of the Department of the Interior.[53] Eighth, tribal courts, as the judicial arms of the local sovereigns in Indian country, are the proper courts to develop the factual records in the first instance when the extent of tribal authority is challenged in federal court.[54] Ninth, tribal resource rights are measured in part by looking to the intent of the tribes—as inherent sovereigns possessing such rights before relations with the United States—at the time treaties or agreements were negotiated with the United States.[55] Last, the fact of independent governmental authority allows courts to draw analogies between tribes and cities, states, and even the United States in order to justify exercises of tribal powers.[56]

One fascinating aspect of this development is the role of pre-contact times. It might initially appear that the powers of Indian tribes, say, 400 years ago, would have contemporary relevance, if at all, only within the walls of an advanced anthropology or philosophy class. In fact, the essence of the Marshall–Cohen view, now endorsed by the Supreme Court, is that those times are not only relevant but controlling. The original status of complete national sovereignty, not action by any European nation or the United States, is the beginning definition of modern tribalism. It is highly significant, in other words, simply that tribes were *once* sovereign in both the internal and external senses. To be sure, that sovereign status has been altered repeatedly by statute, by treaty, and, in a limited context, by implication. But in the cases of the modern era the exceptions have proved far less important than the remarkable and crucial premise—that tribal powers will be measured initially by the sovereign authority that an Indian tribe exercised, or might theoretically have exercised, in a time so different from our own as to be beyond the power of most of us to articulate.

UNITY OF RECOGNITION

Because of the pervasive influence of tribalism in Indian law, it is important to know whether *tribe* is essentially a unitary legal concept or whether each of the hundreds of Indian tribes has substantially different rights and powers with respect to the United States and the states.[57] It is not enough to say, important though the concept may be, that all Indian tribes possessed in the first instance all of the powers of sovereign nations, for that status was altered by alliance with the United States. The transition from an aboriginal legal status common to all tribes to individual relationships with the United States usually took place when a tribe was recognized, normally when a reservation was established. Reservations, however, were created by several different methods so that the form of federal recognition varied among tribes.

Tribes initially were recognized by treaties, a practice that continued until 1871. A majority of tribes have been recognized by other procedural means: bilateral agreements ratified through the normal legislative process rather than by the Senate's advice and consent of treaties; executive orders; unilateral statutes; and recognition by the secretary of interior by means of authority delegated by the Indian Reorganization Act of 1934. Vague terminology was typically employed in the treaties and treaty substitutes at the time of recognition, and Congress has never issued any subsequent specific directive stating whether these differing methods of recognizing tribes were intended to achieve substantially identical ends. The Court was left to decide whether these varying forms of recognition should be given equal dignity.[58]

The controversy has been most acute with respect to the nature and extent of the tribal resource rights accompanying the creation of the different kinds of reservations. When the modern era began, the law governing tribal resources of treaty tribes had been set out with some clarity.[59] States and private parties argued in a number of contexts, however, that nontreaty tribes should not be entitled to equal dignity. The modern Court resolved the issue by effectively demystifying treaties: the other forms of recognition are also the "supreme Law of the Land" under Article VI of the Constitution and carry with them the same generalized kind of rights that accompany treaties.

Antoine v. Washington,[60] decided in 1975, clarified the law of Indian agreements. *Antoine* involved deer hunting on the Colville Reservation in eastern Washington, a region that was set aside by negotiated agreement in 1891.[61] The deer had been taken by tribal members during the state's closed season. The Washington Supreme Court concluded that state law would be inapplicable if a treaty tribe were involved but that an agreement, being only a contract between the United States and the tribe, could not bind the state, which was not a party to the contract. Further, the state court ruled that the Supremacy Clause did not require the state to honor the agreement.[62] The Supreme Court reversed and blended agreements with treaties as the "supreme Law of the Land":

> [The 1871 statute bringing treaty making with Indian tribes to an end] meant no more, however, than that after 1871 relations with Indians would be governed by Acts of Congress and not by treaty. The change in no way affected Congress' plenary powers to *legislate* on problems of Indians, including legislating the ratification of contracts of the Executive Branch with Indian tribes to which affected States were not

parties. . . . These decisions sustained the ratified agreements as the exercise by Congress of its "plenary power . . . to deal with the special problems of Indians [that] is drawn both explicitly and implicitly from the Constitution itself. Article 1, § 8, cl. 3, provides Congress with the power to 'regulate Commerce . . . with the Indian Tribes,' and thus, to this extent, singles Indians out as a proper subject for separate legislation". . . .

Once ratified by Act of Congress, the provisions of the agreements become law, and like treaties, the supreme law of the land. Congress could constitutionally have terminated the northern half of the Colville Indian Reservation on the terms and conditions in the 1891 Agreement, even if that Agreement had never been made. . . . Congress, by its legislation ratifying the 1891 Agreement, constituted those provisions, including Art. 6, "Laws of the United States . . . made in Pursuance" of the Constitution, and the supreme law of the land, "superior and paramount to the authority of any State within whose limits are Indian tribes."[63]

Analytically, the status of reservations created by agreement should have posed no difficult question. Agreements, after all, were introduced as bills in Congress, passed by both houses, and signed by the president. Existing cases provided clear precedent for the result in *Antoine*.[64] Yet the lower court decision, like many others of the time, demonstrates the magnitude of the misconceptions widely held toward Indian tribes.[65] The *Antoine* clarification was a necessary element in consolidating the field of Indian law in a modern context.

The status of tribes recognized by executive orders raised far more difficult questions. Treaty and agreement reservations both rest on explicit constitutional provisions, the Treaty Clause and the Indian Commerce Clause, and can be equated because both trace to congressional authority. There is, however, no express grant of power to the president to act alone in Indian affairs.[66] Some precedent did exist. The executive's ability to make unilateral reservations on the public domain setting aside land from mineral development had been sustained in the leading 1915 case, *United States v. Midwest Oil Co.*. [67] These withdrawals made by President Taft were approved on the ground that Congress had "impliedly acquiesced" to the long-standing presidential practice of making similar reservations. The opinion declined to uphold the reservations upon the basis of independent, inherent executive constitutional right.[68]

The kind of presidential reservations approved in *Midwest Oil* were fundamentally different from executive order reservations for Indian tribes. President Taft removed most known oil and gas reserves on federal public lands from entry and location under existing federal law because of the real threat, in a time of impending war, that all federal reserves would be depleted within a matter of months. Taft's action was a conservation measure to halt the rapid extraction of federal resources. The withdrawals only changed the rules governing the manner in which private parties could obtain future rights in federal minerals. There was virtually no encroachment on state authority and all extractors received actual notice that future extractions would be governed by new principles.[69]

If the Court were to uphold Indian executive order reservations, there would be significantly broader ramifications than was the case with executive withdrawals of public lands for mineral reservations. State police power, including control over wildlife and water resources, would be sharply delimited in favor of tribal control.[70] In addition, private water users often had no actual notice that the creation of an Indian reservation by the president would affect their appropriative rights.[71]

The issue of resource rights on executive order reservations for Indians was presented to the Court in *Arizona v. California I* in 1963.[72] In spite of the differences between Indian and other executive orders, the tribes had important lines of precedent on their side. Executive orders creating reservations for Indians had been cited by the Court in *Midwest Oil* as examples of the executive orders to which Congress had long acquiesced. Further, the Court had unified executive order reservations with treaty reservations for the purposes of the federal statutes dealing with criminal jurisdiction in Indian country.[73]

But those cases did not deal with natural resources, while *Arizona v. California I* raised questions involving the allocation of scarce resources on a grand scale. That case, which involved the largest record ever to come to the Court, effectively divided up water in the Colorado River, the lifeline of the Southwest. Emotions had run high for decades. The asserted Indian rights would claim a major part of the river from California and Arizona and from the citizens they represented. It was not an auspicious setting for the tribes to make the leap from treaties and *Midwest Oil* to a ruling that executive order reservations carry with them reserved water rights.[74]

Yet the Court ruled squarely for the five Indian reservations, small in population but high in potentially irrigable land, along the lower Colorado. Relying upon *Midwest Oil* and *Winters v. United States*,[75] the opinion integrated water rights on Indian executive order reservations with those on other Indian reservations:

> Arizona also argues that, in any event, water rights cannot be reserved by Executive Order. Some of the reservations of Indian lands here involved were made almost 100 years ago, and all of them were made over 45 years ago. In our view, these reservations, like those created directly by Congress, were not limited to land, but included waters as well. Congress and the Executive have ever since recognized these as Indian Reservations. Numerous appropriations, including appropriations for irrigation projects, have been made by Congress. They have been uniformly and universally treated as reservations by map makers, surveyors, and the public. We can give but short shrift at this late date to the argument that the reservations either of land or water are invalid because they were originally set apart by the Executive.[76]

Executive order reservations differ in a few respects from reservations established by Congress. Under the decision in *Sioux Tribe of Indians v. United States*,[77] grants of land by the president can be revoked by the United States without the payment of compensation under the Fifth Amendment. In water litigation, the quantity of water reserved on executive order reservations is the same as for other reservations, but the priority date may be later since the date of the reservation, not the date of aboriginal occupation of the land, will normally apply.[78] Some aspects of mineral taxation are governed by statutes peculiar to executive order reservations.[79] Nevertheless, as the Supreme Court noted in *Merrion v. Jicarilla Apache Tribe*[80] in 1982, these exceptions should not obscure the significance of the meshing of executive order tribes with other tribes in almost all respects: "The fact that the Jicarilla Apache Reservation was established by Executive Order rather than by treaty or statute does not affect our analysis; the Tribe's sovereign power is not affected by the manner in which its reservation was created."

Neither does the recognized form of tribal government normally distinguish the governmental powers of one tribe from another. The major category that might seem to call for a distinction

is the group of tribes that have adopted tribal constitutions under
the Indian Reorganization Act (IRA) of 1934; these number more
than half of all existing tribes. The IRA has been of considerable
importance in spurring a revival of tribal activity, but its significance
in this regard traces mainly to the encouragement, in terms of economic policy directives and funding, that Congress and the BIA
gave to the tribes.[81] The powers mentioned in the act are hardly
remarkable and, with one exception, add nothing to the inherent
authority that the tribes already possessed.[82] Nor does the IRA itself
limit tribal prerogatives; many IRA tribes have provisions requiring
secretarial approval of tribal ordinances, but the 1985 *Kerr-McGee
Corp. v. Navajo Tribe of Indians*[83] opinion made it clear that those
provisions came about as a result of administrative policy during
the 1930s and that nothing in the IRA prevents the removal of such
restrictions from tribal constitutions.[84]

Thus in a series of decisions, some major, some not, the Court
has treated tribes and reservations as a unitary group. Following
the tradition set by Chief Justice Marshall in *Worcester v. Georgia,*[85]
the modern Court has ruled on the powers of the tribe at bar but
has left little doubt that the same results would apply as to other
tribes, absent special provisions in treaties or statutes. This is consistent with substantive congressional policy and with appropriations
procedures, neither of which normally makes distinctions among
tribes based on the procedural method by which they have been
recognized.[86] It is also good judicial practice, for it results in comprehensive doctrine that avoids repetitious litigation.

THE RIGHT TO CHANGE

The tribes have repeatedly raised arguments that implicitly rest
upon a tribal right to change, to evolve from the kinds of legal
institutions and societies that existed in aboriginal times or when
the treaties and treaty substitutes were negotiated. On initial glance,
this right to change might appear to run counter to the Court's
insulation of tribal prerogatives from the changes caused by the
passage of time. It may seem inconsistent, in other words, for the
tribes to be protected against de facto termination and against encroachment due to nonuser of tribal powers and property rights and,

at the same time, for the tribes to assert the right to grow in order to meet the demands of a new time.

The right to change, however, is consistent with, and complements, the protection against the negative effects of the passage of time. At the treaty negotiations tribes requested and received assurances from the United States that tribal lands and societies would be insulated from outside forces—that the United States would build "strong fences." These assurances against encroachment were merged into the Nonintercourse Acts, other protective statutes, and the companion judicial doctrines discussed in Chapter 2. The United States also guaranteed the tribes that tribal societies and governments could continue on the islands comprised in the reservation system. Implicit in this was a promise that tribal communities would be living and growing societies—that they would not somehow be required to remain static. As I will discuss later in this chapter, anthropologists and sociologists recognize that change is a healthy and necessary component within societies. Consistent with these notions, *Winters v. United States*[87] gave early acceptance to this essential tribal prerogative in 1908: "it would be extreme to believe that . . . Congress . . . took from [the Indians] the means of continuing their old habits, yet did not leave them the power to change to new ones." The modern cases have elaborated upon the promise of a right to change in a wide variety of contexts. The recognition of Indian tribes as living, expanding, and adaptive societies amounts to one of the leading developments of the modern era because of its rejuvenating effect on tribalism.

Tribes have asserted the right to develop new forms of governmental institutions, the best examples being formal judicial and taxing systems. Historically, all tribes possessed informal mechanisms to resolve disputes but few had courts.[88] Nevertheless, in several cases the Supreme Court has sanctioned the activities of tribal courts.[89] Similarly, the Court has upheld the evolution of formal tribal taxation institutions. Some tribes had systems of tribute but taxation of members, much less of nonmembers, was foreign to most tribal cultures.[90] A few tribal taxation cases, all involving the comparatively elaborate governments of the Five Civilized Tribes of Oklahoma, were litigated in the late nineteenth and early twentieth centuries, but the matter of tribal taxing power was of mainly

theoretical interest until well after World War II.[91] In the modern
era, these new institutions were validated, first for cigarette taxes,
then for severance taxes on energy companies operating on the
reservations.[92]

The right to change has had an even more dramatic impact in
the resource arena. The prior appropriation doctrine in water law,
which has been adopted in all of the arid western states, where the
many tribes with major water disputes are located, is premised on
defining water rights by the extent of the original appropriation of
water. The watchword of the doctrine—"first in time, first in
right"—establishes seniority at the date of the original diversion of
water and fixes the quantity of water at the level originally diverted.
These vested property rights, superior to all junior appropriations,
are then recorded with the state water resources agency or merged
into a judicial decree. All water users are thus on notice concerning
the amount of water available for their operations. The system grew
out of the necessity of promoting secure rights to diversions of water
in the American West, where water is scarce but essential for farming, ranching, mining, and municipal uses.[93]

In enunciating the famous *Winters* doctrine in 1908, the Court
made it clear that tribes were not limited by the time-bound notions
of state prior appropriation law: tribal rights date from the date of
the reservation, if not earlier, even though no water was then diverted as required by western water law.[94] Nevertheless, Indian
water issues remained mostly inchoate for more than half a century
after *Winters*, largely because few federally funded irrigation projects were constructed for Indians. At the same time heavily subsidized irrigation projects to water the fields of non-Indian farmers
were being constructed throughout the West, often in areas adjacent
to Indian reservations. Only one Indian water case, on relatively
minor issues, reached the Supreme Court between *Winters* in 1908
and *Arizona v. California I* in 1963.[95]

Arizona v. California I reaffirmed the continuing force of the
priority-date ruling of *Winters* in an especially difficult setting, the
conflict over the water of the arid Colorado River Basin. By doing
that the court confirmed that the rigid, time-based hierarchy of the
prior appropriation doctrine had indeed been modified in favor of
unused Indian water rights. The Court then went further. It found
that the quantity of the water reserved by these phantom Indian

appropriations was the amount of water necessary "to satisfy the future as well as the present needs of the Indian reservations." This forward-looking kind of appropriation has few parallels in western water law.[96] Finally, the Court found that the future tribal needs would be defined as that volume of water needed to serve the "practicably irrigable acreage on the reservations." The Court made no express reference as to how a determination of practicably irrigable acreage would be made but the opinion approved the findings of the Special Master (appointed by the Court to hear the complex factual testimony), who relied on the use of modern hydrologic techniques to define the acreage that could be irrigated.[97] The tribe's right, then, is defined by the amount of land that can be watered by modern technology, not by the techniques available when the reservation was established.

Thus *Arizona v. California I* lets time work triply in the tribes' favor—in stark juxtaposition to the prior appropriation system, which locks in water rights at the time of their original use. Indian water rights are given an early date, no later than when the reservation was established, rather than the date when the tribe puts the water to actual use. The rights can expand and include sufficient water for future needs and are not limited to those needs that prevailed at the time the reservation was established. The needs are defined by the quantity of land that up-to-date technology can make usable. To westerners, this is nothing short of heresy.

Subsequent cases have dealt significant procedural setbacks to Indian water rights.[98] None of these opinions involved the quantity of water available to tribes pursuant to the *Winters* doctrine, but most observers agree that the Court's stand in favor of state jurisdiction over future adjudications will result in lower decreed quantities of water for most tribes. Further, the Court has read federal reserved water rights narrowly and suggested obliquely in 1983 that it might have been overly generous with the tribes in *Arizona v. California I.*[99] Nevertheless, the Court has made a point of forcefully stating that it will oversee state court determinations of Indian water rights with "unflagging" vigilance,[100] and, while the developments just discussed will inevitably mean somewhat less reserved water for tribes, there is no doubt that the rights announced in *Arizona v. California I* will lead to adjudications of extensive Indian reserved water rights outside of state law.

The right to change has proved crucial to tribes in another setting. At the time of the Isaac Stevens treaties in the Pacific Northwest during the 1850s, Indians employed a wide variety of fishing devices, including hand-held dip nets, wooden fish traps and weirs, and various spears and hooks made of wood and horn. In some cases, rudimentary gillnets were used. But none of those early devices approached the deadly efficiency of today's light, long, strong, and durable monofilament gillnets. The principle of gill-netting is simple: fish migrating upstream jam their heads through the mesh and are unable to back out. Monofilament nets enhance this capture method not only because of their greater structural integrity as compared to aboriginal net types, but also because the monofilament webbing is less visible to the migrating fish. Gillnets, which are as long as 1,800 feet, can span all or a goodly portion of many coastal rivers.[101]

The use of monofilament gillnets by Indian commercial fishers to capture steelhead was an especially emotional aspect of the Indian fishing rights litigation. Although some non-Indian commercial fish-ers use gillnets for salmon, sportsfishers in California, Washington, and Oregon had waged extensive lobbying campaigns in the state legislatures and achieved bans against the gillnetting of steelhead, the prize sport fish of the region.[102] Adversaries of the tribes argued that tribes should be limited to fishing methods substantially similar to those in use when the treaties were executed; any other result, they accurately asserted, would increase the tribes' ability to take fish far beyond their harvesting capacity when the treaties were signed. One state court expressly ruled that Indian "fishing must also reasonably conform to those types and methods of gathering fish employed by the Chippewa at the time of the 1854 Treaty or to such modern types and methods as are reasonably consistent with those used at the time of the Treaty."[103] In the litigation in the Pacific Northwest, however, the federal district court opinion held that Indian fishers may "utilize improvements in traditional fishing methods, such as, for example, nylon nets and steel hooks."[104]

The Supreme Court upheld the Indian monofilament gillnet fishery when the decision was reviewed in the 1979 Northwest fishing case *Washington v. Washington State Commercial Passenger Fishing Vessel Ass'n.*[105] Four other recent Supreme Court decisions have approved the use of modern fishing gear by Indians.[106] Without this technology, the rulings recognizing treaty fishing rights would have been hollow victories: in these times of intensified fishing pressure and dwindling runs of fish due to dams and other developments in the watersheds, modern gear is a necessity if the tribes are to obtain the amount of fish to which they are entitled under court-ordered apportionment.[107]

A chief legal mechanism for permitting these various evolutions of tribal institutions is a broad characterization of tribal powers; if powers are defined generically, then specific activities are likely to fit within the expansive categorization. Following Chief Justice Marshall's reasoning in *Worcester v. Georgia*,[108] the modern Court has described tribes not as entities with enumerated or delegated powers but as governments possessing in the first instance all of the powers inherent in sovereigns.[109] Sovereign rights in turn have been described in very broad conceptual terms. The Court formulated a power to administer justice without reference to any specific kinds of institutions: tribes have "the right . . . to make their own laws and to be ruled by them."[110] Tribal taxation ordinances fall within the "tribe's general authority, as sovereign, to control economic activity within its jurisdiction, and to defray the cost of providing governmental services by requiring contributions from persons or enterprises engaged in economic activities within that jurisdiction."[111] By defining tribal powers in such abstract terms, rather than in terms descriptive of specific powers actually exercised at the time of federal recognition, the Court has allowed tribes to exercise modern governmental activity and to compete with state and local governments and with private development interests.

The judicial recognition of a right to change in Indian law is consistent with the acceptance by social scientists of the precept that all cultures change and that cultural evolution is both inevitable and healthy. Anthropologists view culture as a system of coping strategies devised by a society to ensure security and survival. These strategies consist of behavioral models for interacting with the physical and social environment as well as conceptual models for making sense of that interaction. By providing ways of thinking about and meeting the problems of existence, cultural systems are adaptive mechanisms, interposed between a society and its physical and social environment.[112]

The basic tendency in all cultural systems is toward change

rather than toward states of equilibrium.[113] New ideas and new ways of doing things continually are finding their way into societies. Further, societies often are forced to alter their coping strategies to meet changed environmental or social conditions. While the changes ultimately incorporated into a cultural system may be the product of innovations from within a society, the most important mechanism of change is cultural borrowing. Those ideas, customs, and practices that fit comfortably into a cultural system will be voluntarily selected and incorporated.[114]

During the last two centuries, by far the most dramatic changes in societies have been triggered by the direct and often prolonged contact between European and non-European cultures.[115] European and then American territorial expansion and cultural aggression have planted the seeds of massive change in traditional societies. While this contact has not always resulted in fundamentally changed cultural practices, it has inevitably led to dramatically altered world views as traditional peoples found themselves part of a world in which they were no longer the center. The struggle of aboriginal peoples to adapt to this cultural onslaught while maintaining their cultural pride and identity has been a recurrent theme in non-Western societies in the last century.[116]

Thus change—whether the result of cultural invention, borrowing, aggression, altered circumstances, or novel ways of thinking about and acting in the world—is engendered in all societies. No society could survive without the ability to absorb new ideas and behaviors and to adapt to changed conditions. The question, then, is not so much whether societies change as how they change. The fundamental nature of change in society and law is demonstrated by the work of E. Adamson Hoebel, who with Karl Llewellyn wrote the widely praised jurisprudential study *The Cheyenne Way*. Hoebel identified four broad functions that law serves in all societies, and one of them is to provide for change:

> The first [function of law] is to define relationships among the members of a society, to assert what activities are permitted and what are ruled out, so as to maintain at least minimal integration between the activities of individuals and groups within the society.
>
> The second is derived from the necessity of taming naked force and directing force to the maintenance of order. It is the allocation of authority and the determination of who may exercise physical coercion as a socially recognized privilege-right, along with the selection of the

most effective forms of physical sanction to achieve the social ends
that the law serves.
The third is the disposition of trouble cases as they arise.
The fourth is to redefine relations between individuals and groups
as the conditions of life change. It is to maintain adaptability.[117]

The implicit acceptance by the Supreme Court of the basic
right of Indian tribes in the United States to change is a core element
in according tribes the ability to survive and prosper in contemporary society.

THE PERMANENCY OF TRIBAL EXISTENCE

A central policy issue in Indian affairs has always been whether
Indian tribes should remain separate or whether they should be
assimilated into the larger society. Policies such as allotment and
termination, for example, were assimilationist. Indians, on the other
hand, press for acceptance, as the philosophical centerpiece of federal Indian policy, of the principle that Indian tribes are permanent
institutions in national policy.[118] Congress has primary constitutional
authority to recognize tribes and determine whether federal finan-
cial support and legal protection will be permanent or temporary.[119]
The Supreme Court, however, rendered decisions in the modern
era that established a slightly different point, that tribes have an
existence independent of any recognition by Congress. As will be
seen, this judicial recognition of the independence and permanency
of tribal existence has served as the vehicle for preserving tribalism
in numerous Indian groups.

Menominee Tribe of Indians v. United States[120] involved the
impact of the Menominee Termination Act on tribal hunting and
fishing rights established by treaty.[121] The litigation necessarily invoked the issue of whether the Menominee Tribe survived termination and whether, therefore, any Indian tribe existed to claim the
special treaty rights. The opinion in the lower court, the Court of
Claims, held that the rights were not diminished by the 1954 act
and explained at considerable length that the act terminated federal
recognition of the Menominee Tribe but that the tribe itself continued to exist after termination.[122] The State of Wisconsin, ap-
pearing as amicus curiae, argued that the Menominee had literally
been "terminated" and that the tribe therefore ceased to exist. At

both oral arguments the Justices showed considerable interest in whether Menominee tribal existence survived termination.[123]

The opinion in *Menominee Tribe*, which held that the treaty rights were not affected by the termination legislation, left little doubt that tribal existence continued after termination. Hunting and fishing rights are tribal rights, and the continuation of the rights necessarily implies the continuation of the tribe itself: indeed, the proceeding was a tribal claim for money damages, with the tribe as the captioned plaintiff.[124] Although the Court reserved judgment on which entity was the tribe for the purpose of regulating hunting and fishing,[125] all of the circumstances, including the attention given to the issue by the parties and the lower court, make it clear that the Court assumed that continued existence of the tribe after the Termination Act was a prerequisite to the continued existence of the treaty rights.

The status of the Menominee Tribe presented legitimately perplexing problems. The word termination tolls out finality. Yet the Court properly read the act liberally to allow for the survival of tribalism. Later opinions agree that termination may sever all or part of the federal–tribal relationship but that it does not literally bring to an end the existence of the tribe. Thus the Ninth Circuit Court of Appeals, in a decision later cited with approval by the Supreme Court, accurately described the effects of the Klamath Termination Act of 1954 in these terms:

> [A]lthough the [Klamath Termination Act] terminated federal supervision over trust and restricted property of the Klamath Indians, disposed of federally owned property and terminated federal services to the Indians, it specifically contemplated the continued existence of the Klamath Tribe. It did not affect the power of the tribe to take any action under its constitution and by-laws consistent with Act.[126]

United States v. John[127] dealt with equally difficult conceptual issues related to tribalism. The Choctaws, whose aboriginal home was in Mississippi, agreed in the Treaty of Dancing Rabbit Creek of 1830 to remove to the Indian Territory.[128] The majority of the tribal members marched west to what is now Oklahoma, but some Choctaws dug in and simply refused to leave Mississippi. In 1918, Congress recognized the Mississippi Band of Choctaws as a discrete Indian group for the first time by appropriating funds for land acquisition and for education, health, and other social services. In

1944 a reservation was proclaimed by the secretary of the interior, and in 1945 the Mississippi Choctaws adopted a constitution and bylaws. The *John* case arose when a Mississippi Choctaw Indian named Smith John allegedly committed the crime of assault with intent to kill. The incident occurred on Choctaw land, and the issue in the case was whether the land was Indian country and thus whether the prosecution was required to proceed in federal court rather than in Mississippi state court.

John held that the area held in trust by the United States for the Mississippi Choctaws was indeed Indian country, that federal jurisdiction existed, and that state jurisdiction was precluded. The Court was not deterred by the fact that most Choctaws had removed west and that historically and ethnologically the Mississippi Choctaws had not acted as a tribe. The opinion found that, since the individual members of the band were all Indians, Congress and the executive branch had the power to deal with them as a tribe for the purpose of federal law. Further, the gap in federal relations with the remnant band between the 1830s and 1918 did not divest Congress of its authority under the Indian Commerce Clause:

> Neither the fact that the Choctaws in Mississippi are merely a remnant of a larger group of Indians, long ago removed from Mississippi, nor the fact that federal supervision over them has not been continuous, destroys the federal power to deal with them. [129]

Taken together, *Menominee Tribe* and *John* hold that tribalism is ultimately a matter of self-definition. Federal recognition may be withdrawn. The tribal unit may change when a catastrophic event occurs, as with the Choctaws, and a tribe may redefine itself ethnologically. [130] But tribalism continues until the members themselves extinguish it. Tribalism depends on a tribe's own will.

This permanency bears directly on the flexibility of federal power. There has been no irrevocable action if the federal government loses touch with a tribe. Since a tribe can continue in existence apart from federal recognition, it can fight back from a denial of federal support, as did the tribes in both *Menominee Tribe* and *John*. Thus the Menominees were restored to full federal recognition within five years of their historic Supreme Court decision, and several other terminated tribes have followed suit. [131] The vindication of the status of the Mississippi Choctaw clarified the standing of other remnant groups. Remnant tribes in the East include the North Carolina Cherokees and the Florida Seminoles. Congress recently recognized the Cow Creek Band, which remained in the hills of southern Oregon when the main body of the tribe was relocated on the Grand Ronde Reservation. Federal recognition has also been extended to a band of Kickapoo Indians that has resided primarily in Mexico since the mid–nineteenth century.[132]

The permanency of tribal existence, then, gives tribes and Congress a continuing option. Tribal existence, wholly independent of any federal action, is maintained as long as a tribe or subgroup has the will to maintain it. In turn, Congress retains authority to deal with the tribe in order to correct old mistakes.

THE HIGHER SOVEREIGN

Congress established a comprehensive matrix of laws regulating Indian affairs and effectively limiting the scope of tribal sovereignty from the beginning days of the Republic. Federal legislation encompassed land transactions, commerce, crimes in Indian country, the liquor traffic, the provision of education and other social services—even religion, as federal funds were used to support the activities of missionaries among the Indians.[133] The Marshall Trilogy legitimized these congressional activities and announced federal powers under the Indian Commerce Clause that "comprehend all that is required" to regulate Indian affairs.[134] Then the far-flung federal administrative structure was instituted in the mid–nineteenth century, and cases in the late nineteenth and early twentieth centuries, notably *United States v. Kagama*[135] and *Lone Wolf v. Hitchcock*,[136] expostulated on the untrammeled, "plenary" nature of federal constitutional power over Indian affairs. The phrase *plenary power* became a pejorative byword among Indians and their advocates for unreviewable, and potentially autocratic, federal legislative and administrative authority.*

*The Court's references to plenary power probably were, and are, intended to mean that congressional power is plenary in the sense that Congress can exercise broad police power, rather than only the power of a limited government with specifically enumerated powers, when legislating on Indian affairs. See F. Cohen, Handbook of Federal Indian Law 217–20 (1982 ed.). Used in this manner, *plenary* refers to general,

The notions of federal supremacy lodged in the plenary power doctrine have long antagonized and frustrated Indian people. They consider outrageous a doctrine that justifies, among other things, strong-arm rules such as the doctrine of discovery that transmutes Indian fee title into a "right of occupancy" not protected by the Fifth Amendment at the moment an explorer's flag is tentatively planted on an isolated shore; the idea that Indian tribes are domestic dependent governments lacking direct access to the international community; the rule that Congress can order the divestiture of tribal land and then transfer it to tribal members in the form of allotments, a "mere change in the form of the investment" that in fact has cost Indians tens of millions of acres of land; and the notion that Indian treaties can be abrogated by Congress without agreement by, or even consultation with, the affected tribes. [137]

None of these by-products of the plenary power doctrine has been shaken by the modern Court nor is any likely to be. But recent opinions have reconceptualized aspects of federal power over Indian property rights, narrowed it, and rendered the term *plenary* (as a synonym for absolute and unreviewable) obsolete. Further, the modern decisions make it abundantly clear that federal power can, and has, cut in both directions: it can also support progressive programs conceived of, and supported by, Indian leaders in order to promote tribal sovereignty and the welfare of Indian people.

Earlier cases had provided a framework for the imposition of principled restraints on the exercise of federal power in Indian law, but the issue had not been sharpened until a series of opinions beginning with *Morton v. Mancari* in 1974. [138] *Mancari* involved a statute favorable to Indians, a provision in the Indian Reorganization Act of 1934 granting an employment preference to Indians for positions in the BIA. The opinion upheld the statute but refused to give absolute deference to Congress. The Court, reconciling Indian law and equal protection principles, adopted a rational basis test: the statute was upheld because it was "tied rationally to the fulfillment of Congress's unique obligation toward the Indians." *Delaware Tribal Business Comm. v. Weeks* [139] also allowed some scrutiny of

---

as opposed to delegated, power. Nevertheless, *plenary* also means absolute or total and has tended to carry that meaning in common usage in Indian policy.

Congress's action, this time in a statute that disadvantaged the Indians in question. The Kansas Delawares sued because they had been excluded from a claims settlement that had been paid to the Oklahoma Delawares. The Court again employed the rational basis test and upheld the statute.

The 1980 *United States v. Sioux Nation of Indians*[140] decision was far more prickly. The Black Hills in South Dakota were included within the Sioux Reservation established by the Fort Laramie Treaty of 1868. After gold was discovered in the Black Hills, the land was confiscated by an 1877 statute.[141] The tribe was allowed by a special 1920 jurisdictional act to seek recovery in the Court of Claims, which held in 1942 that Congress's action was unreviewable: some minimal compensation had been provided when the land was taken and the court refused to look behind that arrangement. The tribe sued again when the Indian Claims Commission Act of 1946 allowed tribal claims for money damages under theories not available to the Sioux when the first claims case had been brought. The second case was held to be barred by the first as a matter of res judicata.[142] In 1978, the tribe obtained passage of a special act allowing a third suit by directing the Court of Claims to hear the case on the merits and to ignore the res judicata defense. Thus the Sioux were able to force judicial attention on the merits, the issue of whether an unconstitutional taking had occurred.

In *Sioux Nation* the Court held that Congress had acted in bad faith and had not sought to make the Sioux whole when the Black Hills were taken.[143] Thus the tribe was entitled to the value of the land and minerals at the time of the taking, plus interest, for a total of more than $100 million. Congress, the Court reasoned, can act in a discrete instance either as a trustee for Indians or in its role of furthering other national interests by limiting Indian rights: it cannot do both at once. When Congress acts as a trustee, its action will be upheld if it acted in good faith. If, on the other hand, Congress was exercising its power of eminent domain, full compensation is required.[144] The courts should undertake a "thorough and impartial examination of the historical record" to determine which hat Congress was wearing. The symbol of the plenary power doctrine, *Lone Wolf v. Hitchcock*, allowed for no such search, relying instead on a near-impermeable presumption of congressional good faith.[145] *Lone Wolf*, which had never been expressly limited, was raked by

Justice Blackmun's majority opinion, which said that the *Lone Wolf* rationale was "discredited" and "had little to commend it as an enduring principle."[146] In *Sioux Nation,* in other words, the Court not only announced that judicial review of congressional actions was appropriate but also exercised this review authority in favor of the tribe.

But *Sioux Nation* had its limits also. It did not hold, nor did it suggest, that the Sioux are entitled to the relief they really cherish— the return of the Black Hills themselves.[147] *Sioux Nation* is a money damages case only and did not cast doubt on Congress's ultimate authority to abrogate the treaty unilaterally by taking the land. Further, the finding of legislative bad faith was made easy by the fact that the contemporary Congress suspected, if it was not convinced, that its nineteenth-century predecessor had in fact overstepped the bounds of good faith.[148] There was no actual conflict between the ruling of this Court and the wishes of this Congress.

The demise of the idea of literally unlimited congressional power in Indian affairs and the employment of a minimal scrutiny test track developments in constitutional law generally. The doctrine of federal sovereign immunity has undergone evolution since *Lone Wolf.* The political question doctrine has been narrowed in scope. Further, plenary power evolved in the context of treaty abrogation, a region of Indian law heavily influenced by international law, which in turn is undergirded by the judiciary's perceived necessity to allow maximum flexibility in the other federal branches in conducting foreign relations. Although international law can be important in explaining doctrine in some contexts, Indian law today is mainly a body of domestic law. The trust relationship, not a body of law looking to the maintenance of absolute executive or congressional power in the delicate international arena, should normally be the focal point when Congress legislates in Indian affairs. The Court recognized this by its reliance on the trust relationship, and not on international law, in *Morton v. Mancari, Delaware Tribe,* and *Sioux Nation,* the three cases that modernized judicial review of congressional action in Indian law.[149]

One can fairly doubt that the renunciation of *Lone Wolf* will spur many adventurous court inquiries into the rationality of congressional action in Indian law. Power may no longer be absolute, but by any mark it remains uncommonly broad. The ancient tradition

in Indian policy of deep federal regulation in affairs of Indian property, jurisdiction, and even culture is not likely to be swept aside
by the latter-day recognition of a slightly expanded role for the
judiciary. No Supreme Court case has yet overturned any statute
as being beyond Congress's authority,[150] and that record may well
remain safe under the new regime, both for statutes that burden
and statutes that benefit Indians. The focus in the courts is likely
to remain on the rules of construction that limit adverse impacts of
legislation on Indians by forcing narrow readings of laws that might
negatively affect Indian interests.

In spite of their likely minimal impact when it comes to courts
actually setting aside federal statutes, the modern cases readjusting
judicial and congressional power may well become reasonably imposing edifices in this field. The scuttling of *Lone Wolf* in the name
of review for rationality amounts to a recognition that the familiar
constitutional framework for ordering congressional action through
limited judicial oversight applies to the making of Indian laws. *Morton v. Mancari, Delaware Tribe,* and *Sioux Nation* are polite but
firm warnings to Congress that care must be taken in-house.

The context should be made clear. Regardless of whatever protections and advances the tribes may have achieved in the courts
in modern times, Congress remains the fount of most of Indian law.
It is on Capitol Hill that it all can be lost and that most of it can be
preserved. The balance there is precarious: the termination era,
only slightly more than a generation past, is a continuing reminder
of that.

One of the greatest developments in Indian policy since termination has gone relatively unnoticed in many quarters: Indians
have learned how to lobby. Highly effective legislative campaigns
have been pursued by individual tribes and by national organizations.[151] Indians and their advocates hold a range of well-placed staff
positions in Congress.[152] A skilled network exists to identify opposition proposals and to react to them promptly and professionally.[153]
None of this obviates what is perhaps the dominant fact—that Indians are a low-income minority group with few votes at the polls.
Tribal rights remain vulnerable to initiatives backed by well-orga-
nized interest groups, including pending proposals to limit Indian
hunting of endangered species for religious ceremonies and to regulate Indian bingo operations. At the same time, the Indian presence

in Washington is incomparably superior to that which existed, for example, just two decades ago. No Indian legislation has been passed over Indian opposition since the Indian Civil Rights Act of 1968.[154]

In this setting, in which there is a sophistication on Indian legal matters in Congress never approached before and in which the issues are often very close, a clarification by the Court of fundamental institutional relationships has the potential of taking on considerable importance.

It is impossible to measure the extent to which the Supreme Court's clarification of the limits on Congress's powers has caused, or will cause, subtle modifications in the legislative process. It is reasonable, however, to believe that some members of Congress will act with a somewhat greater awareness of the federal trust responsibility. Leaving Indian policy aside, we know that doubts about constitutionality can be a legitimately important factor in Congress when it passes on proposed legislation.[155] Since *Delaware Tribe*, tribal representatives have made repeated use of the rational basis test in advocating against bills deemed to be detrimental to Indian interests. The new cases have been argued in the legislative forum with particular vigor in defining Congress's trust duties in regard to confiscatory proposals concerning water, fishing rights, and land—none of which has been enacted.[156] The rule set out in the recent cases is only one tool for Indians, perhaps a minor one. But the calls in Congress are close and the new rule can be expected to matter some, and perhaps a lot in some instances, in the forum that holds ultimate power.

The Court has also given attention to the trust duties of federal officials when dealing with Indian tribes and individuals. In this setting, the modern cases make it clear that the limited review given to congressional action is inapplicable. Agency action is subject, at a minimum, to judicial scrutiny under the Administrative Procedure Act (APA).[157] Moreover, judicial scrutiny of the administration of Indian policy seems to be heightened because of the fiduciary standards required by the trust relationship. In *Morton v. Ruiz*,[158] the Court imposed trust standards on top of the rule making provisions of the APA.[159]

Three modern cases—*Mitchell I*[160] and *Mitchell II*,[161] involving timber harvesting on trust allotments, and *Nevada v. United States*,[162] dealing with water rights to the Pyramid Lake Band of

Paiutes of Nevada—have provided preliminary answers concerning federal trust duties in the management of tribal natural resources. *Mitchell I* is unlikely to have broad impact. The decision found that Section 5 of the General Allotment Act created no trust duty to manage allotted forest lands, but the case was remanded to the Court of Claims for a determination of whether a trust was imposed by other statutes. The Court of Claims then held that the Indian timber management statutes created trust obligations, and the Supreme Court affirmed in *Mitchell II*. The holding in *Mitchell I* is thus made effectively irrelevant by *Mitchell II*, and the holding in *Mitchell II* is unsurprising.

The decision in *Nevada v. United States* was devastating to the Pyramid Lake Band's asserted water rights, but its impact on Indian trust law is less easy to assess. The case involved the United States' failure to argue for tribal reserved water rights to maintain a fishery in a water adjudication instituted in 1912 and made final in 1944. Pyramid Lake comprises most of the band's reservation, and the lake, with its magnificent and rare fishery, shrunk steadily beginning in 1904. The lake level dropped due to diversions to a federal reclamation project from the Truckee River, whose inflow is the only source of water for the lake. The situation reeked with a potential trust conflict because the United States attorney represented both the reclamation water users and the band in the adjudication: the private water users were decreed extensive water rights, and, as mentioned, the band's reserved water rights for the fishery were not even raised with the court, although the United States attorney had been made aware of them.[163]

The Court refused to set aside the 1944 decree. The opinion is bound up with powerful policies involving both finality of adjudications and vested property rights recognized under western water law, and may be limited primarily to that setting.[164] One important principle of Indian trust law, however, was recognized for the first time: when government officials are directed simultaneously to advance both Indian interests and those of competing parties, then the rigid standards applicable to private trusts do not apply in full force.[165] This rule is unavoidable because a governmental trust cannot fairly be equated with a private trust in all circumstances. The private trustee analogy fits well, for example, when Interior Department officials must administer money accounts, parcels of land,

or mineral deposits for tribes or individual Indians.[166] It does not
fit so comfortably, as *Nevada v. United States* recognizes, when a
single federal agency must administer a multipurpose project providing benefits both to Indians and to numerous parties other than
Indians.[167]

The governmental trustee concept set out in *Nevada v. United
States* will probably be applied in a somewhat different fashion when
current administrative decisions, rather than rulings embodied in a
final court decree, are involved. For example, in an earlier proceeding in the Pyramid Lake litigation, District Judge Gesell issued
a widely cited opinion ruling that the Indian trust doctrine required
the Department of Interior to justify with specificity any diversions
of water from Pyramid Lake.[168] It now turns out that Judge Gesell's
assumed premise, that the band possessed senior reserved water
rights, was incorrect.[169] But, in a current conflict concerning an
ongoing multipurpose project involving a tribe's reserved rights,
Judge Gesell's reasoning would still seem to apply. Even if private
trust law is not fully applicable, the government is still a trustee
and has special obligations to the tribe. It follows that some high
level of judicial scrutiny is required. To be sure, after such scrutiny,
a court may conclude that obligations to other parties predominate,
but the special duty to protect Indian resources does not vanish
simply because other interests are involved.

Thus a high obligation may have to be reconciled with other
interests, but courts can nevertheless compel administrators to carry
out current duties with care, competence, and integrity. In *Nevada
v. United States,* the decision had been made decades ago by a
federal court, and powerful reliance interests had built up; the policies based on finality of judicial decrees overrode the policies in
favor of holding government officials strictly accountable for their
actions in regard to Indian beneficiaries. In the absence of such
compelling reliance interests, the courts likely will engage in ex-
acting review of the administration of Indian trust rights.

Although comparatively little has been done to explicate the
enforceable duties of the trustee, the trust relationship has
played a pervasive role in serving as the philosophical basis for a
number of important doctrinal advances. The trust provides an essential part of the rationale for the rules of construction that are so
influential in Indian law.[170] As first explained in *Morton v. Mancari,*

special federal programs benefiting Indians can be justified constitutionally because the classifications are not racial; the programs
may go to individual Indians, but those Indians are properly viewed
not as members of a race but as citizens of a government with whom
the United States has a special government-to-government relationship.[171] The right of tribes to govern themselves in Indian country free of state authority is based in part on the special status of
tribes vis-à-vis the federal government.[172] Thus, in addition to the accountability of federal officials for trust violations, the trust has a
diverse and continuing influence in the development of Indian law.

   Tribalism in the United States, then, traces to ancient, nonfederal sources, but it has become entwined with the federal government. The higher sovereign, faced with few practical constraints,
holds nearly full sway in its ability to sap or energize Indian sovereignty. The power exists to enact everything from the debilitating
allotment and termination programs to the beneficent child welfare
and tax status laws that offer so much promise to Indian people.
With ultimate primacy in Indian law and policy lodged firmly in
Congress, Indian leaders know full well that whether tribal sovereignty will decline or progress will depend in important part on the
tribes' skill in presenting their views in the legislative forum.

4

Territorial Jurisprudence

The hallmark of the modern era, the most ringing shift in emphasis, has been the attention given to questions of jurisdiction, especially in the civil area. The task of erecting bright guideposts of comprehensive doctrine is hindered by the varying circumstances among the tribes, the checkerboarded land patterns in Indian country, the multiplicity of miscellaneous statutes, the dearth of definitive legislative standards for the state–tribal relationship, and the inconsistency of congressional policy from era to era.[1] The most vexing problems, however, trace to people in Indian country, their reasonable expectations, and race-based tensions.

Jurisdictional issues justifiably could be resolved by relatively pat rules on established reservations until about the last two or three decades of the 1800s. Before then, Indian reservations were inhabited almost entirely by Indians. The main exceptions were scattered numbers of missionaries, government officials, and traders, all of whom dealt with Indians on a day-to-day basis. The presence of the states was minimal—indeed, many regions in the West were still in territorial status.[2] Indian reservations logically and equitably could be treated as separate blocks of land for jurisdictional purposes. State or territorial law could stop at the reservation line, where tribal or federal law would pick up. If a tribe sought to regulate or punish a non-Indian, such action was likely to be in accord with reasonable expectations, except where federal law provided otherwise, because the non-Indian probably had come to the reservation for the purpose of dealing with tribal Indians.

Such neat formulations may apply on a small number of modern reservations today but certainly not generically. The allotment policy opened many reservations for settlement. Indian reservations commonly include non-Indian businesses and landowners, sometimes in considerable numbers.

The rights of the states within Indian country are based ultimately on the presence of non-Indian citizens within Indian country. As non-Indians moved in, so too did state law. This is the message of *McBratney v. United States*,[3] the pivotal 1882 decision that first legitimized the application of state law in Indian country by upholding state court jurisdiction over an alleged murder of one non-Indian by another non-Indian. There is no statutory support for the *McBratney* ruling: the Indian Country Crimes Act called for a federal court prosecution. The justification for the result is that some events occur in Indian country that simply do not bear on legitimate tribal or federal concerns.[4] It is not easy, perhaps, to place a murder within that category—the peace within the tribal society has plainly been disturbed, so that the tribe and the United States, as trustee, both seem to have strong interests—but *McBratney* evidences one essential policy choice that the Supreme Court made and continues to honor: absent a highly explicit federal statute to the contrary, state laws prevail over tribal and federal laws in regard to an activity that occurs in Indian country and that is not directly involved with legitimate tribal concerns.[5] This is due to an implicit recognition of the historical and contemporary fact that considerable numbers of people are continually in Indian country for reasons that have little or no connection with Indians.

Matters among non-Indians go to the states and matters among Indians go to the tribes. Those baselines are now set, absent explicit federal provision to the contrary. There are, however, myriad questions in between, including, for example, Can a state tax a non-Indian businessperson who would pass the tax savings along to tribes or individual Indians? Can a tribe tax that businessperson or shut down the operation for health reasons? Does it matter—and, if so, how much—whether the non-Indian does business on fee land? Must a non-Indian businessperson seek review of the tribal council's ruling first in tribal court? Is he or she allowed to seek review of the tribal action in federal court? And what if the complaint at bottom is that the tribal council or tribal court is racist? In turn, these questions require a reconciliation of even broader concerns: How can tribalism be squared with the legal and moral dictates of equal protection and egalitarianism? What is the role of the states in Indian country and of the tribes in the constitutional democracy?

UNITY OF TERRITORY

The problem of defining the geographic bounds of the territory within which tribalism and special federal protections operate has been a matter of concern in Indian law and policy from the beginning. As early as 1758 colonial Pennsylvania guaranteed the Six Nations of the Iroquois Confederation that whites would not encroach into the Ohio Valley, and the British ministry ratified this absolute boundary. The first use of the term *Indian country* traces to the famous Royal Proclamation of 1763, issued by King George III. The proclamation dealt with matters of colonial government and settlement. It also responded to pressing matters of Indian policy. The proclamation set aside the "Indian country" for the tribes and prohibited all land transactions and entry by whites within the region, which was described as "all the Lands and Territories lying to the Westward of the Sources of the Rivers which fall into the Sea from the West and North West." Father Prucha has evaluated the significance of this aspect of the Royal Proclamation:

> The great departure from the past, the new turn in Indian policy found in the Proclamation of 1763, was the boundary line drawn between the lands of the Indians and those of the whites. In earlier colonial days there had been no distinct "Indian Country". Indian ownership of land was recognized—Massachusetts quoted Scripture in support of that principle—and care was taken to regularize the purchase of lands from the natives. In some colonies, indeed, clearly marked reservations were set aside for the Indians, but in many places the Indian families lived side by side with the whites, as they were induced to embrace the white man's way of life and civilization. When the Indians were close at hand, one could go out to buy game from them or sell them household manufactures, a personal, family-size trade expressly guaranteed in colonial legislation. Off to the indefinite west were the unlimited hunting grounds of the Indians and the source of their furs and deerskins. No one saw any need to declare these lands off limits to the whites. There was little occasion at first for a strictly drawn

boundary line to separate the red men in the West from the whites
in the East. It was in the Proclamation of 1763 that the first official
delineation and definition of the Indian Country was made.[6]

The United States faced the same need as England to regularize
commercial trade and land transactions with the tribes and to respond to tribal demands for autonomy. The term *Indian country* was
employed in various imprecise fashions in the early Trade and Intercourse Acts and other early federal statutes. Several of the early
usages included a north–south line of demarcation, with all territory
west of the line being Indian country; the context of the laws in their
entirety, however, suggests that the phrase was intended to apply to
all lands owned and occupied by tribes, including lands east of the
boundary.[7] The first unitary statutory definition of the geography
over which special principles of Indian law applied was contained in
the Trade and Intercourse Act of 1834, which identified Indian country as (1) all lands west of the Mississippi River, outside of the states
of Louisiana and Missouri and the Territory of Arkansas, and (2) any
lands east of the Mississippi, not within any state, the Indian title to
which had not been extinguished.[8]

The definition in the 1834 act was omitted, and thus repealed,
by the compilers of the Revised Statutes in 1874. Although there
was no definition, the term *Indian country* was employed in several
statutes and, not atypically in this field, the "Court was left with
little choice but to continue to apply the principles established under
the earlier statutory language and to develop them according to
changing conditions."[9] The "changing conditions" were indeed imposing and included allotment, the creation of nontreaty reservations, statehood, and acquisition of land from Russia, Great Britain,
and Mexico.[10] As the Court said in 1877:

> Notwithstanding the immense changes which have since taken place
> in the vast region covered by the act of 1834, by the extinguishment
> of Indian titles, the creation of States and the formation of territorial
> governments, Congress has not thought it necessary to make any new
> definition of Indian country. Yet during all this time a large body of
> laws has been in existence, whose operation was confined to the Indian
> country, whatever that may be. And men have been punished by
> death, by fine, and by imprisonment, of which the courts who so
> punished them had no jurisdiction, if the offences were not committed
> in the Indian country as established by law. These facts afford the
> strongest presumption that the Congress of the United States, and

the judges who administered those laws, must have found in the definition of Indian country, in the act of 1834, such an adaptability to the altered circumstances of what was then Indian country as to enable them to ascertain what it was at any time since then.

* * *

It follows from this that all the country described by the act of 1834 as Indian country remains Indian country so long as the Indians retain their original title to the soil, and ceases to be Indian country whenever they lose that title, in the absence of any different provision by treaty or by act of Congress.[11]

Congress finally made one constructive decision on unity of territory. Codifying existing cases, the general revision of the federal criminal laws in 1948 set out a statutory definition of Indian country.[12] The United States Code (18 U.S.C. § 1151) provides that all lands, however owned, within the exterior boundaries of all federal Indian reservations, however created, are Indian country for the purposes of criminal prosecutions. Trust allotments and "dependent Indian communities" are also Indian country under the statute. The full text of Section 1151, one of the most important statutes in the field, reads as follows:

[T]he term 'Indian country', as used in this chapter, means (a) all land within the limits of any Indian reservation under the jurisdiction of the United States Government, notwithstanding the issuance of any patent, and, including rights-of-way running through the reservation, (b) all dependent Indian communities within the borders of the United States whether within the original or subsequently acquired territory thereof, and whether within or without the limits of a state, and (c) all Indian allotments, the Indian titles to which have not been extinguished, including rights-of-way running through the same.

The Indian Country Statute does not deal with civil jurisdiction, which has raised most of the difficult and important questions during the modern era. The Court resolved the issue in a 1975 decision, *DeCoteau v. District County Court,*[13] in which it concluded in a footnote that the definition of Indian country in Section 1151 for crimes "generally applies as well to questions of civil jurisdiction." The Court then reaffirmed the point in more extended discussions in *White Mountain Apache Tribe v. Bracker*[14] and *Ramah Navajo School Bd. v. Bureau of Revenue.*[15] The reasoning is sound. Whether the substantive results may work for or against Indians, there is no logic to distinguishing between criminal and civil cases.

Congress had defined Indian country for criminal cases and, given the tradition of judicial development of common law in the field, especially in the context of Indian country, the Court properly applied the existing congressional determination to the civil side.

The resolution of these issues has had a settling effect because it is typically the territorial concepts embodied in the definition of Indian country that trigger the special principles of Indian law. This was made clear in a pair of companion cases in 1973, *McClanahan v. Arizona State Tax Comm'n*[16] and *Mescalero Apache Tribe v. Jones.*[17] The state tax in *McClanahan* was levied in Indian country and was struck down. The taxes in *Mescalero Apache* were sought to be applied outside of Indian country. The Court effectively found that Indian law is mostly territorially based, that it is not personal law.[18] Distinguishing *McClanahan*, the Court found that "tribal activities conducted outside the reservation present different considerations. . . . Absent express federal law to the contrary, Indians going beyond reservation boundaries have generally been held subject to nondiscriminatory state law otherwise applicable to all citizens of the State."[19]

The geographic boundaries of this territorially based body of law, then, have been fixed with some precision, and in a comprehensive manner that covers most reservations, by employing the criminal law provision, 18 U.S.C. § 1151. Since the field is so heavily influenced by territorial concerns, the Court's relative firmness on this issue is fundamentally helpful. The decisions have stopped short, however, of moving the criminal analysis wholesale over to the civil side. For federal criminal prosecutions, the statute compels an initial determination as to whether the alleged crime occurred within Indian country. If it did, all acres are treated in the same manner, regardless of ownership. This avoids a rule requiring law enforcement officers "to search tract books" in order to determine jurisdiction in criminal cases.[20] In civil cases, to the contrary, the Court has found that tribal jurisdiction is more attenuated on land within Indian country not owned by the tribe or its members.[21]

The Court's refusal to adopt an all-or-nothing approach to civil jurisdiction over non-Indians within Indian country—tribes either have full jurisdiction or lack it entirely—cuts against predictability. This approach, however, is justified in this instance. Nearly absolute rules (broad tribal power and very little state authority) properly can be set when tribal Indians are conducting activities on Indian land. When non-Indians or their lands are implicated, however, the issues become sufficiently more sensitive that a balancing of interests is appropriate. That balancing, which involves most prominently the nature of tribal interests, is the subject of much of what follows.

THE TRIBES, THE STATES, AND THE CONSTITUTION

In *White Mountain Apache Tribe v. Bracker*,[22] which includes the most extensive analysis of jurisdictional doctrine during the modern era, the Court identified for the first time a two-part test governing assertions of state jurisdiction. The approach, which has been employed in each subsequent decision on the question, recognizes "two independent but related barriers" to state jurisdiction. "First, the exercise of such authority may be preempted by federal law. . . . Second, it may unlawfully infringe 'on the right of reservation Indians to make their own laws and be ruled by them.' "[23] I refer to the first barrier as subject matter preemption because it involves the analysis of federal statutes dealing with discrete substantive areas of regulation such as commerce, criminal jurisdiction, health and education, and resource management. Although Congress often limits the operation of such statutes to Indian country as a matter of policy, the essence of the subject matter barrier is the regulatory field covered by the statute.[24] The second barrier, which I call geographical preemption, is purely territorial because it assesses the extent to which state law is ousted due solely to the creation of an Indian reservation by joint federal–tribal action, or unilateral federal action, in a treaty or treaty substitute. Geographical preemption may deny state authority in subject matter areas not addressed explicitly by any federal treaty or statute dealing with Indian policy; the many examples include civil court jurisdiction, taxation, zoning, environmental regulation, and health and safety laws.

The Court has emphasized that the doctrine of tribal sovereignty is relevant to both barriers to state jurisdiction. Tribal sovereignty "informs" subject matter preemption because federal laws often have been enacted to protect and promote Indian self-determination.[25] Tribal self-government is a major interest to be analyzed in regard to the geographical preemption barrier because the tribes' desire to remain apart, and the United States' complementary policy of isolating Indians from the path of settlement, was the central aim of the treaties and treaty substitutes.[26] Importantly, the analysis of the scope of legitimate tribal interests is used to resolve the related issue of tribal civil jurisdiction over non-Indians, where the Court will allow regulation if it is tied to essential tribal interests. Tribal interests have also been significant in the hunting, fishing, and water cases. There is a commonality among all of these areas that we can expect to be recognized more expressly in future cases.[27]

The Court has been inclined to favor the use of the subject matter preemption barrier to resolve assertions of state jurisdiction.[28] This preference probably exists because the legislative guidelines are articulated more fully in the provisions of the subject matter statutes than in the vague language usually employed in the treaties and treaty substitutes establishing Indian country. Thus the Court likely views the subject matter approach as closer to pure statutory construction while geographical preemption, although based on a treaty or treaty substitute, such as a statute, is in fact akin to common law case development in light of the need to discern the implied purposes of the treaties and treaty substitutes.[29]

Since its first explicit reference to federal preemption in Indian cases in *McClanahan v. Arizona State Tax Comm'n*,[30] the Court has constructed a series of general principles, all sensitive to the special status of Indian tribes, that lay the ground rules for both branches of Indian preemption law. First, the preemption analysis in Indian law is distinctive, so that "it [is] generally unhelpful to apply to federal enactments regulating Indian tribes those standards of preemption that have emerged in other areas of the law."[31] Second, preemption of state law in the field of Indian statutes need not be expressly set out in the federal statute but may be implied.[32] Third, there is a general presumption against state jurisdiction in Indian country, operating with greatest force when only Indians are involved.[33] These three rules have set a distinct tone for preemption decisions in Indian law. Thus, to the extent that courts presume that state law is not preempted in most fields,[34] such reasoning does not apply when courts construe Indian statutes. The distinction is based on the special trust relationship with tribes, the policy of promoting tribal self-government in Indian country, and the long-standing federalization of Indian policy, traditions not present in

most fields where preemption issues arise.[35] These general principles have been reflected in the results, which have usually struck
down assertions of state jurisdiction in Indian country.

A fourth principle has been applied to activities outside of Indian country. It effectively reverses the rules governing preemption
in Indian country and merges Indian preemption with the greater
body of preemption law by presuming state jurisdiction unless there
is an express federal statutory provision to the contrary.[36] This opposite approach outside of Indian country is appropriate because
federal policy has been the opposite: although there are instances
of Indian legislation regulating off-reservation activities, Congress
normally has not asserted its powers there. With a lack of tradition
of federal activity outside of Indian country, the rationale for treating
Indian preemption in a distinctive manner dissolves.

These first three rules, which protect tribal government in
Indian country, shed light on the modern Court's treatment of
Worcester v. Georgia.[37] Although the cases have cited *Worcester*
with extraordinary regularity, the Court has said variously that Chief
Justice Marshall's famous opinion has been "modified," that it has
"undergone considerable evolution in response to changed circumstances," and the like.[38] In fact, only one aspect of *Worcester* has
been altered, namely, the language that Cherokee lands were "extraterritorial" to Georgia and that Georgia laws could "have no force"
there. Such a rationale, which could be premised on a constitutional
bar to state jurisdiction in Indian country due to the existence of
tribal sovereignty, would of course be exceedingly protective of
tribal self-government, and the rejection of that reasoning dimin-
ishes tribal prerogatives and elevates state powers.[39]

Each of the several other principles in *Worcester*, however,
remains intact. Its holding on the invalidity of state programs such
as the Georgia laws of the 1820s unquestionably remains good law
today.[40] Further, all of the remaining doctrine established in
Worcester, except the "extraterritoriality" concept, is in force: the
existence of tribal sovereignty before contact with Europeans,[41] the
continuing existence of self-governing status after alliance with the
United States,[42] tribal reserved rights,[43] the rules of construction
for Indian treaties and statutes,[44] and the general exclusion of Indian
reservations from the operation of state law.[45]

These principles guide the modern Court's protective stance

toward Indian self-government. *Worcester* constitutes the head-waters of modern Indian law—one cannot really understand the field without understanding *Worcester*—and it is that legacy that caused the Court to explain at the opening of the modern era that "the basic policy of *Worcester* has remained" and to make similar observations since.[46] The continuing influence of *Worcester*, which drives doctrine toward results that deny state jurisdiction and uphold tribal power, will become apparent as we look more closely at the two branches of Indian preemption law.

Subject Matter Preemption

The use of the first barrier to state jurisdiction, subject matter preemption, has defined the reach of most of the major subject matter statutes in the field. Judicial construction of the Indian traders statutes has been of especial importance because of the potential of these ancient laws, derived from the Trade and Intercourse Act of 1790, to exempt most of the commercial trade with Indians on Indian reservations from state taxation and regulation.[47] In the 1965 opinion in *Warren Trading Post v. Arizona State Tax Comm'n*,[48] the second major decision of the modern era, the Court used the traders statutes to strike down a state gross proceeds tax on a trading post operated by a non-Indian. Fifteen years later, far more difficult questions were resolved against state authority in *Central Machinery Co. v. Arizona State Tax Comm'n*,[49] a 5–4 decision holding that sales of farm equipment to a tribe were exempt from Arizona's gross proceeds tax.

Central Machinery sharply delimited the application of state laws when non-Indian merchants deal with tribes or reservation Indians. Although the farm equipment in *Central Machinery* was used on the reservation, the company had no reservation office. Further, the seller was not licensed under the Indian traders statutes. The Court resolved both of these problems by reading broadly the preemptive force of the traders statutes. In spite of the seller's lack of reservation contacts, the Court found that the seller had "introduce[d] goods . . . in the Indian country" within the meaning of the traders statutes. This being so, the company's lack of a license was immaterial: "[i]t is the existence of the Indian trader statutes, then, and not their administration, that pre-empts the field of transactions with Indians occurring on reservations."[50]

These decisions are of considerable importance for reservation business development. The clarification of the reach of the traders statutes helps settle expectations about commercial dealings in Indian country and provides predictability for businesspeople trading on the reservations.[51] Further, if the states had been permitted to "stack" their taxes on top of tribal taxes, merchants might well refuse to locate on reservations due to the extra burden, with the probable result being that tribes would be forced to pull back their taxes. Under *Central Machinery* and *Warren Trading Post*, businesses have an incentive to do business in Indian country, thus providing badly needed services to tribes and reservation Indians, since they will be exempt from some state taxes and regulation. Tribes can receive revenues, and not destroy that incentive, by imposing their own taxes at a lesser rate than the state taxes. None of this applies when non-Indians sell to non-Indians in an Indian country: state taxes and regulations are fully in force in that situation.[52]

A different kind of result obtains in the field of liquor regulation. The Indian liquor statutes allow for tribal regulation of liquor sales within reservation boundaries[53] but under the Court's 1983 ruling in *Rice v. Rehner*[54] the states can "stack" their liquor licensing requirements on top of tribal requirements for individual Indian sellers. The question of state taxation of liquor was not decided in *Rice v. Rehner* and remains unresolved.[55] *Rice v. Rehner*, the only recent case to allow state jurisdiction in the face of any subject matter statute, is likely to have little impact outside of liquor sales. *Rice* involved an express statutory directive that sales of liquor must be "in conformity with the laws of the state in which such . . . transaction occurs" and was heavily influenced not only by this statutory language but also by long-standing special traditions specific to the sale of liquor.[56]

The Court has construed definitively several other basic statutory programs in the subject matter preemption decisions and has found activities under them to be exempt from state law. Construction of Indian schools, even when carried on by non-Indian contractors, is outside of state tax laws because of the preemptive effect of the Indian education statutes.[57] This means that all or part of the tax savings will be passed along to the tribes. The same result surely will apply to tribal hospitals and probably to other tribal buildings as well.[58]

State law is preempted broadly in regard to activities relating to the development of reservation resources. A non-Indian logging contractor operating on tribal roads and forests was held to be free of most state taxes in *White Mountain Apache Tribe v. Bracker*[59] because of the comprehensive federal scheme governing Indian timber sales, which brought the case within the reasoning in *Warren Trading Post*. Like the other natural resources cases, *White Mountain Apache* was anchored on the fact that "value" was "generated on the reservation," a factor not present in the sale of products such as cigarettes and liquor.[60] Similar factors operating in the fish and wildlife field led a unanimous Court in *New Mexico v. Mescalero Apache Tribe*[61] to hold that state license fees and regulation could not be stacked on top of an active tribal wildlife management program. With these opinions, the Court has effectively resolved against the states their high-stakes attempts to stack their severance taxes on tribal taxes when tribal mineral development occurs.[62]

The Court, then, has strictly construed Indian subject matter statutes against assertions of state jurisdiction. The strength of the law in this field is illustrated well by the dissenting opinion in *Ramah Navajo School Bd. v. Bureau of Revenue,* in which Justice Rehnquist criticized the majority opinion by arguing, accurately, that the tax immunity on Indian lands recognized by the majority opinion is greater than the parallel tax immunity for the United States.[63] The barrier state taxation of school construction on reservation lands recognized in *Ramah Navajo,* however, is just one example of the more favorable treatment that Congress accords to Indian lands as opposed to federal lands. An individual Indian in Indian country is immune from state income taxes, but an employee of the United States residing on public lands is not.[64] Congress has waived tribal sovereign immunity less extensively than it has waived the sovereign immunity of the United States.[65] States may impose severance taxes on the extraction of federal minerals but are barred from taxing the mining of most tribal minerals.[66] State law is applied in a more restrictive manner on Indian lands than it is on federal lands in other subject areas, including wildlife regulation,[67] water law,[68] and civil court jurisdiction.[69]

It is, therefore, no basis for complaint that a tribe might have some specific immunity that the United States does not possess. Such a result is entirely consistent with the general pattern of the subject matter preemption statutes and cases. Acting pursuant to the trust relationship, Congress repeatedly has promoted tribal sovereignty by enacting statutes calling for greater protections from state law for Indian tribes and Indian lands than the United States has provided for itself or for activities conducted on its lands. Indeed, a comparison between the manner in which the immunities of the two governments have become embedded in preemption law is a valuable device by which to underscore the nature and extent of the special traditions in Indian law.

Geographical Preemption

While the barrier to state jurisdiction of subject matter preemption has been employed by the Court to construe many of the major statutory schemes in Indian policy, the second bar, geographical preemption, has been used more sparingly due to the Court's preference for relying on statutory subject matter grounds to deny state law. Geographical preemption has recognized a wide arena for tribal court civil jurisdiction and a narrow ambit for state civil jurisdiction.[70] Geographical preemption also has been used to resolve cases in taxation, where tribes and reservation Indians have been accorded broad-based immunities from state laws[71] but where non-Indian buyers in Indian country have been made subject to state taxes on goods not generated within the reservation even if the non-Indian's transaction is with an Indian or Indian tribe.[72] The Court, however, has not fully explicated the nature and scope of the geographical preemption doctrine, and it is appropriate to do so here.

The opinions make it explicit that federal statutes are the sources of subject matter preemption; the statutes may be informed by notions of tribal sovereignty, but it is a statute regulating some aspect of Indian affairs, coupled with the Supremacy Clause, that prevents state regulatory authority.[73] In the cases relying on geographical preemption there is no subject matter statute, only the general provisions of a treaty or treaty substitute creating Indian country, to serve as the basis for excluding state law. Since the creation of Indian country is the source of geographical preemption, it is necessary to make a principled examination of the manner in which Indian reservations have been created in order to determine the forces that drive the geographical preemption doctrine.

Indian reservations were initially established by negotiated treaties. The tribes came to the bargaining table with existing property rights. They had an ownership interest in the aboriginal lands upon which they lived, hunted, and fished. This tribal land estate is fairly characterized as being of lesser dignity than the real property interest of the federal government: it can be extinguished by the United States unilaterally without compensation.[74] Nevertheless, in spite of the overriding federal authority, Indian aboriginal land holdings legally were secure against private parties and the states.[75] Although the United States could take aboriginal Indian land holdings without payment under the doctrine of conquest, the federal government elected to pursue treaty making in most cases due to a variety of factors including military strategy, pragmatic concerns for creating order, and moral considerations.[76] One element of these treaty negotiations, then, was to consummate land transactions between two parties with existing, shared real property interests.

Another aspect of the treaties, which has been given less attention, was to define the nature of the governmental relationship between the signatories. Again, the tribes came to the negotiations with existing rights—as governments, as well as possessors of interests in land.[77] The aboriginal governmental status of Indian tribes is no legal fiction. Political scientists, anthropologists, historians, and legal scholars from this nation and others agree that there were actual, working Indian governments before contact with Europeans. To be sure, the sophisticated federal structure of the Six Nations of the Iroquois was the clear exception. Other tribes possessed organizations less elaborate than that of the Iroquois and, of course, less elaborate than that of most governments today. In some cases, governmental organization was highly attenuated and relied mainly on the family structure. But Indian tribes set norms, adjudicated disputes, inflicted punishments, and dealt with European and other tribal governments.[78]

The nature of government on the reservations to be established by the treaties was of the first moment to the tribes when treaties were negotiated. They bargained for a separate status outside of the path of settlement and for protection of that status by the United

States. Achieving this measured separatism was a matter of urgency to most of the tribes.[79]

The United States was, in effect, acting as a surrogate for prospective settlers at the treaty negotiations. The government wanted to clear title to most Indian land so that it could be homesteaded.[80] The United States was also a surrogate for future states. It wanted to remove the cloud of Indian sovereign control from most of the West so that new states could govern most lands within their boundaries free of complications with Indians.[81] The United States was seeking to clear tribal governmental claims as well as land claims.

Tribal and federal interests converged in one essential respect. Both sides wanted the tribes isolated. They disagreed, of course, on the size of the domain. The tribes sought to retain as much land and resources as possible, while the United States intended that the units be as limited in size as possible. Some of the reservations were small, others expansive. But the nature of governmental authority on the enclaves was substantially agreed upon once their bounds were set. The reservations would be islands, first within federal territories, later within states. Within the islands, a measured separatism would prevail. The tribes would be left alone to govern themselves in most respects but would receive federal protection against intrusions by outsiders and government support in the form of goods and services. The United States was recognized as a superior party but no such acknowledgment was accorded to future states. Thus separation of tribes on the islands, outside of the path of settlement, met the needs of both sets of negotiators.[82]

No substantial change occured in these arrangements after treaty making was discontinued in 1871, although by that time the balance of military power weighed much more heavily in favor of the United States. Agreements were bilateral transactions similar to treaties, and the motivations of the parties were similar. Executive order reservations grew out of the same set of concerns, for those tribes also had aboriginal land title and governmental status; but negotiations for them were usually carried out in a less formal setting. Tribal leaders typically expressed their need for a reservation to field officers in the Indian Bureau, who would make a recommendation to Interior Department officials in Washington. A secretarial recommendation to the White House would then result in an executive order establishing the reservation.[83] Despite the difference in procedural form, these nontreaty reservations were also devices by which the federal and Indian governments resolved questions of land ownership and jurisdiction. The treaty substitutes, too, were designed by both sides to create islands for the tribes outside of the larger society.[84]

These generalizations about the motives of the United States and of the tribes, and the role they contemplated for the states, cannot be applied to every Indian reservation. This construct, however, reflects the clearly predominant historical and political pattern. Courts in this field traditionally have treated tribes in a unitary fashion when generalizations fairly can be drawn because of Congress's practice of legislating with respect to tribes generally,[85] the Constitution's generic reference to tribes, the desire to avoid repetitious litigation,[86] and the judicial practice of developing general principles to describe the powers of other governments such as states and cities.[87] Absent a special statute or a clear deviation from the historical pattern, the Court properly has utilized the shared intent of the United States and the tribes to establish a measured separatism on the islands as the core concept in resolving questions of geographical preemption.

The nature of Indian treaties and treaty substitutes, and the reservation land areas created by them, can be explored further by examining the place of tribalism within the constitutional allocation of governmental authority.[88]

Indian treaty negotiations are parallel in concept to negotiations with representatives of prospective states over statehood. Both kinds of transactions sought to resolve territorial boundaries, land ownership, and governmental authority. A statehood act is "a 'solemn agreement' which in some ways may be analogized to a contract."[89] A treaty between the United States and an Indian tribe "is essentially a contract between two sovereign nations."[90] The Tenth Amendment reserves to states those sovereign powers not delegated to the federal government in the Constitution. The treaties and treaty substitutes reserve to tribes sovereign powers not expressly or impliedly relinquished to the United States. In theory, state police powers are more permanent than tribal powers because they are constitutionally established, while tribal powers are lodged in treaties and treaty substitutes, which can be altered without recourse to the constitutional amendment process. In practice, however, congressional power to encroach on state prerogatives under the Commerce Clause, spending and taxing clauses, and Section 5 of the Fourteenth Amendment is largely unfettered, just as there are few constitutional restraints on congressional authority over Indian affairs.[91] Tribal and state police powers, in other words, were preserved in the same manner, by reservation in a bilateral agreement; were manifested in different ways, the one by treaty or treaty substitute, the other by constitutional provisions; and are both subject to the commands of Congress, although the political restraints on Congress are much greater in the case of the states. In the judiciary, the main protections for both state and tribal reserved rights are similar rules of construction establishing presumptions against congressional interference with state and tribal sovereignty.[92]

The two sets of transactions have produced disparate results in some respects. States are directly represented in Congress and possess much larger and wealthier citizenries. Accordingly, a greater quantum of reserved state powers remains undisturbed than is the case with reserved tribal powers.[93] Nevertheless, in spite of these differences, treaties and treaty substitutes creating Indian reservations are best understood as organic government documents with legal characteristics similar in many respects to the Tenth Amendment for the states.

Indian tribes are part of the constitutional structure of government. Tribal authority was not created by the Constitution—tribal sovereignty predated the formation of the United States and continued after it—but tribes were acknowledged by the Constitution in the reaffirmation of previously negotiated treaties (most of which were with Indian tribes), the two references to "Indians not taxed," and the Indian Commerce Clause.[94] Relations were then cemented through the treaties and treaty substitutes.

To be sure, although a truly substantial portion of early federal business involved Indian affairs, the Founding Fathers almost certainly assumed that tribes would simply die out under the combined weight of capitalism, Christianity, and military power. But the Framers of the Constitution, who were so seldom wrong on structure, were wrong about Indian tribes. The tribes did not die out, and the modern presidency, Congress, and Supreme Court continue squarely to acknowledge this third source of sovereignty in the

United States. Perhaps the national legislature can unilaterally withdraw all federal recognition of Indian governments, thereby effectively eliminating most actual exercises of tribal power. Still, even
if such an event were to occur, tribal sovereignty would remain alive
because it is independent of federal acknowledgment and exists at
the will of the tribes; as I discussed in chapter 3, no federal termination of tribes is final because Congress can and has reinstituted
recognition of tribes with which federal ties previously had been
severed. Thus, whether under the current system of federal–tribal
relations that has existed for two centuries or under a hypothetical
regime of termination, the rule of law requires that tribes continue
to be reconciled into our constitutional system. Accordingly, while
the Court has recognized that tribal sovereignty traces to an extraconstitutional source, it has found that direct analogies can properly
be made to those governmental entities whose ultimate source of
power is the Constitution:

> To state that Indian sovereignty is different than that of Federal, State,
> or local Governments, does not justify ignoring the principles an-
> nounced by this Court for determining whether a sovereign has waived
> its taxing authority in cases involving city, state, and federal taxes
> imposed under similar circumstances. Each of these governments has
> different attributes of sovereignty, which also may derive from differ-
> ent sources. These differences, however, do not alter the principles
> for determining whether any of these governments has waived a sov-
> ereign power through contract, and we perceive no principled reason
> for holding that the different attributes of Indian sovereignty require
> different treatment in this regard.[95]

Constitutional analysis is helpful in other respects in understanding the treaties and treaty substitutes that must be construed
to resolve competing claims of tribal and state jurisdiction when
geographical preemption is invoked. The Constitution's approval of
existing federal treaties with Indian tribes, the references to "Indians
not taxed," and the clear recognition of federal supremacy over state
authority in Indian affairs under the Indian Commerce Clause all
point to a limited state role in Indian affairs.

Further, the organic governmental side of Indian treaties and
treaty substitutes should be *construed* in the same manner as constitutional provisions. The generalities of the Constitution have been
read to give them life in new generations.[96] Even interpretivists,
who would construe open-ended constitutional guarantees narrowly,

agree that there is a place for implication; courts should conscientiously determine the "sorts of evils" toward which a provision is directed and enforce the prohibition against those evils.[97] In the case of the organic governmental documents establishing Indian country, the goal of creating a measured separatism subject to federal control and protection can fairly be identified as the major aim of both parties on jurisdictional issues. Later changes have been made by Congress, but that shared goal of both parties is the benchmark for construction. Viewed in this light, the Court's recognition of rules providing for insulation against time, a tribal right to change, and special Indian law canons of construction is appropriate, indeed necessary: these doctrines allow principled growth of those organic governmental documents in much the same way as the Constitution evolves.[98]

The concept of starting from the position of tribes as constitutionally recognized entities with reserved governmental rights on islands free of most state authority assists greatly in construing issues of geographical preemption arising under treaties and treaty substitutes. In spite of the relatively well expressed intentions of the parties at the negotiations, these documents themselves are almost always exceedingly vague. There was virtually never any express reference to states, courts, legislatures, jurisdiction, or taxation—even such issues as hunting, fishing, and water rights often went unmentioned. The tribes and the states, then, have done battle over presumptions because the party against whom the presumption operates will usually fail to meet it. The presumption against state jurisdiction and the presumption inherent in the reserved rights doctrine—the notion that tribes possess a governmental power or resource right unless it can be shown to have been abrogated—are essential ground rules if legitimate tribal interests are to be protected on the islands.[99]

The importance of construing the central objectives of the treaties and treaty substitutes to allow for principled change and growth can be appreciated by reviewing the modern cases resolved on the basis of geographical presumption. In *McClanahan v. Arizona State Tax Comm'n*[100] the Court ruled that a reservation Indian is not subject to state income tax for income earned on the reservation. There is no federal subject matter statute dealing with state income taxation of Indians. The words of the Navajo Treaty of 1868 did not bear directly on the issue.[101] The Court, however, recognized the preexisting governmental status of the tribe and found that the treaty was intended "to establish the [reservation] lands as within the exclusive sovereignty of the Navajos under general federal supervision." Later opinions on taxation have reaffirmed this construction.[102]

The results in the field of civil court jurisdiction are similarly based on a conception of treaties and treaty substitutes as organic governmental documents. In *Williams v. Lee,*[103] *Kennerly v. District County Court,* [104] and *Fisher v. District Court*[105] exclusive tribal jurisdiction over reservation-based suits against Indians was upheld in the absence of a subject matter statute or controlling treaty provision. In *Williams* and *Kennerly* the tribal governmental interest was construed to extend to cases involving non-Indian plaintiffs. *Three Affiliated Tribes of the Fort Berthold Reservation v. Wold Engineering*[106] reaffirmed the earlier cases but upheld state jurisdiction in the reverse situation: a tribe, as plaintiff, was allowed to bring suit in state court against a non-Indian over a reservation transaction. Since the tribe itself initiated the suit, no tribal interest was infringed and the rule of exclusive tribal jurisdiction was inapplicable.

The premises for geographical preemption, then, have been developed, but the doctrine has not received as much attention from the Court as subject matter preemption because statutes have been available to resolve most of the cases. Important questions remain to be resolved, especially regarding the final boundaries of state taxation, state environmental and commercial regulation, and state and tribal court jurisdiction. The future course of doctrine in geographical preemption will hold a particular moral significance because the Court must construe the organic documents in which are embedded the essential promises made by the United States to Indian tribes. It is in those documents—drafted by non-Indians in their language to consummate negotiations over complex questions of war, peace, land, and governmental character—that the United States guaranteed protection of fundamental tribal interests. The nature of those interests is the subject of the next section.

THE NEXUS WITH LEGITIMATE TRIBAL INTERESTS

Several threads of doctrine, all of which are integral to defining the special legal and political nature of Indian country, depend upon

an analysis of legitimate tribal interests. In cases where state jurisdiction is asserted and subject matter preemption is raised as a bar,
tribal sovereignty forms the backdrop against which federal statutes
are read. When the analysis rests upon geographical preemption,
tribal and federal courts must determine whether state jurisdiction
would impermissibly infringe upon tribal sovereignty. If a tribe
seeks to assert civil jurisdiction against non-Indians, the question is
whether there is some direct connection between the regulation
and some important tribal interest. In Indian water, hunting, and
fishing cases (which usually turn on whether a state has authority
to regulate Indians), the Court has developed rules that allocate
sufficient resources to meet the needs of the tribes. The validity of
federal legislation, whether it operates to the benefit or detriment
of tribes, depends on whether there is some rational tie between
the congressional action and tribal interests. The opinions seldom
cross-cite among these bodies of doctrine within Indian law, but in
each of these areas crucial issues are resolved or implicated by a
common denominator, an assessment of the existence and scope of
legitimate tribal interests.[107]

The analysis of these and other questions is forced toward a
consideration of tribal interests because most issues look back in
some fashion to the formation of the reservations. Many cases require construction of the treaties or treaty substitutes, pure and
simple. Others involve statutes not directly related to the creation
of Indian country, but most of those laws are premised on the
existence of the reservation system, so that it becomes necessary to
explore the purposes of the transactions establishing the reservations.[108] The identification of legitimate tribal interests is the touch-
stone for refining and specifying the general promises in the old
laws.

The modern decisions have recognized various legitimate tribal
interests that, taken together, have the potential of fulfilling the
major promise made by the United States to Indian tribes—the
guarantee of a measured separatism. As I discussed in the previous
section, the Court has announced a general model of expansive tribal
control and a limited state role in Indian country, but more particularized concepts have been used to define tribal interests in modern times.

First, the opinions recognize an overriding tribal interest in the economic development of the reservations—the measured separatism cannot exist without a viable economic base. There are several aspects to this. Tribes as proprietors own substantial reserved resources. They also possess as governments the authority to regulate and tax resource-related activities within the reservation. Further, the cases recognize a more general tribal interest in promoting reservation business activity, which takes the form of exemptions of Indian and non-Indian businesses from state regulatory and tax authority. The tradition of tribal sovereignty "is reflected and encouraged in a number of congressional enactments demonstrating a firm federal policy of promoting tribal self-sufficiency and economic development." The opinions have been rigorous in assessing negative impacts on reservation development and have disallowed state taxes because the economic burden would ultimately rest on the tribe even though the legal incidence falls on non-Indian businesses.[109]

Second, the Court also has respected contemporary demands on tribal governments by acknowledging a tribal interest in providing services to reservation residents. The authority of tribes to tax non-Indians was justified because "[t]his power enables a tribal government to raise revenues for its essential services."[110] In light of the statutory scheme promoting tribal self-government, the Court has made the telling comment that "'[i]t simply does not make sense to expect the tribes to carry out municipal functions approved and mandated by Congress without being able to exercise at least minimal taxing powers, whether they take the form of real estate taxes, leasehold taxes, or severance taxes.' "[111] This recognition of the responsibilities of tribes today—their duty to act as municipalities and to provide the amenities commonly expected from governments—is central to a definition of legitimate tribal interests.

The cases also stand for a tribe's interest, as a community, in setting norms and adjudicating wrongs in Indian country. The rule of exclusive tribal jurisdiction in civil cases brought by non-Indians against tribal members is a powerful symbol of this concept. Tribal regulatory jurisdiction and tribal court jurisdiction over crimes committed by Indians are other aspects of this prerogative. Importantly, even though private suits may be involved, these are ultimately matters of tribal concern. Individual litigation is conducted pursuant to a body of statutory and common law that reflects community

standards. Tribal jurisdiction thus recognizes the right of tribal councils to enact laws governing reservation relationships and of tribal
judges to find law from tribal traditions and contemporary conditions
if no tribal statute is applicable. Just as tribes, as municipalities,
have the ability to raise revenue to provide community services, so
also do they have the ability and duty to build bodies of law to guide
community relationships.[112]

The Court has announced several limitations on these three
primary tribal interests in achieving economic development, providing governmental services, and resolving community standards.
First, the Court has found that one of the purposes of the treaties
(and of treaty substitutes) was to protect non-Indians from "unwar-
ranted intrusions on their personal liberty." This, of course, formed
the basis of the rule in *Oliphant v. Suquamish Indian Tribe*[113] that
tribes lack inherent authority over non-Indians in criminal matters.
Such considerations probably influenced the development of the
less restrictive doctrine in civil matters allowing tribal regulation of
non-Indians if it directly relates to some important tribal interest.[114]

Another limitation on tribal interests relates more directly to
the contemporary economic setting. In the context of off-reservation
fishing rights, and apparently of water rights as well, special tribal
resource rights are limited to a ceiling necessary to provide a "moderate living."[115] It is difficult to predict how future decisions will
define the nature of this cap, but the Court's language in its only
discussion of the subject suggests that the standard has a narrow
application. Just two examples of circumstances triggering the ceiling were given—when a tribe dwindles to a few members and when
a tribe abandons its fisheries in pursuit of other means of support
(and, presumably, attempts to sell its resource rights). This hardly
suggests that courts are to engage in a comprehensive examination
of the economic circumstances of tribes to determine whether their
members have exceeded a moderate standard of living. Such inquiries would run counter to the desirability of developing unitary
rules applicable to all tribes.[116] In any event, for the foreseeable
future most such examinations would come up dry in light of the
economic conditions in Indian country.

Two other limitations defining legitimate tribal interests in the
economic sphere, however, have a broader impact. They are the
related requirements that tribal activities should be tied to "value

generated on the reservation" and that tribal revenue raising be related to the provision of governmental services. The reservation-generated value consideration was set out first in the *Colville* cigarette tax case, where Justice White's 1980 opinion upheld a state tax on non-Indians in part because the tribe was luring outsiders to the reservation—the tribe was attempting to "market its tax exemption" by selling a product produced off the reservation to persons who had no reservation ties and who did not receive tribal services.[117] These limitations were not applied in later cases involving tribal timber, minerals, and wildlife.[118]

The requirements of reservation-generated value and tribally provided services have an admirable side effect. Both give tribes an incentive to engage in activities—the production of goods and services and the institution of governmental programs. Thus these "limits" in fact encourage tribes to expand reservation operations and to become increasingly substantial, and permanent, entities.

Legitimate tribal interests, in the main, have been construed generously in favor of the tribes over the last twenty-five years. Tribal economic capability, not a specific concern at treaty time, properly has been viewed with sufficient expansiveness so that the legal system offers the reservations the realistic potential to operate as viable home lands in modern times. A broad tribal interest in economic development is called for by the self-determination legislation of the 1970s and 1980s; by the tribes' right to change, to adapt to new social and economic conditions; and by the idea that the treaties and treaty substitutes are organic governmental charters that, like the Constitution, should evolve over time to meet new needs.[119] The policies upon which the rules of construction in Indian law are based—the duties inherent in the trust relationship and the parties' unequal posture as to language and military power—also support an expansive set of tribal interests in a different age.[120] There is still ample room for the states to regulate and raise revenue to meet their proper governmental concerns within Indian country.[121]

Doubtless, legitimate tribal interests could be formulated in other, and perhaps more definitive, terms. My primary aim here is to identify the concept of tribal interests as a useful device by which to bind together aspects of doctrine that are now treated disparately. The choice of legitimate tribal interests as the benchmark of analysis is nondoctrinaire: it simply collects ideas, some of which benefit

tribes and some of which do not, that are embodied in the treaties
and treaty substitutes and that can efficiently and fairly focus judicial
analysis. The tribal interest approach is less cumbersome than the
three-part balancing test—involving state, federal, and tribal concerns—employed in some cases.[122] In any event, the Court has in
fact regularly spent the greater part of its analyses on tribal interests.[123] Focusing the analysis of tribal–state jurisdictional conflicts
in Indian country on an assessment of tribal interests properly puts
the emphasis on the transactions establishing Indian country, which
remain the center point of federal Indian policy and law.

MAJORITY WITHIN A MINORITY: THE QUANDARY OF POLITICAL REPRESENTATION

Many of the most perplexing problems in Indian law involve the
rights of non-Indians, especially residents, in Indian country. Tribes
are moving ahead with newly adopted codes in sensitive areas such
as land use, health, water, and environmental regulation. Increasingly, tribal governments are exercising their taxing authority. Tribal
courts are handling larger caseloads, including litigation involving
non-Indians. Yet claims against tribes are often barred, in both tribal
or federal court, by tribal sovereign immunity.

Non-Indian residents raise a range of objections. Some com-
plain, with considerable stridency, of racism, present or potential,
against them. When confronted with arguments of tribal reliance
interests based on sovereign powers guaranteed by treaty, these
non-Indians counter with a reliance interest of their own; as noted
above, their predecessors were invited to the reservations by homestead or related policies, and there was seldom an indication that
they would be governed by an Indian tribe. Most fundamentally,
however, the non-Indians point to defects in the political process:
because they cannot become tribal members, they lack the ability
to vote in tribal elections, hold tribal office, or participate in decision
making.[124]

When presented with these concerns about political representation, the Court has given them short shrift in the few direct discussions of the issue.[125] Yet, legalities aside, many fair-minded
observers believe that the complaints of non-Indians raise legitimate
policy questions. The lack of political representation plainly worries

lower court judges and some or all members of the Supreme Court.[126] The tribes as well suffer dangers by this perceived unfairness. If non-Indians have no recourse against tribal governments, then inevitably in close cases judges will be tempted simply to eliminate the potential unfairness to non-Indians by holding that tribal jurisdiction does not exist in the first place. This may have occurred already in a few difficult lower court cases.[127]

In one sense no explanation for tribal authority over resident non-Indians can be fully satisfactory. The quandary of political representation dramatizes the anomalous position Indian tribal governments hold in this country. One cannot completely reconcile classic political rights, as enjoyed by citizens in other political units in the United States, with the kind of rights that exist within Indian tribal governments for the fundamental reason that Indian tribal governments are literally foreign: they exist outside of the Constitution.[128]

This is not to say that we must proceed wholly without analogy. The concerns of reservation non-Indians can all be answered on a certain level. Racism is not present here—Indian tribes are political, not race-based, entities.[129] Homestead patents are just deeds that involved only title to real property and carried with them no express or implied warranties as to political control.[130] So, too, can the difficult political issues be explained, especially by drawing comparisons with international law.[131] People commonly are regulated and taxed in jurisdictions in which they have no political rights: when they travel to another state or foreign country; when they work in another city, state, or country; and when they own a second home in another state, county, or nation. Under this kind of analysis, even the most fundamental political right—that of citizens to vote in the jurisdiction of their residence—has not been denied to non-Indian residents in Indian country: they can vote in state, county, and city elections. In any event, their claim to participate in local tribal affairs is imperfect because they lack citizenship in the local government, the tribe.

Our jurisprudence, then, has recognized tribal authority as being both preconstitutional and extraconstitutional. These principles are premises for the conclusions that American Indian governments can be, for example, theocratic, hereditary, and race-based in citizenship. Powerful moral and historical considerations support this special tribal status. European nations recognized similar notions half a millennium ago, and in the United States all three federal branches have acknowledged the special attributes of Indian tribal sovereignty from the beginning.[132]

All of this is not likely, however, to remove the philosophical disquiet. The United States has gone to extraordinary lengths to provide a democratic form of governance and to guarantee protections against racial discrimination. Obviously, Indians have been denied access to the political process and have been subjected to racism aplenty, but the democratic process and all modern protections against discrimination are now fully available to them.[133] When Indian tribal governments act, however, some of the system's guards do not apply. How can we be sure that non-Indians within Indian territorial jurisdiction will be treated squarely? What is the proper rule of the judiciary?

My general formulation, which I will set out in more detail below, is that federal judicial review of tribal action is often appropriate and perhaps should be expanded. Procedure, however, should be sharply distinguished from substance. Courts should play a prudential role and recognize broad tribal authority over non-Indians as a necessary predicate for achieving the measured separatism promised in the treaties and treaty substitutes. Respecting substantive tribal authority over non-Indians while allowing limited federal review in individual cases of alleged injustices is the best method of substantially reconciling the legitimate interests of both tribes and non-Indians. Importantly, this prudential judicial role is appropriate because there are several other viable checks against arbitrary tribal action.

One area of exploration on procedural issues is the continuing viability of *Santa Clara Pueblo v. Martinez*.[134] *Santa Clara*, which held that a tribal member is barred by tribal sovereign immunity from obtaining federal judicial review of a tribal council decision concerning membership in the tribe, is in some respects one of the modern decisions most favorable to the tribes. It recognized the preconstitutional and extraconstitutional status of tribes, employed the canons of construction strictly in favor of tribal prerogatives, and gave an expansive reading to tribal sovereign immunity.[135]

The *Santa Clara* opinion, however, accomplishes little to provide a fair resolution of the legitimately troubling situation of reservation non-Indians. Title I of the Indian Civil Rights Act of 1968

(ICRA) imposes free exercise, due process, and equal protection constraints on tribes but *Santa Clara* refused to imply any federal remedies, finding that only tribal forums are available to enforce the ICRA. The one remedy expressly provided by the ICRA, the writ of habeas corpus to review tribal criminal prosecutions, is irrelevant for non-Indians, since tribes lack criminal jurisdiction over them.[136] Thus *Santa Clara* results in the anomaly of a federal civil rights act that provides only very limited federal remedies to enforce it.

Santa Clara does leave open federal judicial review in some circumstances outside of criminal cases. First, although the Court has foreclosed most suits against tribes and tribal officials, in some instances relief may be obtained against tribal officials acting outside the scope of their official duties.[137] Second, non-Indians can presumably raise offsetting claims, arising from the same transaction, when they are sued by tribes.[138] Third, a federal forum may be available against federal officials if they have reviewed the tribal action that is the basis of the grievance.[139]

There is another instance, of considerable importance to the rights of non-Indians in Indian country, in which *Santa Clara* does not block federal review. In 1985, the Court found in *National Farmers Union Ins. Cos. v. Crow Tribe of Indians*[140] that a party in a private civil tribal court action can, after fully exhausting tribal remedies, invoke federal-question jurisdiction and obtain a determination by a federal district court as to whether the tribe possesses jurisdiction. The case involved a non-Indian defendant in a personal injury case arguing that the tribal court lacked sufficient contacts under the "tribal interest" test.

The 1985 decisions demonstrate that non-Indians can obtain federal review of many major questions of tribal power. *National Farmers* allowed an insurance company to obtain a ruling on the jurisdiction of the tribal court. *Kerr-McGee Corp. v. Navajo Tribe,*[141] in which mineral companies were able to avoid tribal sovereign immunity by seeking a declaration as against tribal officials, permitted a test of tribal power to levy severance taxes. These kinds of questions involving the scope of tribal judicial and regulatory authority have been among the most pressing issues raised by non-Indians in Indian country; the existence of a federal remedy in this context is a major step toward meeting the legitimate interests of non-Indians.

The rule in *Santa Clara,* however, still appears to prohibit federal courts from looking at alleged individual acts of discrimination by tribal officials. Take the examples of *National Farmers* and *Kerr-McGee.* Companies in those circumstances are allowed to test the scope of tribal jurisdiction, but if they lose on that question they appear to have no recourse if a tribal judge or jury openly and clearly favors the Indian party or if a tribal tax administrator enforces the tax code only against non-Indian companies. Since the equal protection and due process provisions of the Constitution do not apply to tribes, the only basis for a cause of action is the ICRA— and the Court in *Santa Clara* has announced that no federal cause of action, other than habeas corpus, lies to enforce the ICRA.

The matter cannot be finally resolved by stating that instances of arbitrary and discriminatory conduct by tribal officials may be rare. The overriding fact remains that *Santa Clara* is perceived as a fundamental barrier to a just legal process in Indian country by creating the specter of tribal powers that cannot be checked outside of the tribe. The legislative history of the ICRA gives substantial indications that Congress intended for federal courts to be available to enforce the rights enumerated in the ICRA.[142] At the same time, it bears repeating that there are powerful counterbalancing considerations—abridgments of tribal sovereignty should be construed strictly, as the thrust of the opinion in *Santa Clara* recognized.[143]

Perhaps a better approach, however, and one more consonant with Congress's will, is that federal courts should have jurisdiction to engage in limited judicial review when ICRA rights are allegedly abridged by tribal institutions. Reviewing courts would be required to respect tribal traditions and reservation conditions.[144] Tribal decisions could be overturned only upon a showing based on an elevated test, such as the arbitrary and capricious standard.[145] The requirement of exhaustion of tribal remedies should be rigorously observed.[146] Exhaustion means all recourse that a reasonable person familiar with the system would pursue.[147] In Indian tribes, for example, tribal councils, which are typically small, relatively informal units, often perform some of the functions of courts in the Anglo-American system. Thus exhaustion of remedies in the Indian context, in order to be appropriately sensitive to the special qualities of tribal legal institutions, will often entail a serious attempt to enlist the aid of the tribal council.

Ultimately, limited federal review as proposed here accords tribal governments much the same kind of deference, premised on a presumption of regularity, that federal courts accord state institutions. Such an approach is appropriate because tribes are exercising local sovereignty in much the same way that states do outside of Indian country. This is the real message of the 1985 decision in *National Farmers*, where the Court, citing authority involving state courts and plainly conceptualizing tribes as direct analogues to states, made these concluding comments in requiring that the tribal court should first decide the question of tribal jurisdiction before any review by the federal court:

> We believe that examination should be conducted in the first instance in the Tribal Court itself. Our cases have often recognized that Congress is committed to a policy of supporting tribal self-government and self-determination. That policy favors a rule that will provide the forum whose jurisdiction is being challenged the first opportunity to evaluate the factual and legal bases for the challenge. Moreover the orderly administration of justice in the federal court will be served by allowing a full record to be developed in the Tribal Court before either the merits or any question concerning appropriate relief is addressed. The risks of the kind of "procedural nightmare" that has allegedly developed in this case will be minimized if the federal court stays its hand until after the Tribal Court has had a full opportunity to determine its own jurisdiction and to rectify any errors it may have made. Exhaustion of tribal court remedies, moreover, will encourage tribal courts to explain to the parties the precise basis for accepting jurisdiction, and will also provide other courts with the benefit of their expertise in such matters in the event of further judicial review.[148]

Federal review of this kind would be a minor incursion on tribal sovereignty and would meet legitimate concerns about unfair treatment by tribes of both Indians and non-Indians. It would amount to a safety valve allowing serious injustices, real and perceived, to be heard. The admitted intrusion on tribal sovereignty would be outweighed by the benefits from the defusing.

So let us suppose that it is good policy and law to allow limited federal judicial review of alleged arbitrary, and possibly racist, conduct by tribal institutions. The question remains how courts should approach the task of defining substantive powers of Indian tribes over non-Indians.

The settled principles of preconstitutional and extraconstitutional tribal status, coupled with the promise of a viable, evolving separatism in the treaties and treaty substitutes, justify race-based tribal governments without political representation by nonmembers. The courts should respect these precepts and provide latitude to tribes by generously construing tribal powers over nonmembers. Congress, not the courts, should make alterations based on expediency.[149]

The Court has recognized its special institutional obligation to protect minority rights. This duty is evidenced by the *Carolene Products* footnote, by the desegregation decisions, and by other decisions protective of racial minorities, and has recently been expanded upon in John Hart Ely's *Democracy and Distrust*.[150] Beginning with the Marshall Trilogy the tradition has been especially rich in Indian law.[151] The Court has forthrightly acknowledged the need for protecting Indians from the states: "Because of the local ill feeling, the people of the States where they [Indians] are found are often their deadliest enemies."[152] In *Williams v. Lee*,[153] the first case of the modern era, the Court flatly stated: "The cases in this Court have consistently guarded the authority of Indian governments over their reservations." In 1984 the Court reaffirmed its "traditional solicitude for the Indian tribes."[154] A continuing theme of the modern opinions is for the Court to affirm the existence of Indian rights, with the caveat that Congress can make adjustments pursuant to its power over Indian affairs.[155]

I well appreciate the apparent irony of citing *Carolene Products* and Dean Ely in support of the proposition that courts should broadly construe the powers of tribes over nonmembers: Ely and other process theorists hold that the essential function of the Constitution is to insure access to all aspects of the political process. Superficially, a process-based analysis seems to call for granting non-Indians rights within tribal governments or, at the least, strictly construing tribal powers over non-Indians. Process theory, however, seems to me not to support the rights of the non-Indian minority in Indian country. First, process theory is constitutional theory, and the Constitution does not limit Indian tribes on the questions at issue here. Thus the policies so firmly embedded in the Constitution are simply inapplicable. Second, to the extent that participational rights have a value independent of the Constitution (and they do) or to the extent that they have been applied to the tribes by statute, this is a situation in which the "minority" of non-Indians is in fact a majority. Process theory is nothing if not an attempt to analyze constitutional law systemically. The non-Indian minority in Indian country may not have direct participational rights in tribal government, but non-Indians have political clout in the Department of Interior, Congress, and state governments due to their superior numbers and economic position. Non-Indians in Indian country, then, should be treated as a majority for the purpose of process-based analysis: the courts should fulfill their traditional obligation of protecting minority rights, in this case Indian tribal rights.

There are other institutional reasons why the Court should play a prudential role by broadly construing tribal powers, even when non-Indians are involved, and leaving Congress to make corrections if necessary. Most fundamentally, no one now knows whether alleged abuses against non-Indians are either serious or widespread. As I discussed earlier, judicial opinions in Indian law usually involve just one tribe but apply generically to all tribes. Thus if a court is influenced by an individual flagrant abuse and departs from principle to deny tribal powers, the rights of all tribes are implicated. The same is true of presumed but unproven abuses that a judge may unconsciously employ as a backdrop in a particular case. Whether abuses exist and, if they do, whether they are sufficiently serious to warrant curtailing tribal powers are matters that Congress is best equipped to resolve. A legislature is not bound by the facts of just one case. Congress has investigative and oversight powers designed to produce a comprehensive record. Institutionally, the courts are best suited to the judiciary's traditional role of holding firmly to historic principles that are protective of tribal prerogatives.

Further, events are rapidly occurring in the field that justify a judicial stance protective of broad substantive tribal authority over non-Indians. The possibility of abuses by tribes against non-Indians is lessened by several developments. As I discussed earlier in this chapter, federal judicial review is left open to curtail many abuses of tribal power without denying the existence of tribal power. The Department of the Interior has asserted its power to oversee tribal codes that would regulate or tax non-Indians. Some tribes have set up advisory boards that allow nonvoting reservation residents to influence policy on matters affecting them. Others have established special assessment districts that extend the vote to all persons within the districts. Regional courts of appeals have been established in the Pacific Northwest and in Oklahoma so that an intertribal appellate court can hear appeals, removed from the pressures of the reservation where the case arises. A movement of sweeping importance is the boom in intergovernmental agreements, in which states or local governments have settled jurisdictional arrangements with tribes by negotiation. In several recent instances, state legislatures have enacted laws at the joint request of tribes and states to settle differences.[156]

These are all enormously healthy developments because they allow for pragmatic, on-the-ground dispute resolution by the parties actually involved. The courts should allow this process to continue, confident that the judiciary's historic prudential role of protecting rights of American Indians will be crafted into specific shapes by legislation, administrative action, and, most important, negotiation. Ultimately, if the process does continue, then tribal governments will at long last be given the chance to conquer the effects of time that have stilled tribal activity for so long.

Conclusion

The field of Indian law rests mainly on the old treaties and treaty substitutes. To understand them, one must reach back to aboriginal sovereignty and forward to the epochal changes that have occurred since in law and civilization. But the inquiry usually returns to these unique documents and their unique promises.

The decisions of the modern era have given contemporary content to these old laws. The cases stand for a rule of general exclusion of state law and general applicability of tribal law within Indian country. That rule, which is not absolute, depends in individual situations upon the existence of a relationship to one of several legitimate tribal interests, including an interest in development of tribal resources, broadly defined; an interest in the provision of community and social services by the tribes or by Indian or non-Indian entrepreneurs; and an interest in dispute resolution by the tribes themselves. The decisions of the last quarter of a century also stand for the idea that this promise of a measured separatism normally should not be eroded by the press of civilization or the passage of time. At the same time, tribes have the right to grow and to take on the accoutrements of modern society in order to implement legitimate tribal interests.

Although not all of the aspects of the treaties and treaty substitutes have been enforced, in my view the net result of the decisions of the modern era has been to allow the measured separatism to proceed in a fair and reasonably expansive way. The tribes will be able to obtain sufficient fish and game for subsistence, religious, and commercial purposes. Water—the sine qua non of any society in the dry West—will be available in sufficient quantities for nearly all tribes. The state–tribal tax and business development cases allow a modest but meaningful shelter on reservations; it will protect Indian enterprises and entice some non-Indian business to Indian country, thereby providing revenues to the tribes and encouraging the growth of support services in communities that often lack even the most basic amenities. Tribes can exert control over many aspects of law and order on their reservations. At long last they can also control the education and custody of their young people.

These islands, then, which for generations have epitomized not much more than a wrenching rural poverty, are steadily moving toward a fulfillment of the ultimate promise, that they be homelands. Generalizations on this score are treacherous because there are so many tribes and because the conditions among them vary so widely. But if you talk with Indian people you find that conditions in Indian country have improved since the 1960s, even since 1980. This is due most prominently to the will of Indian people, but they in turn have relied most prominently on the law.

There are no exact answers as to why the law has responded as it has. Surely nothing was inevitable about it. Indian law in, say, 1959, plainly could have moved toward a judicial termination of Indian tribes or toward a legal context in which Indian tribes would be not much more than toy governments.

After my long journey through this body of law, I have reached my own conclusion as to why the field has developed as it has, as to the deepest reasons why the Court has refused to allow American Indian tribes to be engulfed by the passage of time.

These old laws emanate a kind of morality profoundly rare in our jurisprudence. It is far more complicated than a sense of guilt or obligation, emotions frequently associated with Indian policy. Somehow, those old negotiations—typically conducted in but a few days on hot, dry plains between midlevel federal bureaucrats and seemingly ragtag Indian leaders—are tremendously evocative. Real promises were made on those plains, and the Senate of the United States approved them, making them real laws. My sense is that most judges cannot shake that. Their training, experience, and, finally,

their humanity—all of the things that blend into the rule of law—
brought them up short when it came to signing opinions that would
have obliterated those promises.

No, this is no perfect body of law. But the thrust of it has hewed
to principle in the face of agonizingly powerful forces to abandon
principle in the name of societal change. Now, two and a half decades
after *Williams,* most branches of Indian law have stabilized.

This relative stability should now itself be honored. To the
tribes, their chief task always has been not just to survive but to
build traditional and viable homelands for their people. The original
promise of a measured separatism might have allowed that goal to
be reached, but the work was interrupted by a century of assimilationist policies and their effects. Perhaps, at last, the tribes can
begin to withdraw from the judicial system and train their energies
on fulfilling their historic task of creating workable islands of Indi-
anness within the larger society.

Supreme Court Cases in Indian Law during the Modern Era

1958 Term
1. Williams v. Lee, 358 U.S. 217 (1959), upholding exclusive tribal judicial jurisdiction over actions involving contracts entered into on an Indian reservation between a non-Indian plaintiff and an Indian defendant.

1959 Term
2. Federal Power Comm'n v. Tuscarora Indian Nation, 362 U.S. 99 (1960), construing the Federal Power Act, 16 U.S.C. §§ 796 (2) and 797 (e) (1982), as authorizing a licensee of the Federal Power Commission to take lands owned in fee simple by an Indian tribe upon the payment of just compensation.

1961 Term
3. Seymour v. Superintendent, 368 U.S. 351 (1962), upholding exclusive federal judicial jurisdiction over prosecutions for offenses covered by the Major Crimes Act that are committed by an Indian on lands held in fee patent by a non-Indian within the exterior boundaries of an Indian reservation.
4. Metlakatla Indian Community v. Egan, 369 U.S. 45 (1962), upholding the secretary of the interior's authority to license the manner in which the Metlakatlan Indians fish on lands reserved for the use of the tribe by the Act of March 3, 1891.

5. Organized Village of Kake v. Egan, 369 U.S. 60 (1962), striking down the authority of the secretary of the interior to authorize fishing by Thlinget Indians, for whom no reservation had been set aside, in a manner contrary to state law.

1962 Term

6. Arizona v. California, 373 U.S. 546 (1963), upholding the authority of the United States to reserve water rights for Indian reservations originally established by executive order; defining the quantity of water reserved for Indian reservations as being enough water to satisfy the future, as well as present, needs of the reservations, including enough water to irrigate all of the practicably irrigable acreage on the reservations.

1964 Term

7. Warren Trading Post v. Arizona State Tax Comm'n, 380 U.S. (1965), striking down the imposition of a state gross receipts tax on income earned by a federally licensed trader on sales to Indians on a reservation.

1965 Term

8. Arizona v. California, 383 U.S. 269 (1965), ordering the secretary of the interior and states of Arizona, California, and Nevada to furnish the Court with a list of their present perfected rights (including Indian reserved rights) and claimed priority dates to waters in the Colorado River.

1967 Term

9. Poafpybitty v. Skelly Oil Co., 390 U.S. 365 (1968), upholding an Indian landowner's standing to sue to enforce an oil and gas lease, approved by the secretary of the interior, for use on land held by the Indian under a trust patent.

10. Peoria Tribe of Indians v. United States, 390 U.S. 468 (1968), holding the United States liable for the investment that would have been earned on the proceeds from the sale of lands ceded by the tribe had those lands been sold at their public auction value, as required by the Treaty of May 30, 1854.

11. Menominee Tribe of Indians v. United States, 391 U.S. 404 (1968), upholding the Menominee Tribe's retention of its treaty hunting and fishing rights despite the Termination Act of 1954.

12. Puyallup Tribe v. Department of Game, 391 U.S. 392 (1968), upholding the state's authority to regulate the manner in which a tribe exercises its off-reservation treaty fishing rights where such regulations are reasonable and necessary to conserve fish and wildlife resources and are nondiscriminatory.

1968 Term

13. Makah Indian Tribe v. Tax Comm'n, 393 U.S. 8 (1968) (per curiam), dismissing, for lack of a substantial federal question, the tribe's appeal of the Washington Supreme Court's holding that application of a state cigarette tax to wholesalers who distribute cigarettes to retailers doing business on the reservation did not violate the Indian Commerce Clause, U.S. Const., art. III, § 8, cl. 3.

1969 Term

14. Tooahnippah v. Hickel, 397 U.S. 598 (1970), striking down the secretary of the interior's authority to disapprove an Indian's testamentary disposition of trust property on the secretary's subjective belief that the disposition is not "just and equitable."

15. Choctaw Nation v. Oklahoma, 397 U.S. 620 (1970), upholding the Cherokee, Chickasaw, and Choctaw Nations' title to lands underlying a ninety-six mile navigable stretch of the Arkansas River.

1970 Term

16. Kennerly v. District Court, 400 U.S. 423 (1971), striking down asserted state judicial jurisdiction over civil contract actions brought by a non-Indian against an Indian concerning a transaction occurring on the reservation.

17. United States v. Southern Ute Tribe, 402 U.S. 159 (1971), barring, as res judicata, the tribe's claim for compensation for lands ceded pursuant to the Act of June 15, 1880.

1971 Term

18. Affiliated Ute Citizens v. United States, 406 U.S. 128 (1972), upholding the termination of the federal government's supervision of trust property held by individual mixed-blood Utes after the secretary of the interior's issuance of a termination proclamation.

1972 Term

19. United States v. Jim, 409 U.S. 80 (1972), upholding Congress's authority to redistribute mineral royalties generated by tribal lands to a larger class of Indian beneficiaries without incurring a Fifth Amendment obligation to compensate the original, smaller class of Indian beneficiaries.

20. Mescalero Apache Tribe v. Jones, 411 U.S. 145 (1973), upholding the imposition of a state gross receipts tax on income earned from a tribal business conducted on off-reservation lands where the tax does not discriminate against Indians.

21. McClanahan v. Arizona State Tax Comm'n, 411 U.S. 164 (1973), striking down the imposition of a state tax on income earned on a reservation by a tribal member who resides on the reservation.

22. Keeble v. United States, 412 U.S. 205 (1973), construing the Major Crimes Act as entitling Indian criminal defendants to a jury instruction on a lesser-included offense that is not an offense enumerated in the act.

23. United States v. Mason, 412 U.S. 391 (1973), upholding a federal administrator's authority to rely on prior Supreme Court cases that the Court has not later overruled or questioned in discharging the government's fiduciary obligations to Indians.

24. Mattz v. Arnett, 412 U.S. 481 (1973), upholding the continued existence of the Klamath River Reservation despite the Act of June 17, 1892, which opened the lands within the reservation to settlement under the homestead laws.

1973 Term

25. Department of Game v. Puyallup Tribe, 414 U.S. 44 (1973), striking down, as discriminatory against Indians, a state regulation that completely banned net fishing for steelhead trout.

26. Oneida Indian Nation v. County of Oneida, 414 U.S. 661 (1974), upholding federal judicial jurisdiction over an action brought by a tribe claiming that political subdivisions of the state were interfering with the tribe's possessory rights to aboriginal lands.

27. Morton v. Ruiz, 415 U.S. 199 (1974), striking down a regulation of the Bureau of Indian Affairs (BIA) that denied general assistance to unassimilated Indians living in an Indian community near their native reservation.

28. Morton v. Mancari, 417 U.S. 535 (1974), upholding a BIA reg-

ulation providing for Indian preference in promotional opportunities within the agency.

1974 Term

29. United States v. Mazurie, 419 U.S. 544 (1975), upholding Congress's authority to delegate to tribal governments the authority to regulate the distribution of alcoholic beverages on a reservation.

30. Antoine v. Washington, 420 U.S. 194 (1975), upholding Congress's authority to enact legislation limiting a state's power to regulate tribal hunting and fishing rights on lands ceded by the tribe.

31. DeCoteau v. District County Court, 420 U.S. 425 (1975), construing the Act of March 3, 1891, as having disestablished the Lake Traverse Indian Reservation.

32. Chemehuevi Tribe of Indians v. Federal Power Comm'n, 420 U.S. 395 (1975), construing § 4 (e) of the Federal Power Act (16 U.S.C. §§ 791a–823 (1982)) as not authorizing the Federal Power Commission to issue licenses for the construction of thermal-electric power plants.

1975 Term

33. Fisher v. District Court, 424 U.S. 382 (1976) (per curiam), upholding exclusive tribal jurisdiction over an adoption proceeding where all of the parties to the proceeding were members of the tribe and resided on the reservation.

34. Colorado River Water Conservation Dist. v. United States, 424 U.S. 800, (1976), upholding the dismissal of an action brought by the United States in federal court to adjudicate federal and Indian reserved water rights when there is a concurrent adjudication of the same issues in state court.

35. Moe v. Confederated Salish & Kootenai Tribes, 425 U.S. 463 (1976), striking down the imposition of a state cigarette tax on on-reservation sales by Indians to Indians; upholding the imposition of a state cigarette tax on on-reservation sales by Indians to non-Indians.

36. Northern Cheyenne Tribe v. Hollowbreast, 425 U.S. 649 (1976), upholding the authority of Congress to transfer mineral rights from individual Indian allottees to their tribe without compensation where the act authorizing allotment of tribal lands

severed the mineral and surface estates.

37. Bryan v. Itasca County, 426 U.S. 373 (1976), striking down the imposition of a state tax levied on personal property located on a Public Law 280 reservation.

1976 Term

38. Delaware Tribal Business Comm. v. Weeks, 430 U.S. 73 (1977), upholding the exclusion of the Kansas Delawares from an act distributing judgment funds to the Delaware Tribe.

39. Rosebud Sioux Tribe v. Kneip, 430 U.S. 584 (1977), construing the acts of April 23, 1904, March 2, 1907, and May 30, 1910, as having disestablished a portion of the Rosebud Sioux Reservation.

40. United States v. Antelope, 430 U.S. 641 (1977), upholding the first degree murder conviction of an Indian under the Major Crimes Act where the conviction of a non-Indian for the same offense in state court would have placed a higher burden of proof upon the state.

41. Puyallup Tribe, Inc. v. Department of Game, 433 U.S. 165 (1977), upholding the state's authority to regulate the tribe's on-reservation treaty fishing rights when such regulations are reasonable and necessary for the conservation of fish.

1977 Term

42. Oliphant v. Suquamish Indian Tribe, 435 U.S. 191 (1978), striking down tribal jurisdiction over crimes committed by non-Indians on a reservation.

43. Untied States v. Wheeler, 435 U.S. 313 (1978), upholding successive tribal and federal prosecutions of an Indian for crimes arising out of the same offense committed on a reservation.

44. Santa Clara Pueblo v. Martinez, 436 U.S. 49 (1978), holding the writ of habeas corpus to be the exclusive remedy available for alleged violations of the Indian Civil Rights Act.

45. United States v. John, 437 U.S. 634 (1978), striking down state jurisdiction over the prosecution of an Indian for an offense included in the Major Crimes Act and committed on lands purchased for the Mississippi Choctaws, a remnant band of the Choctaw Tribe.

1978 Term

46. Washington v. Confederated Bands of the Yakima Indian Nation, 439 U.S. 463 (1979), upholding the authority of an optional

Public Law 280 state to assert partial jurisdiction over an Indian reservation.

47. Wilson v. Omaha Indian Tribe, 442 U.S. 653 (1979), construing 25 U.S.C. § 194 (1982) as shifting the burden of persuasion to non-Indian parties, except states, involved in land ownership disputes against an individual Indian or tribe.

48. Washington v. Washington State Commercial Passenger Fishing Vessel Ass'n, 443 U.S. 658 (1979), upholding the Pacific Northwest tribes' treaty right to take up to 50 percent of the harvestable fish passing through the tribes' usual and accustomed fishing places.

1979 Term

49. United States v. Clarke, 445 U.S. 253 (1980), striking down the authority of Alaska municipalities to acquire individual Indian allotments by inverse condemnation.

50. United States v. Mitchell, 445 U.S. 535 (1980), construing the General Allotment Act as creating only a limited trust relationship that does not impose a fiduciary obligation on the United States to manage the allottees' timber resources properly.

51. Andrus v. Glover Construction Co., 446 U.S. 608 (1980), construing the Buy Indian Act (25 U.S.C. § 47 (1982)) as requiring the department of the interior to advertise for bids pursuant to the Federal Property and Administrative Services Act (41 U.S.C. §§ 251–60 (1982)) before entering into road construction contracts.

52. Washington v. Confederated Tribes of the Colville Indian Reservation, 447 U.S. 134 (1980), upholding the imposition of state cigarette and sales taxes on on-reservation sales by a tribe to nonmembers of the tribe.

53. White Mountain Apache Tribe v. Bracker, 448 U.S. 136 (1980), striking down the imposition of state motor carrier license and fuel use taxes on a non-Indian corporation engaged in logging activities on a reservation pursuant to a contract with the tribe.

54. Central Machinery Co. v. Arizona State Tax Comm'n, 448 U.S. 160 (1980), striking down the imposition of a state gross receipts tax on on-reservation sales by a non-Indian to a tribe, where the non-Indian seller is not licensed to trade with Indians and has no permanent place of business on the reservation.

55. United States v. Sioux Nation of Indians, 448 U.S. 371 (1980),

upholding the United States' obligation to compensate the tribe for taking the Black Hills in 1877.

1980 Term

56. Montana v. United States, 450 U.S. 544 (1981), striking down the tribe's authority to regulate non-Indians' hunting and fishing on a state-owned navigable watercourse traversing the reservation.

1981 Term

57. Merrion v. Jicarilla Apache Tribe, 455 U.S. 130 (1982), upholding the tribe's authority to impose a severance tax on oil and gas producation on reservation land.

58. Ramah Navajo School Bd. v. Bureau of Revenue, 458 U.S. 832 (1982) , striking down the imposition of a state gross receipts tax on a non-Indian corporation constructing school facilities on reservation land.

1982 Term

59. Arizona v. California, 460 U.S. 605 (1983), barring, on the basis of finality, an increase in tribes' water rights based on additions to the tribes' practicably irrigable acreage, except as to lands judicially determined to have extended the reservation boundaries.

60. New Mexico v. Mescalero Apache Tribe, 462 U.S. 324 (1983), upholding exclusive tribal regulatory jurisdiction over hunting and fishing by members and nonmembers within the reservation.

61. Nevada v. United States, 463 U.S. 110 (1983), barring, on the basis of res judicata, the tribe's assertion of a reserved water right to maintain Pyramid Lake.

62. United States v. Mitchell, 463 U.S. 206 (1983), construing various timber management statutes as imposing a fiduciary duty on the United States to manage individual Indian allottees' timber resources properly.

63. Arizona v. San Carlos Apache Tribe, 463 U.S. 545 (1983), upholding the dismissal of an action brought in federal court by an Indian tribe to adjudicate its reserved water rights when there is a concurrent adjudication of the same issue in state court.

64. Rice v. Rehner, 463 U.S. 713 (1983), upholding concurrent tribal

and state regulation of on-reservation sales of alcoholic beverages.

1983 Term
65. Solem v. Bartlett, 104 S. Ct. 1161 (1984), construing the Cheyenne River Act as having opened a portion of the Cheyenne
River Sioux Reservation to settlement by non-Indians, but as
not having disestablished the opened lands from the
reservation.
66. Escondido Mutual Water Co. v. La Jolla Band of Mission Indians, 104 S. Ct. 2105 (1984), upholding the authority of the
secretary of interior to impose mandatory conditions on Federal
Energy Regulatory Commission licenses for construction, operation, and maintenance of hydroelectric project works located
on Indian reservations; finding that Indian reserved water rights
are not protected reservations within the meaning of the Federal
Power Act.
67. Three Affiliated Tribes of the Fort Berthold Reservation v. Wold
Engineering, 104 S. Ct. 2267 (1984), upholding concurrent
tribal and state judicial jurisdiction over actions brought by an
Indian tribe against a non-Indian defendant for claims arising
in Indian country.

1984 Term
68. United States v. Dann, 105 S. Ct. 1058 (1985), holding that the
Shoshone Tribe's aboriginal title to lands in several western
states was extinguished when, pursuant to a judgment awarded
the tribe by the Indian Claims Commission, the United States
placed $26 million in an interest-bearing trust account for the
tribe.
69. County of Oneida v. Oneida Indian Nation, 105 S. Ct. 1245
(1985), upholding the tribe's federal common law right of action
for a violation of its possessory rights to aboriginal lands that
occurred in 1795.
70. Kerr-McGee Corp. v. Navajo Tribe, 105 S. Ct. 1900 (1985),
upholding the authority of a non-IRA tribe to impose possessory
interest and business activity taxes on mineral production within
the reservation without the approval of the secretary of interior.
71. Montana v. Blackfeet Tribe of Indians, 105 S. Ct. 2399 (1985),
striking down the imposition of a state tax on tribal royalty
interests in mineral leases on reservation land.

72. National Farmers Union Ins. Cos. v. Crow Tribe of Indians, 105 S. Ct. 2447 (1985), construing 28 U.S.C. § 1331 (1982) as conferring jurisdiction on federal district courts to hear actions alleging that a tribal court has exceeded its jurisdiction after the appellant has exhausted tribal court remedies.

73. Mountain States Tel. & Tel. Co. v. Pueblo of Santa Ana, 105 S. Ct. 2587 (1985), construing § 17 of the Pueblo Lands Act of 1924 as authorizing the conveyance of the nineteen New Mexico Pueblos' land upon the approval of the secretary of the interior.

74. Oregon Dept. of Fish & Wildlife v. Klamath Indian Tribe, 105 S. Ct. 3420 (1985), upholding the authority of the state to regulate tribal members' hunting and fishing on former tribal lands ceded by the tribe in 1901.

1985 Term

75. California State Bd. of Equalization v. Chemehuevi Indian Tribe, 106 S. Ct. 289 (1985) (per curiam), upholding the authority of the state to require the tribe to collect an excise tax on tribal cigarette sales to non-Indians where the incidence of the tax falls upon the purchasers.

76. South Carolina v. Catawba Indian Tribe, 106 S. Ct. 2039 (1986), holding that the Catawba Indian Tribe Division of Assets Act of 1959 requires the application of the state statute of limitations to the tribe's land claim.

77. Bowen v. Roy, 106 S. Ct. 2147 (1986), holding that the right of Indian parents to exercise their religion under the Free Exercise Clause was not violated by the government's use of their child's Social Security number.

78. United States v. Dion, 106 S. Ct. 2216 (1986), holding that Congress, in the Eagle Protection Act, set out a clear and plain intent to abrogate the treaty rights of Indians to hunt eagles.

79. United States v. Mottaz, 106 S. Ct. 2224 (1986), holding that a suit against the United States by an Indian, claiming that the sale of her allotment interests was void, was barred by the 12-year statute of limitations period of the Quiet Title Act, 28 U.S.C.A. § 2409a (1982).

80. Three Affiliated Tribes of the Fort Berthold Reservation v. Wold Engineering, 54 U.S.L.W. 4654 (1986), holding that Public Law 280 preempted state's disclaimer of jurisdiction over suits brought by Indian tribes against non-Indians in state court.

Notes

INTRODUCTION

1. 358 U.S. 217 (1959).

2. On the rules when Indian country is not involved, see E. Scoles & P. Hay, Conflict of Laws 257–58, 262–68 (5th ed. 1984). The *Williams* Court twice stated that "exclusive" jurisdiction was lodged in the Navajo tribal court. Williams v. Lee, 358 U.S. 217, 220, 221–22 (1959). The rule was justified as a protection of tribal self-government. Id. at 223. See also, e.g., Three Affiliated Tribes of the Fort Berthold Reservation v. Wold Engineering, 104 S. Ct. 2267 (1984); Kennerly v. District Court, 400 U.S. 423 (1971). Other cases applying the rule of exclusive tribal court jurisdiction are collected in F. Cohen, Handbook of Federal Indian Law 342 n.106 (1982 ed.) [hereinafter cited as F. Cohen].

3. See, e.g., Williams v. United States, 327 U.S. 711 (1946) (Assimilative Crimes Act, 18 U.S.C. § 13, applicable to crimes committed in Indian country); New York ex rel. Ray v. Martin, 326 U.S. 496 (1946) (upholding prosecution in state court of crime committed by a non-Indian against a non-Indian in Indian country); Tulee v. Washington, 315 U.S. 681 (1942) (treaty Indian fisherman not required to purchase state fishing license); United States v. Powers, 305 U.S. 527 (1939) (adjudication of water rights on Indian allotment).

4. See, e.g., Tee-Hit-Ton Indians v. United States, 348 U.S. 272 (1955); Alcea Band of Tillamooks v. United States, 341 U.S. 48 (1951). On the Indian claims process, see F. Cohen, supra note 2, at 562–72.

5. See Williams v. Lee, 358 U.S. 217 (1959) (collection case); Oliphant

v. Suquamish Indian Tribe, 435 U.S. 191 (1978) (criminal jurisdiction over non-Indians); National Farmers Union Ins. Cos. v. Crow Tribe of Indians, 105 S. Ct. 2447 (1985); Dry Creek Lodge, Inc. v. Arapahoe & Shoshone Tribes, 623 F.2d 682 (10th Cir. 1980), cert. denied, 449 U.S. 1118 (1981); UNC Resources, Inc. v. Benally, 514 F. Supp. 358 (D.N.M. 1981); UNC Resources, Inc. v. Benally, 518 F. Supp. 1046 (D. Ariz. 1981) (all personal injury cases).

6. Menominee Tribe of Indians v. United States, 391 U.S. 404 (1968) (Menominee County, Wisconsin); Puyallup Tribe v. Department of Game, 391 U.S. 392 (1968) (Puyallup River); Department of Game v. Puyallup Tribe, 414 U.S. 44 (1973) (Puyallup River); Puyallup Tribe, Inc. v. Department of Game, 433 U.S. 165 (1977) (Puyallup River); Washington v. Washington State Commercial Passenger Fishing Vessel Ass'n, 443 U.S. 658 (1979) (Puget Sound); Blumm, Hydro-Power vs. Salmon: The Struggle of the Pacific Northwest's Anadromous Fish Resources for a Peaceful Coexistence with the Federal Columbia River Power System, 11 Envtl. L. 211, 280–90 (1981) (Columbia River); United States v. Michigan, 653 F.2d 277 (6th Cir. 1981), cert. denied, 454 U.S. 1124 (1982) (Great Lakes).

7. United States v. Mazurie, 419 U.S. 544 (1975) (state licensing of on-reservation tavern); Merrion v. Jicarilla Apache Tribe, 455 U.S. 130 (1982) (tribal severance tax on on-reservation mineral leases); Montana v. Blackfeet Tribe of Indians, 105 S. Ct. 2399 (1985) (state tax on tribal royalty interests from on-reservation mineral leases).

8. See, e.g., National Farmers Union Ins. Cos. v. Crow Tribe of Indians, 105 S. Ct. 2447, 2454 (1985); Kerr-McGee Corp. v. Navajo Tribe, 105 S. Ct. 1900, 1903 (1985); Rice v. Rehner, 463 U.S. 713, 723 (1983); Arizona v. San Carlos Apache Tribe, 463 U.S. 545, 563 (1983); New Mexico v. Mescalero Apache Tribe, 462 U.S. 324, 333 (1983); Ramah Navaho School Bd. v. Bureau of Revenue, 458 U.S. 832, 837 (1982); Montana v. United States, 450 U.S. 544, 564 (1981); White Mountain Apache Tribe v. Bracker, 448 U.S. 136, 142, 151 (1980).

9. This historical progression is discussed in more detail in Ch. 1, infra.

10. See, e.g., Clinton, State Power Over Indian Reservations: A Critical Comment on Burger Court Doctrine, 26 S.D.L. Rev. 434, 446 (1981) ("[I]nheriting a clear constitutional history under the Indian commerce clause opposed to state jurisdiction and a long legacy of doctrinal simplicity and clarity which for the most part excluded the force of state law from Indian country for Indians and non-Indians alike, the Burger Court has produced a complex legal structure which threatens to undermine the process of Indian self-government and encourage the progressive expansion in Indian country of the very state authority and control that the framers sought to preclude"); R. Barsh & J. Henderson, The Road: Indian Tribes and

Political Liberty 201 (1980) ("Federal Indian law is fortunate to have had the benefit of a major conceptual decision, Worcester v. Georgia, but the Court has drifted away from it and abandoned precedent and order"); Newton, Federal Power over Indians: Its Sources, Scope, and Limitations, 132 U. Pa. L. Rev. 195 (1984) (criticism of the modern Court's use of the plenary power doctrine); Laurence, The Indian Commerce Clause, 23 Ariz. L. Rev., 203, 206 (1981) ("[The recent Indian jurisdiction] decisions, like the older cases, make clear the treatment of precise fact patterns but do little to further the evolution of a unified analytical framework"); Pelcyger, Justices and Indians: Back to Basics, 62 Or. L. Rev. 29, 30 (1983) ("In this very vital area—governmental authority over reservation activities of non-Indians—the Court has been anything but consistent and predictable. Each new decision in this area seems to turn on finer points and to raise more questions"); Barsh, The Omen: Three Affiliated Tribes v. Moe and the Future of Tribal Self-Government, 5 Am. Ind. L. Rev. 1, 1 (1977) ("The Court lacks direction. Opinions are internally contradictory, inconsistent with one another, and often in conflict with political, historical, and economic facts").

11. Much of this book deals with broad philosophical directions that cannot always be characterized as hard rules. The Court, however, has laid down a number of reasonably specific principles, examples of which follow.

Tribal powers: Tribes lack inherent criminal authority over non-Indians, Oliphant v. Suquamish Indian Tribe, 435 U.S. 191 (1978); tribes possess civil regulatory jurisdiction over non-Indians on tribal lands, Merrion v. Jicarilla Apache Tribe, 455 U.S. 130 (1982); tribes may tax transactions involving non-Indians which occur "on trust lands and significantly involv[e] a tribe or its members," Washington v. Confederated Tribes of the Colville Indian Reservation, 447 U.S. 134, 152–54 (1980); tribes may regulate conduct of non-Indians on non-Indian land within reservation boundaries "when that conduct threatens or has some direct effect on the political integrity, the economic security, or the health or welfare of the tribe," Montana v. United States, 450 U.S. 544, 566 (1981); tribes possess sovereign immunity, Santa Clara Pueblo v. Martinez, 436 U.S. 49, 58 (1978); tribes hold exclusive possession to their aboriginal lands until it is transferred away or expressly extinguished by Congress, County of Oneida v. Oneida Indian Nation, 105 S. Ct. 1245 (1985).

The federal-tribal relationship: Congress possesses broad authority over Indian affairs and may enact special legislation favoring Indians without violating the equal protection requirement because Indian legislation is based on a government-to-government relationship, not upon race, Morton v. Mancari, 417 U.S. 535, 551–55 (1974); for the reasons just discussed, Congress also has broad authority to enact legislation that may disadvantage Indians, United States v. Antelope, 430 U.S. 641, 645–47 (1977); Congress's authority over Indians is not unlimited and must be "tied rationally to the fulfillment of Congress' unique obligation toward the Indians," Delaware Tribal Business Comm. v. Weeks, 430 U.S. 73, 85 (1977); tribal laws enacted according to inherent tribal sovereignty are not subject to approval by the secretary of the interior, Kerr-McGee Corp. v. Navajo Tribe of Indians, 105 S. Ct. 1900 (1985); federal district courts possess federal question jurisdiction, 28 U.S.C. § 1331 (1982), to review tribal court decisions on the extent of tribal authority, National Farmers Union Ins. Cos. v. Crow Tribe of Indians, 105 S. Ct. 2447, 2452 (1985).

Tribal-state relationship: The definition of Indian country in the criminal statutes, 18 U.S.C. § 1151 (1982), generally applies as well to questions of civil jurisdiction, DeCoteau v. District County Court, 420 U.S. 425, 427 n.2 (1975); tribal courts have exclusive jurisdiction over normally transitory actions brought by non-Indians against Indians arising in Indian country, Williams v. Lee, 358 U.S. 217 (1959); Kennerly v. District Court, 400 U.S. 423 (1971); tribes are not barred from suing non-Indians in state court for causes of action arising in Indian country, Three Affiliated Tribes of the Fort Berthold Reservation v. Wold Engineering, 104 S. Ct. 2267, 2274–75 (1984); matters of title to Indian lands are inherently federal, and suit may be brought in federal court, Oneida Indian Nation v. County of Oneida, 414 U.S. 661, 666–67 (1974); states may tax Indians in Indian country only upon the express approval of Congress, Montana v. Blackfeet Tribe of Indians, 105 S. Ct. 2399, 2403 (1985).

Resource rights: Tribes possess broad treaty hunting and fishing rights, amounting to as much as 50 percent of the harvestable runs, and such rights are not lost by the creation of states after the execution of the treaties, Washington v. Washington State Commercial Passenger Fishing Vessel Ass'n, 443 U.S. 658 (1979); tribes possess reserved water rights, sufficient to meet their future needs and to develop all practicably irrigable acreage within the reservation, and such rights are not subject to state law, Arizona v. California, 373 U.S. 546, 595–601 (1963); under the McCarran Amendment, 43 U.S.C. § 666a (1982), state courts have jurisdiction to determine Indian water rights in general stream adjudications, and federal courts should normally defer to state courts in such situations, Arizona v. San Carlos Apache Tribe, 463 U.S. 545 (1983).

Many of these rules still require clarification of critical phraseology, but law is not physics and it is often impossible to structure rules to meet all possible circumstances; on balance, it seems to me that the above rules have decided important controversies with considerable precision. The Court also has laid down balancing tests in a number of areas. Balancing tests are inherently ambiguous but some situations intrinsically call for balancing. In my view, the Court has developed reasonably workable tests to determine when Indian reservations have been disestablished, see Solem

v. Bartlett, 104 S. Ct. 1161 (1984); to determine when state regulatory jurisdiction has been preempted in Indian country, see Ch. 4, infra; and to provide for the construction of statutes affecting Indians, see Ch. 2, infra. In terms of comprehensive unification of doctrine, the Court has also made a major accomplishment in tying together the law affecting treaties, statutes, agreements, and executive orders, see Ch. 3, infra. As noted, this book will deal with additional, more abstract, concepts developed by the Court that, in most instances, protect the legitimate interests of the tribes and further the coherent development of this body of law.

    12. See Ch. 4, infra.

    13. See T. Berger, Fragile Freedoms: Human Rights and Dissent in Canada 219 (Rev. ed. 1982). See also Aboriginal Peoples and the Law: Indian, Metis and Inuit Rights in Canada (B. Morse ed. 1985).

    14. See, e.g., R. Broome, Aboriginal Australians: Black Response to White Dominance 1778–1980 (1982); W. Eberhard, China's Minorities: Yesterday and Today (1982); C. von Furer-Haimendorf, Tribes of India: The Struggle for Survival (1982); C. Dozier, Nicaragua's Mosquito Shore: The Years of British and American Presence (1985); R. Stone, Dreams of Amazonia (1985); Arvelo-Jiménez, The Political Struggle of the Guayama Region's Indigenous Peoples, 36 J. Int'l Aff. 43 (1982); Dow, Ethnic Policy and Indigenismo in Guatemala, 5 Ethnic and Racial Studies 140 (1982); Gross, The Indians and the Brazilian Frontier, 36 J. Int'l Aff. 1 (1982); Guiart, One of the Last Colonies; New Caledonia, 36 J. Int'l Aff. 105 (1982); Kellman, The Yanomamis: Their Battle for Survival, 36 J. Int'l Aff. 15 (1982); Salomon, The Andean Contrast, 36 J. Int'l Aff. 55 (1982); Smith, Liberal Ideology and Indigenous Communities in Post-Independence Peru, 36 J. Int'l Aff. 73 (1982); Varese, Restoring Multiplicity: Indianities and the Civilizing Project in Latin America, 9 Latin Am. Persp. 29 (1982); Williams, Land Rights and the Manipulation of Identity: Official Indian Policy in Brazil, 15 J. Latin Am. Stud. 137 (1983).

    15. See generally Symposium on Law and Indigenous Populations, 27 Buffalo L. Rev. 581 (1978).

CHAPTER 1. THE CHALLENGE OF THE MODERN ERA

    1. The extent to which native villages in Alaska are self-governing sovereigns in the fashion of the tribes in the lower forty-eight states remains unclear. See generally D. Case, Alaska Natives and American Laws (1984). In 1977 there were approximately 133 nonrecognized Indian communities in the United States. See American Indian Policy Review Commission, 94th Cong., 1st Sess., 1 Final Report 467 (Comm. Print 1977). The Interior Department has since established a process for determining whether recognition should be granted to nonrecognized tribes, 25 C.F.R. Part 83

(1985). For a listing of the 109 tribes that were initially terminated, see F. Cohen, Handbook of Federal Indian Law 811 (1982 ed.) [hereinafter cited as F. Cohen]. Several of those tribes have since been restored to federal status. Id. at 818.

2. F. Cohen, supra note 1, at 471 (total current land holdings); H.R. Rep. No. 2503, 82d Cong., 2d Sess. 60–74 (1953) (analysis of land recognized by treaties and other methods).

3. Future treaty making with Indian tribes was terminated in 1871 by a rider to the Indian Appropriations Act, ch. 120, 16 Stat. 566 (1871) (codified at 25 U.S.C. § 71 (1982)), in response to the growing opposition of House members to their practical exclusion from control over Indian affairs. See F. Cohen, supra note 1, at 105–07. The statute expressly provides that existing treaties continue in effect. Agreements, like treaties, have been recognized by the Supreme Court as the "supreme Law of the Land." Antoine v. Washington, 420 U.S. 194, 201–02 (1975), quoted in text in Ch. 3, note 63, infra.

4. See F. Cohen, supra note 1, at 477–81, 498–99.

5. For statistics on executive order land, see H.R. Rep. No. 2503, 82d Cong., 2d Sess. 60 (1953); 67 Cong. Rec. 10913 (1926). Federal authority in the field of Indian law is lodged in Congress pursuant to the Indian Commerce Clause, U.S. Const. art. I, § 8, cl. 3, but unilateral executive orders creating Indian reservations have been upheld on the ground that Congress "acquiesced" to them. See Ch. 3, notes 66–76, infra. By 1953 most executive order land had been confirmed by statute and less than 3 million acres were held under executive order only. See H.R. Rep. No. 2503, 82d Cong., 2d Sess. 60–74 (1953).

6. The citation to the General Allotment Act is ch. 119, 24 Stat. 388 (codified as amended at 25 U.S.C. §§ 331–334, 339, 341–42, 348–49, 354, 381 (1982)). The quotation in the text is from Comm'r. Ind. Aff. Ann. Rep., H.R. Exec. Doc. No. 1, 44th Cong., 2d Sess. 381, 387 (1876). On the allotment era, see notes 65–74, infra.

7. On state ownership of beds of navigable watercourses within Indian reservations, see Montana v. United States, 450 U.S. 544 (1981). On subsurface rights, see, e.g., Northern Cheyenne Tribe v. Hollowbreast, 425 U.S. 649, 658–60 (1976) (subsurface estate of allotted reservation lands reserved and held by United States in trust for the tribe); F. Cohen, supra note 1, at 531–33.

8. On economic issues relating to allotments and leasing, see generally Chambers & Price, Regulating Sovereignty: Secretarial Discretion and the Leasing of Indian Lands, 26 Stan. L. Rev. 1061 (1974); Comment, Too Little Land, Too Many Heirs—The Indian Heirship Land Problem, 46 Wash. L. Rev. 709 (1971). The matter of multiple ownership of allotments will be alleviated to some degree by the Indian Land Consolidation Act of

1982, 25 U.S.C. §§ 2201–2210 (1982). On jurisdictional difficulties, see, e.g., Seymour v. Superintendent, 368 U.S. 351, 358 (1962) (The Indian country statute, 18 U.S.C. § 1151 (1982), should be construed to avoid "an impractical pattern of checkerboard jurisdiction" so that "law enforcement officers operating in the area [will not be required] to search tract books in order to determine" jurisdiction in individual cases).

9. See text at Ch. 14, note 156, infra.

10. See, e.g., United States v. Washington, 520 F.2d 676, 693 (9th Cir. 1975), cert. denied, 423 U.S. 1086 (1976) (Burns, J., concurring).

11. The importance of the treaties and treaty substitutes is discussed later in this chapter and in chapter 4, infra.

12. Special legislation has been enacted on a wide range of subjects dealing with individual issues affecting specific tribes. Common areas of attention include enrollment, see, e.g., Act of June 4, 1920, ch. 224, § 3, 41 Stat. 752 (Crow Tribe of Montana); land acquisition, see, e.g., Pueblo Lands Act of 1924, ch. 331, 43 Stat. 636 (Pueblo Indians of New Mexico); and claims distributions, see, e.g., Act of Dec. 31, 1975, Pub. L. No. 94–189, 89 Stat. 1093 (Sac and Fox Nation).

13. Exceptions to this are some recent statutes that deal in quite detailed fashion with organic issues because of the importance and high visibility of the subject matter. See, e.g., Alaska Native Claims Settlement Act of 1971, 43 U.S.C. §§ 1601–28 (1982). Ten years later, Congress was even more specific about federal–state relations when it passed the Maine Indian Claims Settlement Act of 1980, Pub. L. No. 96–420, 94 Stat. 1785 (codified at 25 U.S.C. §§ 1721–35b (1982)).

14. Northwest Ordinance of July 13, 1787, art. 3, reenacted by the First Congress of the United States at ch. 8, 1 Stat. 50, 52 (Aug. 7, 1789).

15. Ch. 119, 24 Stat. 388 (codified as amended at 25 U.S.C. §§ 331–34, 339, 341–42, 348–49, 354, 381 (1982) (commonly referred to as the Dawes Act). See notes 67–75, infra.

16. Act of June 18, 1934, ch. 576, 48 Stat. 984 (codified as amended at 25 U.S.C. §§ 461–79 (1982). See note 76, infra.

17. H.R. Con. Res. 108, 67 Stat. B132 (1953), quoted in F. Cohen, supra note 1, at 171–72.

18. Act of Aug. 15, 1953, ch. 505, 67 Stat. 588 (§ 7 repealed and reenacted as amended 1968) (codified as amended at 18 U.S.C. § 1162 (1982), 25 U.S.C. §§ 1321–26 (1982), 28 U.S.C. § 1360 (1982)). See generally Bryan v. Itasca County, 426 U.S. 373 (1976); Goldberg, Public Law 280: The Limits of State Jurisdiction over Reservation Indians, 22 UCLA L. Rev. 535 (1975).

19. Indian Self-Determination and Education Assistance Act of 1975, Pub. L. No. 93–638, 88 Stat. 2203 (codified at 25 U.S.C. §§ 450–450n, 455–458e (1982)).

20. Some of these laws deal only with federally recognized tribes. See also, e.g., Ch. 3, note 86, infra.

21. See Ch. 2, notes 34–36, infra.

22. See, e.g., 18 U.S.C. §§ 13, 1151–53, 1165, 3242, 3243 (1982). See generally Clinton, Criminal Jurisdiction over Indian Lands: A Journey Through a Jurisdictional Maze, 18 Ariz. L. Rev. 503 (1976).

23. 25 U.S.C. §§ 70 to 70v–3 (1982) (repealed Sept. 30, 1978). See generally F. Cohen, supra note 1, at 562–74.

24. Pub. L. No. 90–284, §§ 201–701, 82 Stat. 73, 77–81 (codified at 25 U.S.C. 1301–03 (1982)). See generally Santa Clara Pueblo v. Martinez, 436 U.S. 49 (1978).

25. Act of Nov. 8, 1978, Pub. L. No. 95–608, 92 Stat. 3069 (codified at 25 U.S.C. §§ 1901–63 (1982)). See generally Guerrero, Indian Child Welfare Act of 1978, 7 Am. Ind. L. Rev. 51 (1979).

26. The foundation for federal Indian law was laid long before the formation of the Republic. The basic concepts of original Indian title and tribal sovereign status originated as principles of sixteenth-century international law in the writings of scholars such as Francisco de Victoria. See F. Victoria, De Indis et de Jure Belli Relectiones 128 (J. Bate trans. 1917) (orig. ed. 1557). These precepts were adhered to by the European colonial powers in their earliest dealings with Indians, see S. Tyler, A History of Indian Policy 18–19 (1973), and were integrated into American jurisprudence. See, e.g., Worcester v. Georgia, 31 U.S. (6 Pet.) 515 (1832); Cohen, The Spanish Origin of Indian Rights in the Law of the United States, 31 Geo. L.J. 1 (1942). One recent piece of scholarship traces theories of Indian rights to the Middle Ages. See Williams, The Medieval and Renaissance Origins of the Status of the American Indian in Western Legal Thought, 57 S. Cal. L. Rev. 1 (1983).

27. The Commerce Clause, U.S. Const. art. I, § 8, cl. 3, authorizes Congress "to regulate Commerce with foreign Nations, and among the several States, and with the Indian Tribes." The principal architect of the Indian Commerce Clause, James Madison, argued that the provision would eliminate the problems encountered under the Articles of Confederation—claims by states to authority over Indian relations and lands—by committing the primary power over Indian affairs to the federal government. See, e.g., J. Madison, Journal of the Federal Convention 190, 549 (E. Scott ed. 1898). This view was affirmed by Chief Justice Marshall in Worcester v. Georgia, 31 U.S. (6 Pet.) 515, 561 (1832), which held that the Indian Commerce Clause committed the "whole intercourse between the United States and [the Cherokee] nation" exclusively to the federal government.

While recent decisions of the Court have found that federal power over commerce with the Indian tribes is the primary constitutional source of federal authority over Indian affairs, see, e.g., McClanahan v. Arizona

State Tax Comm'n, 411 U.S. 164, 172 n.7 (1973), the Court has rejected the argument that the Indian Commerce Clause alone precludes all state authority. Moe v. Confederated Salish & Kootenai Tribes, 425 U.S. 463, 481 n.17 (1976). See also Ch. 4, note 39, infra.

28. The presence and power of the Indian tribes before and after Independence was an unavoidable fact that was given considerable attention by the new nation. See, e.g., F. Prucha, American Indian Policy in the Formative Years 43–50 (1962); W. Washburn, The Indian in America 126–45 (1975). Thus a primary objective of early Indian policy was maintaining peace with the tribes by restraining aggressive frontiersmen from encroaching on Indian lands while ensuring the orderly advance of the frontier. See, e.g., 1 S. Morison, H. Commager, & W. Leuchtenburg, The Growth of the American Republic 362–65 (6th ed. 1969). The strategy chosen was in large part inherited from English colonial policy: the goals were "conciliation of the Indians by negotiation, a show of liberality, express guarantees of protection from encroachment beyond certain set boundaries and a fostered and developed trade." F. Prucha, supra, at 44. See generally A. Debo, A History of the Indians of the United States 84–100 (1970).

To a large extent, the history of Indian relations before the twentieth century is the history of this interaction between national governments and the frontiersmen or local governments: the central governments of the European and American nations tailored their policies to protect Indian rights and property and thereby achieve a modicum of peace on the frontier, but unscrupulous traders, avaricious settlers, and speculators preferred to exploit the tribes. See F. Prucha, supra, at 34–40; Cohen, The Spanish Origin of Indian Rights in the Law of the United States, 31 Geo. L.J. 1 (1942). These realities help explain the statutory scheme and often have been a backdrop to the court decisions. See, e.g., United States v. Sioux Nation, 448 U.S. 371, 376–84 (1980); United States v. John, 437 U.S. 634, 638–45 (1978); United States v. Kagama, 118 U.S. 375, 383–84 (1886); Worcester v. Georgia, 31 U.S. (6 Pet.) 515, 551–55 (1832). See also C. Miller, The Supreme Court and the Uses of History 24 (1969) ("In disputes concerning American Indian tribes the courts have also considered and often decided cases principally on the basis of historical materials").

29. The ambiguities on this issue are evident in National Farmers Union Ins. Cos. v. Crow Tribe of Indians, 105 S. Ct. 2447 (1985), holding that federal district courts possess federal question jurisdiction under 28 U.S.C. § 1331 (1982) to determine whether tribal courts have exceeded their jurisdiction. The opinion noted that Section 1331 comprehends claims based on federal common law (without concluding that the issue of tribal jurisdiction is so based) and then stated:

Federal law, implemented by statute, by treaty, by administrative regulations, and by judicial decisions, provides significant protection for the individual, territorial, and political rights of the Indian tribes. The tribes also retain some of the inherent powers of the self-governing political communities that were formed long before Europeans first settled in North America.

Id. at 2451.

The federal question in *National Farmers* was whether the Crow Tribe's aboriginal sovereignty was sufficiently abridged by the Crow treaty with the United States that the tribe relinquished its civil jurisdiction over non-Indians on the facts at issue. See generally chapters 3, 4, infra. Thus the federal question in *National Farmers,* which is typical of most Indian litigation in this respect, is best understood as being based on federal treaties and statutes as construed by the courts, not on court decisions standing alone. Line-drawing here is obviously a delicate matter since the treaties and treaty substitutes are usually so vague and the scope of judicial construction so broad, but Indian legal issues normally trace, at least in part, to some federal enactment. A leading example of true federal common law is the origin of the rule that Indian tribes may not transfer real property without the approval of the United States. The principle was first announced in Johnson v. McIntosh, 21 U.S. (8 Wheat.) 543 (1823), which set aside purported transfers made by tribes in 1773 and 1775. The Court later explained that the rule in Johnson v. McIntosh arose from federal common law. County of Oneida v. Oneida Indian Nation, 105 S. Ct. 1245, 1251–52 (1985). Congress codified the rule against transfer in the Nonintercourse Act of 1790. See 25 U.S.C. § 177 (1982).

30. Washington v. Washington State Commercial Passenger Fishing Vessel Ass'n, 443 U.S. 658, 675 (1979) (Pacific salmon and steelhead); United States v. Michigan, 653 F.2d 277 (6th Cir. 1981), aff'g, 471 F. Supp. 192 (W.D. Mich. 1979) (Great Lakes fishing); McClanahan v. Arizona State Tax Comm'n, 411 U.S. 164, 174–75 (1973) (Navajo taxation); Oliphant v. Suquamish Indian Tribe, 435 U.S. 191, 207–09 (1978) (criminal jurisdiction over non-Indians); Arizona v. California, 373 U.S. 546 (1963) (Colorado River water rights).

31. Exec. Order establishing Cocopah Reservation, Sept. 27, 1917, printed in 4 Indian Affairs; Laws and Treaties 1001 (C. Kappler ed.) (1929). The other executive orders at issue in the litigation are cited at Arizona v. California, 373 U.S. 546, 596 nn.99–100 (1963).

32. See Act of August 7, 1789, ch. 7, 1 Stat. 49 (establishing the Department of War, with responsibility over Indian affairs); Act of August 7, 1789, ch. 8, 1 Stat. 50 (providing for the government of the Northwest Territory and guaranteeing that "utmost good faith shall always be observed toward the Indians"); Act of August 20, 1789, ch. 10, 1 Stat. 54 (appropriating funds to negotiate treaties with Indians and providing for the appointment of commissioners at such negotiations); and Act of Sept. 11,

1789, ch. 13, 1 Stat. 67 (providing a salary for the superintendent of Indian affairs with the northern department). Shortly thereafter, Congress enacted the comprehensive first Trade and Intercourse Act, Act of July 22, 1790, ch. 33, 1 Stat. 137.

33. Early ratified treaties are collected in 7 Stat. On the period of 1789–1817, see 1–3 J. of the Exec. Proc. of the Senate (D. Green ed. 1828). Hayden states that "[t]here can be no doubt that from the very beginning the Senate exercised to the full the powers in treaty-making and in foreign affairs granted to it by the Constitution. . . . Foreign affairs and relations with the Indian tribes were among the most important of the subjects with which the new government had to deal. Through the constant exercise of its treaty-making powers the Senate exerted a powerful influence in both fields of activity." R. Hayden, The Senate and Treaties, 1789–1817, at 103 (1920).

34. We have conducted this research in painstaking—a word I use advisedly—detail, but it seems pointless to provide readers with all of the citations to cases analyzing old laws not related to the subject of this book. The modern cases construing old Indian laws, of course, are cited in the Appendix and discussed throughout. The following will provide a flavor of the kinds of old laws reviewed by the Court since 1970.

The laws enacted before 1800 construed by the Supreme Court between 1970 and 1981 fell into these subject areas: (1) Indian law; (2) Shipping, see, e.g., Douglas v. Seacoast Products, Inc., 431 U.S. 265 (1977) (construing Enrollment and Licensing Act, ch. 8, §§ 1, 2, 4, 1 Stat. 305, 307 (1793), current version at 46 U.S.C. ch. 12 (1982)); (3) Money and finance, see, e.g., United States v. Moore, 423 U.S. 77 (1975) (construing Act of March 3, 1797, ch. 20, § 5, 1 Stat. 515; Act of March 2, 1799, ch. 22, § 65, 1 Stat. 676, current version at 31 U.S.C. § 3713(a) (1982)); (4) Judiciary, see, e.g., United States v. Mauro, 436 U.S. 340 (1978) (construing Judiciary Act, ch. 20, § 14, 1 Stat. 81 (1789), current version at 28 U.S.C. § 2241 (1982)); and (5) Postal Service, see, Brennan v. United States Postal Service, 439 U.S. 1345, 1347 (1978) (construing Act of Feb. 20, 1792, ch. 7, § 14, 1 Stat. 236, adopting Act of Oct. 18, 1782, 23 J. Cont. Cong. 672–73, current version at 18 U.S.C. § 1693 (1982)).

Most of the laws enacted between 1800 and 1850 fell within the following subject areas: (1) Indian law; (2) Statehood and state boundaries, see, e.g., Texas v. Louisiana, 410 U.S. 702 (1973) (construing Act of April 8, 1812, ch. 50, §§ 1–6, 2 Stat. 701; Act of July 5, 1848, ch. 94, 9 Stat. 245; Treaty of Amity, Settlement, & Limits, Feb. 22, 1819, United States–Spain, 8 Stat. 252, T.S. 327; Treaty of Limits, April 5, 1831, United States–Mexico, 8 Stat. 372, T.S. 202; Convention Between the United States and the Republic of Texas, Oct. 12, 1838, 8 Stat. 511, T.S. 356; Joint Resolution for the Admission of Texas, No. 1, Dec. 29, 1845, 9 Stat. 108); (3) Navigation, see, e.g., United States v. California, 436 U.S. 32, 34 (1978) (construing Act of Sept. 9, 1850, ch. 50, §§ 1–3, 9 Stat. 452); and (4) Shipping, see, Douglas v. Seacoast Products, Inc., 431 U.S. 265 (1977) (construing Act of April 20, 1836, ch. 55, 5 Stat. 16, current version at 46 U.S.C. § 325 (1982)).

The significant increase in constructions of laws enacted between 1850 and 1875, as opposed to the earlier time periods, is due almost entirely to the surge in civil rights litigation construing civil rights laws enacted in the late 1860s and 1870s. The Court construed the post–Civil War Reconstruction statutes 117 times in 101 different cases. See, e.g., Sixty-Seventh Minnesota State Senate v. Biens, 406 U.S. 187 (1972) (construing Act of April 9, 1866, ch. 31, § 3, 14 Stat. 27; Act of May 31, 1870, ch. 114, § 18, 16 Stat. 144, current versions at 42 U.S.C. § 1988 (1982); Act of April 20, 1871, ch. 22, § 1, 17 Stat. 13, current version at 42 U.S.C. § 1983 (1982)). The Court also construed laws from the 1850–75 period in the following subject areas: (1) Indian law; (2) Banks and banking, see, e.g., Camp v. Pitts, 411 U.S. 138 (1973) (construing National Bank Act, ch. 106, §§ 12, 17, 18, 13 Stat. 102, 104 (1864), current version at 12 U.S.C. §§ 26, 27 (1982)); (3) Mining, see, e.g., Andrus v. Charlestone Stone Products Co., 436 U.S. 604 (1978) (construing Act of July 26, 1866, ch. 262, § 9, 14 Stat. 253, current version at 30 U.S.C. § 51 (1982); Act of July 9, 1870, ch. 235, § 17, 16 Stat. 218, current version at 30 U.S.C. § 52 (1982); General Mining Act, ch. 152, §§ 1, 5, 17 Stat. 91, 92, current version at 30 U.S.C. §§ 22, 28 (1982)); (4) Patents, see, e.g., Diamond v. Chakrabarty, 447 U.S. 303 (1980) (construing Act of July 8, 1870, ch. 230, § 24, 16 Stat. 201, current version at 35 U.S.C. § 101 (1982)); and (5) Public lands, see, e.g., Leo Sheep Co. v. United States, 440 U.S. 668 (1979) (construing Union Pacific Act, ch. 120, §§ 1–19, 12 Stat. 489 (1862)).

Thus, while the Court made 117 interpretations of the Reconstruction Statutes from 1970–1981, it construed Indian laws 54 times during the same period. The next most frequently construed area of the law is shipping law, but the Court made only 10 constructions of shipping laws enacted before 1875.

35. I have just offered a statistical approach toward analyzing the impact of the treaties and treaty substitutes on modern litigation. See note 34, supra. Another way to make the point is to list just some of the major recent cases that were resolved by a construction of the old laws. See, e.g., County of Oneida v. Oneida Indian Nation, 105 S. Ct. 1245 (1985); Three Affiliated Tribes of the Fort Berthold Reservation v. Wold Engineering, 104 S. Ct. 2267 (1984); Montana v. United States, 450 U.S. 544 (1981); Washington v. Washington State Commercial Passenger Fishing Vessel Ass'n, 443 U.S. 658 (1979); Oliphant v. Suquamish Indian Tribe, 435 U.S. 191 (1978); McClanahan v. Arizona State Tax Comm'n, 411 U.S. 164 (1973); Puyallup Tribe v. Department of Game, 391 U.S. 392 (1968); Arizona v. California,

373 U.S. 546 (1963); Williams v. Lee, 358 U.S. 217 (1959). The old laws were major factors, although not the sole basis of resolution, in other leading cases. See, e.g., Solem v. Bartlett, 104 S. Ct. 1161 (1984); United States v. Mitchell, 103 S. Ct. 2961 (1983); White Mountain Apache Tribe v. Bracker, 448 U.S. 136 (1980); Santa Clara Pueblo v. Martinez, 436 U.S. 49 (1978); Bryan v. Itasca County, 426 U.S. 373 (1976); United States v. Mazurie, 419 U.S. 544 (1975); Menominee Tribe of Indians v. United States, 391 U.S. 404 (1968); Warren Trading Post v. Arizona State Tax Comm'n, 380 U.S. 685 (1965). Further, the old laws controlled each of the classic nineteenth- and early-twentieth-century cases discussed in notes 85–89, infra.

36. On the preconstitutional and extraconstitutional status of tribes, see Ch. 3, infra. Analogies can be drawn between Indian reservations, on the one hand, and federal public land systems, states, cities and counties, and even foreign nations, on the other, but each of those comparisons is incomplete. See Ch. 4, notes 66–69, infra. In general, the legal powers of the United States, states, and foreign nations are all greater than those of tribes. The legal powers of cities and counties, especially in rural areas, are often less. For our purposes here, however, it is more important to understand that the nature of each of those governments is different from that of Indian tribes.

37. In attempting to determine the themes of Indian treaties and treaty substitutes as organic wholes, I have benefited from scholarship analyzing the Constitution in a somewhat similar fashion. See C. Black, Structure and Relationship in Constitutional Law (1969); J. Ely, Democracy and Distrust: A Theory of Judicial Review (1980).

38. These problems are explored in V. Deloria & C. Lytle, The Nations Within: The Past and Future of American Indian Sovereignty 7–11 (1984).

39. On aboriginal tribal sovereignty before contact with Europeans, see, e.g., Worcester v. Georgia, 31 U.S. (6 Pet.) 515, 542–48 (1832); Ch. 3, infra.

40. See, e.g., Johnson v. McIntosh, 21 U.S. (8 Wheat.) 543, 574 (1923) (describing Indian tribes as "the rightful occupants of the soil, with a legal as well as just claim to retain possession of it"); Oneida Indian Nation v. County of Oneida, 414 U.S. 661, 667 (1974) ("It very early became accepted doctrine in this Court that although fee title to the lands occupied by Indians when the colonists arrived became vested in the sovereign—first the discovering European nation and later the original States and the United States—a right of occupancy in the Indian tribes was nevertheless recognized. That right, sometimes called Indian title and good against all but the sovereign, could be terminated only by sovereign act"). See also Cohen, Original Indian Title, 32 Minn. L. Rev. 28 (1947); Ch. 2, notes 33–40, infra.

41. The different terms used to provide for reservations are discussed in F. Cohen, supra note 1, at 475–77.

42. Treaty with the Apache, July 1, 1852, 10 Stat. 979.

43. Treaty provisions are discussed in F. Cohen, supra note 1, at 65–67. On federal service programs to Indians, see id., Ch. 13.

44. See, e.g., Treaty with the Kiowa and Comanche Tribes, Oct. 21, 1867, 15 Stat. 581 (guarantee of "absolute and undisturbed use and occupation" by the tribes on reservation lands, id. at art. 2, 15 Stat. 582); Treaty of Fort Sumner with the Navajo Tribe, June 1, 1868, 15 Stat. 667 (guarantee that "no persons except those herein so authorized to do . . . shall ever be permitted to pass over, settle upon, or reside in, the territory described in this article," id. at art. 2, 15 Stat. 668; Treaty of Fort Laramie with the Sioux, April 29, 1868, 15 Stat. 635 (guarantee that no unauthorized persons "shall ever be permitted to pass over, settle upon, or reside in" the reservation, id. at art. 2, 15 Stat. 636).

45. Treaty with the Omaha, March 16, 1854, 10 Stat. 1043; Treaty with the Menominee, May 12, 1854, 10 Stat. 1064.

46. Washington v. Washington State Commercial Passenger Fishing Vessel Ass'n, 443 U.S. 658, 699 (1979) (Powell, J., dissenting) (citations omitted).

47. See, e.g., Cherokee Nation v. Georgia, 30 U.S. (5 Pet.) 1, 17–18 (1831) (federal duty of protection); Worcester v. Georgia, 31 U.S. (6 Pet.) 551, 556–57 (1832) (separatism).

48. These documents can be obtained on microcopy from the National Archives and Records Service and are catalogued as follows: Record Group 75: Microcopy T494, Documents Relating to the Negotiation of Ratified and Unratified Treaties with Various Tribes of Indians, 1801–69 [hereinafter cited as "Record Group 75"].

49. See, e.g., Treaty of Dancing Rabbit Creek with the Choctaw Nation, Sept. 27, 1830, 7 Stat. 333, Letter from Andrew Jackson in Journal of Proceedings Connected with the Negotiation of a Treaty (Aug. 23, 1830) (Record Group 75, supra note 48, Roll 2: Ratified Treaty No. 160). See also note 57, infra.

50. See A. Debo, A History of the Indians of the United States 101–35 (1970) [hereinafter cited as A. Debo]; G. Foreman, Indian Removal 19–22, 229–30 (1932) [hereinafter cited as G. Foreman].

51. E.g., R. Satz, American Indian Policy in the Jacksonian Era 6 (1975). Satz recounts that

> George Washington envisioned a "Chinese Wall" to keep Whites and Indians apart. Thomas Jefferson, after the Louisiana Purchase in 1803, contemplated making a permanent exchange of vacant land in the newly acquired area for Indian land in the East. James Madison considered similar measures in his effort to pacify the Indians after the War of 1812. John C. Calhoun, James Monroe's talented Secretary of War,

was a strong advocate of Indian removal and convinced Monroe to adopt the policy in 1825.

Id. See also I F. Prucha, The Great Father 183–89 (1984); B. Sheehan, Seeds of Extinction: Jeffersonian Philanthropy and the American Indian 241–50 (1973). In any event, it was not until after the War of 1812 that treaty making became primarily concerned with the removal of tribes to western territories. F. Cohen, supra note 1, at 79. The removal policy was not inspired entirely by greed for land or by hatred of the Indians. Many people genuinely interested in the welfare of the Indians believed that, however unconscionable the means, securing to the Indian people permanent homelands in the West was a humanitarian end. See R. Satz, supra, at 14–30; I F. Prucha, supra, at 179–81.

52. Historical accounts of Jackson as the consummate Indian-hater are probably as overstated as they are colorful, see, e.g., R. Satz, supra note 51, at 9; Prucha, Andrew Jackson's Indian Policy: A Reassessment, 56 J. Am. Hist. 527–39 (1969). Nevertheless, Jackson's "deeply rooted conviction" in the "legitimate sphere of state sovereignty," 2 J. Richardson, Messages and Papers of the Presidents 452, 457–58 (1902), and his fervent belief in frontier expansion as America's manifest destiny remain unquestioned. See A. Debo, supra note 50, at 101–11; F. Prucha, American Indian Policy in the Formative Years 233–49 (1982); R. Satz, supra note 51, at 9–11. See generally Abel, The History of Events Resulting in Indian Consolidation West of the Mississippi, 1 Ann. Rep. of the Am. Hist. A. 233–450 (1908). Further, as an army officer and territorial governor often involved in the negotiation of treaties with tribes, Jackson came to view treating with the Indians within the territorial limits of the United States as "an absurdity." 2 Correspondence of Andrew Jackson 279–81 (J. Basset ed. 1927). As president, Jackson defined his task in managing Indian affairs as devising "a plan whereby the government could provide for 'justice to the Citizen, the interest and security of the United States, and the peace and happiness of the Indians.'" R. Satz, supra note 51, at 10. His grand design for these inevitably irreconcilable objectives was the Indian Removal Act. Act of May 28, 1830, ch. 148, 4 Stat. 411. Tribes agreeing to remove to the trans-Mississippi territories would receive title to a permanent, federally protected homeland in exchange for their eastern land holdings, while those desiring to remain in the East would receive individual allotments and come under state law. G. Foreman, supra note 50, at 231–32. I F. Prucha, supra note 52, at 244–49; R. Satz, supra note 51, at 10–11.

53. See, e.g., S. Beckham, Requiem for a People (1971) (removal of Oregon coastal Indians to Siletz Reservation). On the confederation of western tribes, often on new lands, see generally F. Cohen, supra note 1, at 92–98.

54. J. Richardson, supra note 52, at 458. Satz reports that on numerous occasions Jackson even called for the "consolidation of the southern tribes in the West with the possibility of their becoming a 'member of the United States.' " R. Satz, supra note 51, at 11.

55. Treaty with the Chippewas, Ottawas, and Potawatamies, June 5 & 17, 1846, 9 Stat. 853, Speech of Commissioner in Journal of Proceedings (Nov. 12, 1845) (Record Group 75, supra note 48, Roll 4: Ratified Treaty No. 247).

56. Treaty of Lapwai with the Nez Perce, June 9, 1863, 14 Stat. 647, Statements by Commissioners in Journal of Proceedings Connected with the Negotiation of a Treaty (June 4–5, 1863) (Record Group 75, supra note 48, Roll 6: Ratified Treaty No. 323).

57. Treaty of Dancing Rabbit Creek with the Choctaw Nation, Sept. 27, 1830, 7 Stat. 333, letter from Andrew Jackson in Journal of Proceedings connected with the Negotiation of a Treaty (Aug. 23, 1830) (Record Group 75, supra note 48, Roll 2: Ratified Treaty No. 160). See also Treaty with the Potawatamie Nation, June 5 & 17, 1846, 9 Stat. 853, Speech of Commissioner in Journal of Proceedings connected with the Negotiation of a Treaty (June 3, 1846) (Record Group 75, supra note 48, Roll 4: Ratified Treaty No. 247) ("It is a treaty that will make you all rich and happy. It will remove you from a country where you are surrounded by the Sioux on one side; by the people of the Iowas on the other (who are encroaching on you like the waves of the great sea); and where the fire water is hissing at you (like a deceiving spirit) on the other side. . . . This treaty will remove you to a new home: one of your own choice and selection. The same land selected by your chiefs while at Washington. You will, when there, be . . . near Fort Leavenworth where your Great Father could protect you with a strong arm from all bad men, whether red or white"); Treaty with the Quapaw Indians, May 13, 1833, 7 Stat. 424, Speech of Commissioner in Council Meeting Connected with the Negotiation of a Treaty (May 13, 1833) (Record Group 75, supra note 48, Roll 3: Ratified Treaty No. 186) ("Brothers . . . [your Great Father] will assist you in building houses and give your women wheels and looms and learn them to spin and weave and make cloth to clothe your children. You will have a permanent home . . . open your ears to the counsel of your Great Father and you will find him forever your friend and protector").

58. Jackson, his Indian commissioners, and their successors forcefully drove home this point. Anticipating that very few tribal Indians would care to submit to state law, government negotiators spared no threats of its imposition when it came to coaxing the Eastern tribes to accept new homelands west of the Mississippi. See, e.g., Treaty of Dancing Rabbit Creek with the Choctaw Nation, Sept. 27, 1830, 7 Stat. 333, Statement by Commissioners in Journal of Proceedings Connected with the Negotiation of a

Treaty (Sept. 18, 1830) (Record Group 75, supra note 48, Roll 2: Ratified Treaty No. 160):

> Brothers . . . Are you willing to remain here and live as white men? Are you willing to be sued in courts, there to be tried and punished for any offenses you may commit? To be subjected to taxes—to work upon roads, and attend in musters? For all these you must do. If under this state of things it is believed you can be contented and happy, then dwell upon the lands where you live. But if you are satisfied that under such a condition of things you cannot be happy, consent to remain beyond the Mississsippi, where you will be away from the white people, and from their laws, and be able to live under your own.

And if mild persuasion did not succeed, more direct coercion usually did:

> If you take [the treaty offer] your people will be made comfortable and happy forever . . . in your own country. . . . Should you refuse to take it neither this or any other offer will ever be made to you again. . . . What then will be your situation and condition—you will have to pay back to the United States the $6000 your chiefs spent in going to Washington to do nothing. You will have to begin to pay back a very large sum of annuity money which was improperly paid to you. . . . You will in fact have very little annuity money left for your people, you will be very poor. The bad Sioux, the waves of population from Iowa, and the firey water will like a serpent destroy your people. In a few years you will *implore* your Great Father to remove you. You will then be willing to remove (the few that remain among you) without either money or annuity. For such will be your distress that you will be satisfied with a removal on any condition. . . . You will be found on your knees asking for a mouthful of something to eat for yourselves and children.

Treaty with the Potawatamie Nation, June 5 & 17, 1846, 9 Stat. 853, Speech of Commissioner in Journal of Proceedings Connected with the Negotiation of a Treaty (June 3, 1846) (Record Group 75, supra note 48, Roll 4: Ratified Treaty No. 247).

59. Treaty with the Red Lake and Pembina Bands of Chippewa Indians, April 13, 1864, 13 Stat. 689, Speech of Hse-Ne-Wab in Council Meeting Connected with the Negotiation of a Treaty (April 13, 1864) (Record Group 75, supra note 48, Roll 7: Ratified Treaty No. 330). See also, e.g., Treaty with the Confederated Tribes of Sac and Fox, Oct. 1, 1859, 15 Stat. 467, Speech of Chief Kev Kuch in Council Meeting Connected with the Negotiation of a Treaty (July 16, 1859) (Record Group 75, supra note 48, Roll 6: Ratified Treaty No. 312) ("We wish to improve our condition, to have houses, hogs and stock of all kinds. . . . We also wish to have school for purposes of educating our children").

60. Treaty of Prairie du Chien with the Chippewa, Ottawa, and Po-

tawatamie, July 29, 1829, 7 Stat. 320, Speech of Wau-Kann-Tshah-Wau-Kee-Kgan (Whirling Thunder) in Journal of Proceedings Connected with the Negotiation of a Treaty (July 27, 1829) (Record Group 75, supra note 48, Roll 2: Ratified Treaty No. 155). See also, e.g., Treaty of Green Bay with the Potawatamie, Chippewa, Ottawa, and Winnebago Tribes, Aug. 25, 1828, 7 Stat. 315, Speech of Little Priest in Journal of Proceedings Connected with the Negotiation of a Treaty (Aug. 24, 1828) (Record Group 75, supra note 48, Roll 2: Ratified Treaty No. 153) ("You think nothing of the land because the Great Spirit made you with paper in one hand and pen in the other and although he made us at the same time, he did not make us like you. We think of nothing but what is on the land.").

61. Treaty with the Confederated Tribes of Sac and Fox, Oct. 1, 1859, 15 Stat. 467, Speech by Sac Chief in Council Meeting Connected with the Negotiation of Treaty (July 1, 1859) (Record Group 75, supra note 48, Roll 6: Ratified Treaty No. 312). See also H. Malone, Cherokees of the Old South: A People in Transition 57–173 (1956).

62. See, e.g., Treaty of Dancing Rabbit Creek with the Choctaw Nation, Sept. 27, 1830, 7 Stat. 333, Choctaw Response to letter of President Jackson delivered in Council Meeting (Aug. 25, 1830) (Record Group 75, supra note 48, Roll 2: Ratified Treaty No. 160) ("Father . . . we humbly beg leave to represent to you that we have arrived to the age of maturity, and that we may continue to act on this important occasion as will be best calculated to obtain so desirable objects: peace, quietness, and a perpetual home"); Treaty with the Potawatamie Nation, June 5 & 17, 1846, 9 Stat. 853, Reply on behalf of Indian delegation by R. Elliot in Journal of Proceedings Connected with the Negotiation of a Treaty (Nov. 12, 1845) (Record Group 75, supra note 48, Roll 4: Ratified Treaty No. 247) ("A white man is called wise who endeavors to get himself a good home and to make his family comfortable. This is all we wish to do. . . . We look at the path behind us as well as the one before us. We trust [our Great Father] will do the same"); Id. at Speech of Ne-Ar-Ne in Journal of Proceedings (June 4, 1846) ("You tell us this home is to be a permanent one and we hope this will be so. Our women and children have heard this and it made their hearts glad to think they will have a home forever").

63. Treaty with the Quapaw Indians, May 13, 1833, 7 Stat. 424, Speech of Head Chief of Quapaw Tribe in Council Meeting Connected with the Negotiation of a Treaty (May 10, 1833) (Record Group 75, supra note 48, Roll 3: Ratified Treaty No. 186).

64. Treaty of Butte des Morts with the Chippewa, Menominee, and Winnebago Tribes, Aug. 11, 1827, 7 Stat. 303, Statements by Chief in Journal of Proceedings Connected with the Negotiation of a Treaty (Aug. 9, 1827) (Record Group 75, supra note 48, Roll 2: Ratified Treaty No. 148). Thus as tribal chiefs and headmen sought to retain lands for their people,

they also were aware that promises of perpetual tribal homelands would be empty without contemporaneous guarantees that their people would be secured in those homelands against white encroachment. See, e.g., Treaty with the Quapaw Indians, May 13, 1833, 7 Stat. 424, Speech of Head Chief of Quapaw Tribe in Council Meeting Connected with the Negotiation of a Treaty (May 13, 1833) (Record Group 75, supra note 48, Roll 3: Ratified Treaty No. 186) ("If the white people trouble us in the country to which we are to move, we hope our Great Father will send them from us"); Treaty with the Cherokee Nation, February 27, 1819, 7 Stat. 195, Letter from Head Chief Path Killer in connection with Negotiation of a Treaty (June 12, 1818) (Record Group 75, supra note 48, Roll 1: Ratified Treaty No. 106) ("Our Father the president promised . . . he would draw a line and blaze the trees as a boundary between us and [the white man] so that if any of your people should intrude on us . . . he would put them on their own side. It is my wish to . . . never leave that promise behind").

65. Kinney has found reference to the allotment of Indian land as early as 1633. J. Kinney, A Continent Lost—A Civilization Won 82–83 (1937). On early-nineteenth-century allotments, see id. at 83–94; M. Young, Redskins, Ruffleshirts, and Rednecks—Indian Allotments in Alabama and Mississippi (1961). The Manypenny administration is discussed in F. Cohen, supra note 1, at 98–102.

The existence of these early allotments shows that the General Allotment Act of 1887, ch. 119, 24 Stat. 388 (currently codified at scattered sections of 25 U.S.C. (1982)) did not arise full-blown. Comparatively, however, the allotting of land proceeded slowly until the 1887 act. In the years prior to 1887, about 584,000 acres were allotted. Nearly 5 million acres of tribal land were allotted to individual Indians between 1887 and 1900 alone. D. Otis, The Dawes Act and the Allotment of Indian Lands 87 (1973). In total, more than 35 million acres were allotted between 1887 and 1934. During this same period, Indian allottees transferred nearly 27 million acres of allotted lands to non-Indians. Thirty-eight million acres of unallotted tribal lands were declared "surplus" to Indian needs and were ceded to the federal government for sale to non-Indians. The government opened to homesteading outrightly another 22 million acres of "surplus" tribal lands. As a result, total Indian landholdings dropped from 138 million acres in 1887 to 52 million in 1934. II F. Prucha, supra note 51, at 896.

66. The 1871 act, ch. 120, 16 Stat. 566, is discussed in note 3, supra. On the BIA boarding schools, see, e.g., F. Prucha, American Indian Policy in Crisis—Christian Reformers and the Indian, 1865–1900, 265–291 (1976); I F. Prucha, supra note 51, at 687–711; M. Szasz, Education and the American Indian 8–11 (2d ed. 1977).

67. Act of Feb. 8, 1887, ch. 119, 24 Stat. 388 (codified as amended at 25 U.S.C. §§ 331–34, 339, 341–42, 348–49, 354, 381). Kelly states that "the

concept of autonomous Indian enclaves remained fixed in federal policy"
until the passage of the 1887 act. L. Kelly, The Assault on Assimilation—
John Collier and the Origins of Indian Policy Reform 147 (1983).

68. F. Prucha, supra note 66, at v.

69. Quoted in S. Tyler, A History of Indian Policy 104 (1973). Roosevelt
borrowed the phrase from Merrill Gates, past president and secretary of
the board of Indian commissioners, who had used it at the Lake Mohonk
Conference of 1900. F. Prucha, supra note 66, at 257 n.67. Although the
results of allotment and assimilation are widely perceived as being disastrous
for Indians, most historians emphasize that the 1887 act was widely supported by those whites who sympathized with the Indian cause. See, e.g.,
J. Kinney, supra note 65, at 208–13; D. Otis, supra note 64, at 8–39.

70. Individual acreages are provided for in 25 U.S.C. § 331 (1982).
The Burke Act of 1906 is found at ch. 2348, 34 Stat. 182 (codified at 25
U.S.C. § 349 (1982)); other provisions concerning restrictions on allotments
are discussed in F. Cohen, supra note 1, at 619–21. On competency commissions, see, e.g., Institute for Government Research, The Problem of
Indian Administration 100–05, 115, 172–76, 470–72 (L. Meriam ed. 1928).
The surplus lands provision is set out at ch. 119, § 5, 24 Stat. 388 (1887).
Proceeds from surplus land sales went to the tribes. See generally Solem
v. Bartlett, 104 S. Ct. 1161 (1984); DeCoteau v. District County Court,
420 U.S. 425 (1975). Subsequently, tribes were allowed to seek recovery
in the Indian Claims Commission if compensation for surplus land sales
was inadequate. F. Cohen, supra note 1, at 565–66.

71. On the loss of Indian land due to the allotment policy, see note
65, supra; A. Josephy, Now That the Buffalo's Gone 131–32 (1982).

72. A. Debo, supra note 50, at 276–77, (emphasis in original).

73. See, note 65, supra.

74. On the checkerboard pattern and fractionated heirships, see note
8, supra. The leasing of Indian land to non-Indians during the allotment
era, often at below-market prices, has received widespread criticism. See,
e.g., J. Kinney, supra note 65, at 214–48; I F. Prucha, supra note 51, at
671–73; F. Prucha, supra note 66, at 258–62.

75. W. Washburn, Red Man's Land/White Man's Law: A Study of the
Past and Present Status of the American Indian 75–76 (1971). On tribal
courts during this era, see generally W. Hagan, Indian Policy and Judges—
Experiments in Acculturation and Control (1966). On the role of the Bureau
of Indian Affairs, see, e.g., W. Washburn, supra note 71, at 169 ("In the
later nineteenth century, . . . the white power began to overwhelm and
break the autonomy of the Indian nations, and the Indian agent—repre-
senting the Great Father in Washington—began to infringe on the prerogatives of Indian leaders"). On the period between 1887 and 1934, see
generally A. Josephy, supra note 71, at 84–86; Americanizing the American

Indians (F. Prucha ed. 1973); F Hoxie, A Final Promise: The Campaign to Assimilate the Indians, 1880–1920 (1984).

76. The IRA is found at ch. 576, 48 Stat. 984 (1934) (codified as amended at 25 U.S.C. §§ 461–79 (1982)). The IRA and its leader, John Collier, remain controversial. Tribes were generally encouraged to exercise governmental authority on a number of fronts, with the result that a strong tribal presence emerged on most reservations for the first time since the nineteenth century. On the other hand, the tribal councils recognized by the Department of the Interior sometimes did not represent traditional elements within the tribes. As a result, on some reservations today there are disputes over leadership, with the government-recognized councils challenged by "shadow" traditional governments. See generally V. Deloria & C. Lytle, supra note 38; L. Kelly, supra note 67; K. Philp, John Collier's Crusade for Indian Reform (1977).

77. See generally Wilkinson & Biggs, The Evolution of the Termination Policy, 5 Am. Ind. L. Rev. 139 (1977).

78. See, e.g., F. Cohen, supra note 1, at 673–77.

79. See notes 72, 74, 75 supra.

80. On the homestead policy, which has been described as one of the most progressive land policies undertaken by any nation, see generally P. Gates, History of Public Land Law Development 387–434 (1968).

81. See, e.g., Solem v. Bartlett, 104 S. Ct. 1161, 1165 (1984) ("Another reason why Congress did not concern itself with the [jurisdictional] effect of surplus land acts on reservation boundaries was the turn-of-the-century assumption that Indian reservations were a thing of the past. . . . [T]he Indian tribes would enter traditional American society and the reservation system would cease to exist") (footnote omitted).

82. 21 U.S. (8 Wheat.) 543 (1823) (tribes possess title right of occupancy to aboriginal lands but alienation of Indian title permissible only with federal approval).

83. 30 U.S. (5 Pet.) 1 (1831) (Indian tribes characterized as "domestic, dependent nations" with a relationship to the United States that "resembles that of a ward to his guardian").

84. 31 U.S. (6 Pet.) 515 (1832) (Indian tribes possess inherent sovereignty and are substantially free from state jurisdiction).

85. 109 U.S. 556 (1883) (murder of one Indian by another punishable only by the tribe because Congress had not expressly provided for federal court jurisdiction). The result in *Crow Dog* was obviated two years later when Congress passed the Major Crimes Act, ch. 341, § 9, 223 Stat. 385 (currently codified as amended at 18 U.S.C. 1153 (1982)).

86. 163 U.S. 376 (1896) (Indian tribes not limited by the grand jury requirement because tribal powers preexisted the Constitution and were not restricted by the Fifth or Fourteenth amendments). Several provisions

of the Bill of Rights were later made applicable to tribes by the passage of the Indian Civil Rights Act of 1968, Pub. L. 90–284, title II, 82 Stat. 77 (codified at 25 U.S.C. §§ 1301–03 (1982).

87. 118 U.S. 375 (1886) (upholding the federal prosecution of crimes committed by Indians on reservations pursuant to the Major Crimes Act, supra note 85).

88. 104 U.S. 621 (1882) (upholding state jurisdiction over the murder of a non-Indian by a non-Indian in Indian country in spite of the provisions of the General Crimes Act, 18 U.S.C. § 1152 (1982), which directed that federal criminal jurisdiction "shall extend to the Indian country" with exceptions not applicable to the facts of *McBratney,* see Ch. 4, note 4, infra.).

89. 187 U.S. 553 (1903) (upholding federal sale of tribal land even though 1867 treaty requirement of consent of three-fourths of all adult male Indians to any land sale was not met).

90. Kagama v. United States, 118 U.S. 375, 383–84 (1886) (emphasis in original).

91. One reflection of the decline in the national significance of Indian policy since the mid-nineteenth century is reflected in Congress's abandonment of treaty making in 1871, 25 U.S.C. § 71 (1982), and the abolition of the two standing Committees on Indian Affairs in the Senate and House of Representatives in 1946. See F. Cohen, supra note 1, at 159. Until the late 1970s, Indian matters were relegated to subcommittees. Id. Today, after several years of existence of a temporary committee in the Senate, there is once again a permanent Select Committee on Indian Affairs in the Senate (S. Res. 127, 98th Cong., 2d Sess., 130 Cong. Rec. S 6673 (No. 75, June 6, 1984)). In the House, however, there is no longer even a subcommittee: Indian issues are heard by panels of the House Committee on Interior and Insular Affairs. Official Congressional Directory, 99th Congress, 297, 330–31 (1985).

Of course, during the last fifteen years several Indian issues have proved to be of major state, regional, even national interest. The leading examples are the legislation over Alaska land claims, e.g., M. Berry, The Alaska Pipeline: The Politics of Oil and the Native Land Claims (1975); the Eastern land claims, e.g., McLoughlin, Giving It Back to the Indians, 239 Atl. Monthly 70 (Feb. 1977); the fishing controversies in several states, e.g., C. Williams & W. Neubrech, Indian Treaties—American Nightmare (1976); and Indian water issues in the West, e.g., Hundley, The "Winters" Decision and Indian Water Rights: A Mystery Reexamined, 13 W. Hist. Q. 17 (1982). The relative prominence of these and other issues, however, does not begin to rival the central policy position that Indian affairs occupied in the early days of the Republic.

92. See Brown v. Board of Education, 347 U.S. 483 (1954) (school desegregation).

93. The equal footing doctrine was employed by the Court to justify state jurisdiction in Indian country in several nineteenth-century cases. See Draper v. United States, 164 U.S. 240, 243 (1896); Ward v. Race Horse, 163 U.S. 504, 514–15 (1896); United States v. McBratney, 104 U.S. 621, 624 (1882). All of those cases, however, can be explained on other grounds, e.g., New York ex rel. Ray v. Martin, 326 U.S. 496, 500–01 (1946), quoted in Ch. 4, note 4, infra, and the applicability of the equal footing doctrine was squarely rejected as to Indian reservations in United States v. Winans, 198 U.S. 371, 382–84 (1905). See also Winters v. United States, 207 U.S. 564, 577–78 (1908). Nevertheless, several cases continued to justify the extension of state jurisdiction to Indian country based on the equal footing doctrine. See, e.g., Tooisgah v. United States, 186 F.2d 93, 96–97 (10th Cir. 1950); State v. Towessnute, 89 Wash. 478, 487, 154 P. 805, 809 (1916). As recently as 1963, the Washington Supreme Court used the equal footing doctrine to support a broad-based denial of federal power over Indian affairs: "[T]reaties do not impair the police powers of the state. . . . The United States may grant such rights in the soil while lands are held in territorial status without conflict with the subsequent admission of states upon equal footing." State v. McCoy, 63 Wash. 2d 421, 434–36, 387 P. 2d 942, 950–52 (1963).

94. 25 U.S.C. § 71 (1982), discussed in note 3, supra. See, e.g., United States v. Blackfeet Tribe, 364 F. Supp. 192, 194 (D. Mont. 1965).

95. 8 U.S.C. § 1401(b) (1982). See e.g., Red Hawk v. Joines, 129 Or. 620, 629, 278 P. 572, 576 (1929) ("[I]n view of the [Act of June 2, 1924] . . . tribal relations are thereby declared abolished and citizenship conferred in its place").

96. 31 U.S. (6 Pet.) 515, 563–96 (1832).

97. These cases are collected in Ch. 2, infra.

98. See, e.g., State v. Wallahee, 143 Wash. 117, 118, 255 P. 94, 95 (1927) ("[T]he United States government was the sovereign and did not undertake to part with its sovereign rights by [treaties]. . . . [T]he Yakima tribe was not an independent nation nor a sovereign entity of any kind, the Indians being mere occupants of the land"). See also note 102, infra; Bean, The Limits of Indian Tribal Sovereignty: The Cornucopia of Inherent Powers, 49 N.D.L. Rev. 303 (1973).

99. See, e.g., McClanahan v. Arizona State Tax Comm'm, 14 Ariz. App. 452, 455–56, 484 P.2d 221, 224–25 (1971), rev'd, 411 U.S. 164 (1973); Warren Trading Post Co. v. Moore, 95 Ariz. 110, 117, 387 P.2d 809, 814 (1963) rev'd sub nom. Warren Trading Post Co. v. Arizona State Tax Comm'n, 380 U.S. 685 (1965); Tenorio v. Tenorio, 44 N.M. 89, 102–104, 98 P.2d 838, 846–47 (1940); Trujillo v. Prince, 42 N.M. 337, 341, 350, 78 P.2d 145, 147, 153 (1938); Red Hawk v. Joines, 129 Or. 620, 634, 278 P. 572, 577 (1929). The Supreme Court itself made a similar suggestion in

Organized Village of Kake v. Egan, 369 U.S., 60, 72–74 (1962), but the Court later made it clear that *Kake* did not stand for a presumption of state jurisdiction as to reservation lands. McClanahan v. Arizona State Tax Comm'n, 411 U.S. 164, 176 n.15 (1973).

100. The effects of this approach, which was rejected in McClanahan v. Arizona State Tax Comm'n, 411 U.S. 164, 169–73 (1973), are discussed further in the text in Ch. 4, notes 47–69, infra.

101. See United States v. Wright, 53 F.2d 300, 307 (4th Cir. 1931):

[N]o act of Congress in [the Indians'] behalf would be valid which interfered with the exercise of the police power of the state. In such a situation, a law to be sustained must have relation to the purpose for which the federal government exercises guardianship and protection over a people subject to the laws of one of the states; i.e., it must have reasonable relation to their economic welfare.

See also State v. McCoy, 63 Wash. 2d 421, 387 P.2d 942 (1963), quoted in note 93, supra.

102. See, e.g., Settler v. Yakima Tribal Court, 419 F.2d 486, 489 (9th Cir. 1969), cert. denied, 398 U.S. 903 (1970); Colliflower v. Garland, 342 F.2d 369, 378–79 (9th Cir. 1965).

103. Bad Horse v. Bad Horse, 163 Mont. 445, 517 P.2d 893, 897, cert. denied, 419 U.S. 847 (1974). See also, e.g., Brough v. Appawora, 553 P.2d 934, 935 (Utah 1976), vacated and remanded, 431 U.S. 901 (1977) ("The Ute nation, of the long-ago treaty, no longer exists, and the descendants of the inhabitants of that nation are now citizens of the United States. When a nation ceases to exist, its treaties are no longer of any force or effect"). State v. Towessnute, 89 Wash. 478, 481–82, 154 P. 805, 807 (1916) ("The premise of Indian sovereignty we reject. . . . At no time did our ancestors in getting title to this continent ever regard the aborigines as other than mere occupants, and incompetent occupants, of the soil . . . . The Indian was a child, and a dangerous child).

104. Oliver, The Legal Status of American Indian Tribes, 38 Or. L. Rev. 193, 231 (1959).

105. Higgins, International Law Considerations of the American Indian Nations by the United States, 3 Ariz. L. Rev. 74, 82 (1961). Higgins concluded that invoking the doctrine would be "unappealing" since the "very conditions which changed were—partly intentionally, partly unintentionally—effected by a party to the treaty contract, i.e., the United States." Id. at 84.

106. 129 F. Supp. 15, (D.S.D. 1955), aff'd, 231 F.2d 89 (8th Cir. 1956).

107. 129 F. Supp. at 17 (emphasis supplied).

108. Iron Crow v. Oglala Sioux Tribe, 231 F.2d 89, 99 (8th Cir. 1956).

109. Barta v. Oglala Sioux Tribe, 259 F.2d 553, 556 (8th Cir. 1958).

110. Native American Church v. Navajo Tribal Council, 272 F.2d 131, 134–35 (10th Cir. 1959).

111. Morgan v. Colorado River Indian Tribe, 103 Ariz. 425, 428 n.1, 443 P.2d 421, 424 n.1 (1968) (citations omitted).

112. A. Miller, Social Change and Fundamental Law 11 (1981). The manner in which law is to meet the needs of changing times and circumstances is an issue that arises in any legal system. But while continuity and change are essential attributes of most bodies of law, different legal–political systems have balanced the need for continuity and change in different ways. See, e.g., G. Calabresi, A Common Law for the Age of Statutes 3–5 (1982). In this country, the common law courts have been the principal instruments for balancing competing considerations of continuity and change by setting cases against the backdrop of contemporary realities. See, e.g., G. Calabresi, supra, at 13; B. Cardozo, The Growth of the Law 56–80 (1924); W. Friedmann, Law in a Changing Society 24–34 (1959).

Jurists generally accept the proposition that the common law would almost certainly no longer exist if courts had not from time to time taken note of changes in the social fabric and laid down new principles to meet the needs and problems posed by those changes. See W. Friedmann, supra, at 26. One writer has succinctly expressed this view by characterizing American law as "Darwinian rather than Newtonian, [as] it follows the laws of life rather than of mechanics." A. Miller, supra, at 4. See generally, L. Friedman, A History of American Law (1973); Hart, Positivism and the Separation of Law and Morals, 71 Harv. L. Rev. 593 (1958).

113. While Congress is a legislative body with only those powers expressly granted to it by the Constitution, state governments have all powers not explicitly or implicitly prohibited by the Constitution. U.S. Const. amend. X. See generally L. Tribe, American Constitutional Law 224–27 (1978). Just prior to the Civil War, political and judicial thought had begun to recognize and define the inherent need of governments to protect the health, safety, and welfare of its citizens from unrestrained exercise of individual liberties. See, e.g., Charles River Bridge Co. v. Warren Bridge Co., 36 U.S. (11 Pet.) 420 (1837); E. Corwin, Liberty Against Government 88 (1948). This came to be known as the "police power" concept, encompassing the right of state and local governments to protect the "health, safety, morals or general welfare of people within their jurisdiction." J. Nowak, R. Rotunda & J. Young, Constitutional Law 429 (2nd ed. 1983).

114. Worcester v. Georgia, 31 U.S. (6 Pet.) 515, 560–61 (1832) ("[T]he settled doctrine of the law of nations is, that a weaker power does not surrender its independence—its right to self-government, by associating with a stronger, and taking its protection. A weak state, in order to provide for its safety, may place itself under the protection of one more powerful, without stripping itself of the right of government, and ceasing to be a state").

115. In *Worcester*, Marshall announced virtually every basic doctrine in Indian law: federal plenary power ("The whole intercourse between the United States and this nation is, by our Constitution and laws, vested in the government of the United States," id. at 561); the trust relationship ("From the commencement of our government, Congress has passed acts to regulate trade and intercourse with the Indians; which treat them as nations, respect their rights, and manifest a firm purpose to afford that protection which treaties stipulate," id. at 556–57); the reserved rights doctrine ("[T]he Indian nations possessed a full right to [their] lands . . . until that right should be extinguished by the United States, with their consent," id. at 560); and the general exclusion of state law from Indian country ("The Cherokee nation, then, is a distinct community, occupying its own territory, with boundaries accurately described, in which the laws of Georgia can have no force," id. at 561).

116. E.g., R. Barsh & Y. Henderson, The Road: Indian Tribes and Political Liberty 56–61 (1980); Walters, Review Essay: Preemption, Tribal Sovereignty, and Worcester v. Georgia, 62 Or. L. Rev. 127 (1983).

117. Worcester v. Georgia, 31 U.S. (6 Pet.) 515, 559–60 (1832).

118. Id. at 542, 561.

119. Id. at 559–61.

120. Id. at 559–62.

121. Id. at 556–57.

122. Id. at 542–43, 546–47, 555–57.

123. Id. at 542–45.

124. In discussing the evolution of Indian law since *Worcester*, the Court described the notions in *Worcester* as "platonic." McClanahan v. Arizona State Tax Comm'n, 411 U.S. 164, 172 (1973).

125. See, e.g., National Farmers Union Ins. Cos. v. Crow Tribe of Indians, 105 S. Ct. 2447, 2452 n.14 (1985); Montana v. Blackfeet Tribe of Indians, 105 S. Ct. 2399, 2402 (1985); County of Oneida v. Oneida Indian Nation, 105 S. Ct. 1245, 1251 (1985); Three Affiliated Tribes of the Fort Berthold Reservation v. Wold Engineering, 104 S. Ct. 2267, 2271 (1984); Rice v. Rehner, 463 U.S. 713, 718 (1983); New Mexico v. Mescalero Apache Tribe, 462 U.S. 324, 331 (1983); Merrion v. Jicarilla Apache Tribe, 455 U.S. 130, 140 (1982); White Mountain Apache Tribe v. Bracker, 448 U.S. 136, 141 (1980); United States v. Wheeler, 435 U.S. 313, 331 (1978); Oliphant v. Suquamish Indian Tribe, 435 U.S. 191, 207 (1978); McClanahan v. Arizona State Tax Comm'n, 411 U.S. 164, 168 (1973).

126. Since 1970, *Worcester* has been cited by state and federal courts more than virtually any other case handed down by the Supreme Court between 1789 and the end of the Civil War. The only cases cited more often are Marbury v. Madison, 5 U.S. (1 Cranch) 137 (1803); McCulloch v. Maryland, 17 U.S. (4 Wheat) 316 (1819); and United States v. Perez, 22

U.S. (9 Wheat) 579 (1824). See Shepard's United States Citations—Cases, Case Edition Supplements (1971–85).

CHAPTER 2. INSULATION AGAINST TIME

    1. 31 U.S. (6 Pet.) 515, 563–96 (1832) (McLean, J., concurring).

    2. Id. at 593–94.

    3. 25 F. Cas. 422 (C.C.D. Ohio 1835) (No. 14,795). See also State v. Foreman, 160 Tenn. (8 Yer.) 256 (1835).

    4. At issue in *Worcester* were a number of Georgia laws that purported to extend state authority over the Cherokees. 31 U.S. (6 Pet.) at 542, 577–78. See generally G. Foreman, Indian Removal 229–30 (1932). The 1802 Trade and Intercourse Act is cited as Act of March 30, 1802, ch. 13, 2 Stat. 139. The Ohio laws are described at United States v. Cisna, 25 F. Cas. at 422.

    5. 25 F. Cas. at 424. The passage in full reads as follows:

> The law of 1802 is constitutional, and so the supreme court have decided. That this act had a constitutional operation upon the Wyandott Nation admits of no doubt; and it remains to be considered whether the situation of this tribe has become so changed as to render this law inoperative as to them. The territory of the Wyandotts, as before stated, is limited to twelve miles square, and it is surrounded by a dense white population, which have daily intercourse with the Indians. Stores and taverns are kept within the reservation by the Indians or those connected with them, which are as much resorted to for trade and other purposes, by the surrounding white population, as similar establishments in any other part of the country. The treaties made with this tribe have not been abrogated, and they hold their possessory right to the soil on the same tenure as other tribes with whom treaties have been made. And a sub-agent of the government still resides among them, through whom the government holds its official intercourse with the tribe. The Wyandotts have made rapid advances in the arts of civilization. Many of them are very intelligent; their farms are well improved, and they generally live in good houses. They own property of almost every kind, and enjoy the comforts of life in as high a degree as many of their white neighbors.

    6. The opinion emphasized that federal and state actions concerning the assimilation of the Wyandotts were so clear that the federal acts "may be presumed" to amount to an abrogation of the relative provisions of the Trade and Intercourse Act. 25 F. Cas. at 425. Today, it is settled that federal acts involving Indians are strictly construed against implied repeals. See, e.g., Morton v. Mancari, 417 U.S. 535, 551 (1974); Menominee Tribe of Indians v. United States, 391 U.S. 404, 412–13 (1968). See generally pp. 46–52, infra.

Justice McLean also read federal power under the Indian Commerce Clause very narrowly in United States v. Bailey, 24 F. Cas. 937 (C.C. Tenn. 1834) (No. 14,495), where the opinion struck down the Indian Country Crimes Act of 1817, providing for certain crimes committed on Indian reservations, ch. 92, 3 Stat. 383 (current version at 18 U.S.C. § 1152 (1982)). The Court later upheld the Indian Country Crimes Act, but it construed the fact situation in *Bailey*, involving the murder of a non-Indian by another non-Indian, to be outside of the scope of the act. See United States v. McBratney, 104 U.S. 621 (1882). The Supreme Court has since considered the Indian Commerce Clause to be considerably broader than McLean's view. See, e.g., United States v. Antelope, 430 U.S. 641, 645 & n.6 (1977).

7. 72 U.S. (5 Wall.) 737 (1866). For the citation of *Cisna* to the Court, see the summary of the parties' briefs, 18 L.Ed. at 671.

8. 104 U.S. 621 (1882). See also Forty-Three Gallons of Cognac Brandy, 11 F. 47, 51–52 (C.C.D. Minn. 1882) (Relying upon *Cisna* and stating, "If Indians occupy a territory of very limited extent, surrounded by a white population which necessarily have daily intercourse with them, and it becomes impracticable to enforce the law, the federal jurisdiction must cease").

9. The Indian Country Crimes Act, 18 U.S.C. § 1152 (1982), provides that the general criminal laws of the United States "shall extend to the Indian country." Three exceptions are enumerated, but none of them applies to the situation in *McBratney*, the murder of one non-Indian by another non-Indian. Reasons for the Court's finding that federal jurisdiction did not apply in spite of the language of the act are discussed in F. Cohen, Handbook of Federal Indian Law 264–66 (1982 ed.) [hereinafter cited as F. Cohen]. See also Ch. 4, note 4, infra.

10. 20 R.I. 715, 40 A. 347 (1898). See also, e.g., State v. Doxtater, 47 Wis. 278, 2 N.W. 439 (1879).

11. See, e.g., New York ex rel. Ray v. Martin, 326 U.S. 496 (1946); Oklahoma Tax Comm'n v. United States, 319 U.S. 598, 603 (1943).

12. 411 U.S. 164, 173 n.12 (1973).

13. 425 U.S. 463 (1976).

14. The statute imposed the tax upon purchasers rather than upon the Indian sellers. That provision was approved as to non-Indian purchasers, as was a state requirement that the Indian sellers keep records of the transactions. Id. at 482–83. The Court struck down a personal property tax, vendor license fee, and tax on cigarette sales by Indians to Indians. Id. at 480–81.

The taxing system approved by the Court has allowed other states to collect taxes in Indian country on cigarette sales by individual Indians to non-Indians. In addition, *Moe* was used as precedent for upholding taxes in a somewhat more difficult situation, where tribes, not just individual tribal members, were involved in the sales. Washington v. Confederated Tribes of the Colville Indian Reservation, 447 U.S. 134 (1980). See Ch. 4, notes 60, 117, infra.

15. Situated on 1.25 million picturesque acres in northwestern Montana, the Flathead Reservation lies on the western slope of the Continental Divide in a broad, fertile valley bounded on the north by Flathead Lake, one of the largest freshwater lakes in the West. The soaring Cabinet Mountains and Mission Range stand, respectively, as the western and eastern bounds of the glacial valley. The region also includes a sizeable prairie and numerous lakes, reservoirs, creeks, and rivers. See generally O. Johnson, Flathead and Kootenay: The Rivers, the Tribes and the Region's Traders 29–33 (1969).

The Treaty of Hell Gate, 12 Stat. 975, ordained the present Flathead Reservation, along with part of the Bitteroot Valley, for "the use and occupation" of the Salish & Kootenai tribes. Id. at art. II, para. 1, 12 Stat. 975–76. Following the passage of the General Allotment Act in 1887, Ch. 1, note 67, supra, each tribal member was accorded 40, 80, or 160 acres of land; any land not homesteaded reverted to the tribe. In 1910 the reservation was opened for settlement by non-Indians, and presently more than half of its 1.25 million acres is held in fee by either Indian or non-Indian landowners. Of the remaining land, about 51,000 acres are held by allottees and about 562,000 acres are tribal trust land. See generally Bureau of Indian Affairs, Department of the Interior, American Indian Tribes of Montana and Wyoming 43–55, 117–18 (1978); Moe v. Confederated Salish & Kootenai Tribes, 425 U.S. 463, 466–67 (1976).

16. Confederated Salish & Kootenai Tribes v. Moe, 392 F. Supp. 1297, 1317–24 (D. Mont. 1975) (three-judge court) (Smith, J., dissenting).

17. Id. at 1323–24.

18. Moe v. Confederated Salish & Kootenai Tribes, 425 U.S. 463, 476 (1976). The Kansas Indians, 72 U.S. (5 Wall.) 737 (1866), is discussed in the text accompanying note 7, supra.

19. Id. at 476. In *McClanahan*, the Court noted that state law did have some impact on the Navajo Reservation, citing education and health expenditures, the Navajos' right to vote in state elections, and the tribal members' right to use state courts. 411 U.S. at 173 n.12. The Court then expressly approved the *Kansas Indians* test that "'[c]onferring rights and privileges on these Indians cannot affect their situation, which can only be changed by treaty stipulation, or a voluntary abandonment of their tribal organization.' The Kansas Indians, 5 Wall. at 757." Id. The *Kansas Indians* test should not be read literally. In addition to voluntary abandonment and treaty stipulations, tribal protections from state law plainly can be terminated by statute. See F. Cohen, supra note 9, at 17–19. Had *Kansas Indians*

not been written during the treaty era, when most relationships with tribes were conducted bilaterally, the Court presumably would have expressly recognized Congress's power to act by unilateral statute.

20. See text accompanying Ch. 4, notes 144–56, infra.

21. An example of the partial application of state law is Public Law 280, enacted in 1953 (Act of Aug. 15, 1953, Pub. L. 83–280, 67 Stat. 589, codified as amended at 28 U.S.C. § 1360, 18 U.S.C. § 1162, and 25 U.S.C. §§ 1321–26 (1982)). See Ch. 1, note 18, supra. On partial federal recognition of tribes, see also Joint Tribal Council of the Passamaquoddy Tribe v. Morton, 528 F.2d 370, 376–80 (lst Cir. 1975). On Congress's power to terminate the federal–tribal relationship entirely, see F. Cohen, supra note 9, at 811–18.

22. See Williams v. Lee, 358 U.S. 217, 223 (1959) ("The cases in this Court have consistently guarded the authority of Indian governments over their reservations. . . . If this power is to be taken away from them, it is for Congress to do it").

23. Most of the pending cases are identified, with estimates as to acreage, in Library of Congress, Congressional Research Service, Indians: Land Claims by Eastern Tribes (Oct. 2, 1978). The Interior Deptartment is now evaluating for litigation a great many additional claims by tribes and individual Indians. See Bureau of Indian Affairs Statute of Limitations Claims List, 48 Fed. Reg. 13,698 (Mar. 31, 1983); 48 Fed. Reg. 51,204 (Nov. 7, 1983).

24. Strong policy considerations have always nourished and fortified these age-old common law statutes and court-made doctrines. The Statute of Limitations was justified by Lord Coke "as calculated so to impose diligence on, and vigilance in, him that was to bring his actions so that, by one constant law, certain limitations might serve, both for time present, and for all times to come." 2 Inst. 95. Equitable doctrines were long ago recognized as essential for the orderly development of the United States by insuring the security of land titles. Lewis v. Marshall 30 U.S. (5 Pet.) 470, 476–77 (1831). Buswell said that for the "dominion of things" to remain certain and preserve peace in the society, "the laches of those who are dilatory in pursuing their just remedies, should be punished, and that those who are indolent shall impute to themselves the punishment." H. Buswell, Statute of Limitations (1889). Estoppel was, and is today, well founded upon a need for certainty, precluding parties from unsettling what has been "fittingly determined." M. Bigelow, The Law of Estoppel 6 (6th ed. 1913). Waiver, a rule of judicial policy, is the "legal outgrowth of judicial abhorrence . . . of a person's taking inconsistent positions and gaining advantages thereby through the aid of the courts." Pabst Brewing Co. v. Milwaukee, 126 Wis. 110, 116, 105 N.W. 563, 566 (1905).

25. 424 U.S. 382 (1976).

26. Id. at 390 ("[Respondents] argue that the ordinances of the Northern Cheyenne Tribe could not deprive the Montana courts of the jurisdiction they exercised over tribal matters prior to organization of the Tribe in 1935. ... [The tribal ordinance of 1935] implements an overriding federal policy which is clearly adequate to defeat state jurisdiction over litigation involving reservation Indians. Accordingly, even if we assume that the Montana courts properly exercised adoption jurisdiction prior to the organization of the tribe, a question we do not now decide, that jurisdiction has now been preempted").

27. 400 U.S. 423 (1971).

28. Under Public Law 280, as originally enacted in 1953, see Ch. 1, note 18, supra, jurisdiction could be transferred to states other than the designated "mandatory" states, but "affirmative legislative action" by such "optional" states was required to effect transfers. 400 U.S. at 425. See generally Washington v. Confederated Bands of the Yakima Indian Nation, 439 U.S. 463 (1979). Montana was an optional state, and its legislature had never taken affirmative legislative action so that Kennerly could not be decided on that basis. 400 U.S. at 427. The act was amended in 1968 to allow a transfer of tribal jurisdiction to a state upon a majority vote of enrolled Indians on the reservation in question, 25 U.S.C. § 1326 (1982), but the Blackfeet Tribal Council had never submitted the action to a vote of the tribe; thus the facts of Kennerly could not be decided on the basis of the 1968 amendment. 400 U.S. at 429. Therefore, under Public Law 280, either as originally written or as amended in 1968, the voluntary action of the tribal council at issue in Kennerly was insufficient to transfer jurisdiction to the state. See 400 U.S. at 429 ("[l]egislative action by the Tribal Council does not comport with the explicit requirements of the Act"). Two judges disagreed on the ground that denying the will of the council would "substantially [frustrate] productive self-government by reservation Indians because it unjustifiably reduces the options available to them with respect to state court jurisdiction" 400 U.S. at 431 (Stewart, J., dissenting).

29. For example, in Moe v. Confederated Salish & Kootenai Tribes, 425 U.S 463 (1976), the tribal members on the Flathead Reservation had paid cigarette taxes before they were challenged and overturned in court. The lower court opinion makes this clear. Confederated Salish & Kootenai Tribes v. Moe, 392 F. Supp. 1297, 1324 (D. Mont. 1975) (three-judge court) (Smith, J., dissenting). The Supreme Court opinion, however, made no reference to the potential waiver issue. Similarly, we know from later litigation by Indians to recover back taxes, Topash v. Commissioner of Revenue, 291 N.W. 2d 679, 680 (Minn. 1980), that Indians in Minnesota had paid the personal property taxes struck down in Bryan v. Itasca County, 426 U.S. 373 (1976). For another suggestion that many reservation Indians paid taxes later found to be beyond the states' jurisdiction, see Staff of

American Indian Policy Review Commission, Report on Federal, State, and Tribal Jurisdiction 103–06 (1976).

30. Arizona v. California, 373 U.S. 546, 601 (1963), discussed in note 52, infra. The result has been different when Indian rights have actually been decreed. See Nevada v. United States, 463 U.S. 110 (1983), discussed in text accompanying notes 44–46, infra. The tribes were unable to exercise their water rights in large part because of federal policy that heavily subsidized non-Indian development through the reclamation program but provided for few Indian reclamation projects. National Water Comm'n, Water Policies for the Future 145–47, 474–75 (1973); 2 R. Clark, Waters and Water Rights 255–79 (1967); Sax, Selling Reclamation Water Rights: A Case Study in Federal Subsidy Policy, 64 Mich. L. Rev. 13 (1965); Ellis & DuMars, The Two-Tiered Market in Western Water, 57 Neb. L. Rev. 333 (1978).

31. Washington v. Washington State Commercial Passenger Fishing Vessel Ass'n, 443 U.S. 658 (1979). The Indian catch before the 1979 decision is discussed in Wilkinson & Conner, The Law of the Pacific Salmon Fishery: Conservation and Allocation of a Transboundary Common Property Resource, 32 U. Kan. L. Rev. 17, 98 & n.438 (1983). Indian fishing had been discontinued entirely at several of their usual and accustomed fishing places. United States v. Washington, 384 F. Supp. 312, 358, 393 (W.D. Wash. 1974). The Court's refusal to give weight to the settled expectations of non-Indians was in one sense easier here than in the other cases discussed in this section because the Court expressly found that the state regulation was "often-discriminatory" against Indians. 443 U.S. at 669.

32. 455 U.S. 130 (1982).

33. 21 U.S. (8 Wheat.) 543 (1823).

34. The first four enactments of the Indian Trade and Intercourse Acts were temporary. See Act of July 22, 1790, ch. 33, 1 Stat. 137; Act of Mar. 1, 1793, ch. 19, 1 Stat. 329; Act of May 19, 1796, ch. 30, 1 Stat. 469; Act of Mar. 3, 1799, ch. 46, 1 Stat. 743. The first permanent Trade and Intercourse Act was the Act of Mar. 30, 1802, ch. 13, 2 Stat. 139. See also Act of May 6, 1822, ch. 58, 3 Stat. 682; Act of June 30, 1834, ch. 161, 4 Stat. 729 (repealed in part) (codified as carried forward and amended at 18 U.S.C. §§ 1152, 1160, 1165 (1982), 25 U.S.C. §§ 177, 179–80, 193–94, 201, 229–30, 251, 263, 264 (1982)). See generally F. Prucha, American Indian Policy in the Formative Years: The Indian Trade and Intercourse Acts, 1790–1834 (1962). The classic piece on Indian title, which discusses the writing of sixteenth-century Spanish scholar Francisco de Victoria and other early thinkers as well as the doctrine's development in England and the United States, is Cohen, Original Indian Title, 32 Minn. L. Rev. 28 (1947). The leading recent article is Clinton & Hotopp, Judicial Enforcement of the Federal Restraints of Indian Land: The Origins of the Eastern Land Claims, 31 Me. L. Rev. 17 (1979). See also F. Cohen, supra note 9, at 50–59, 486–93, 508–28.

35. Oneida Indian Nation v. County of Oneida, 414 U.S. 661 (1974).

36. Id. at 667–68.

37. Wilson v. Omaha Indian Tribe, 442 U.S. 653, 665 (1979). In United States v. Dann, 105 S. Ct. 1058 (1985), the Court held that Indian title had been extinguished when the United States placed funds for compensation, pursuant to an award of the Indian Claims Commission, into a trust account in the Treasury.

38. Mohegan Tribe v. Connecticut, 638 F.2d 612, 614–15 & n.3 (2d Cir. 1980), cert. denied, 101 S. Ct. 3124 (1981); Narragansett Tribe of Indians v. Southern Rhode Island Land Dev. Corp., 418 F. Supp. 798, 804 (D.R.I. 1976); Schaghticoke Tribe of Indians v. Kent School Corp., 423 F. Supp. 780, 784–85 (D. Conn. 1976).

39. 105 S. Ct. 1245 (1985).

40. Id. at 1252 (emphasis in original). Justice Stevens, joined by Chief Justice Burger and Justices White and Rehnquist, concluded in dissent that the claim was barred by laches. The majority did not rule on the laches issue since it had not been raised on appeal, but analyzed the question in a footnote and stated that "the application of laches would appear to be inconsistent with established federal policy." Id. at 1257 n.16.

41. 430 U.S 584 (1977).

42. The Court's extended analysis of the legislative history is found at 430 U.S. at 586–603.

43. 430 U.S. at 603, 604–05. The opinion in DeCoteau v. District County Court, 420 U.S. 425 (1975), involving similar issues on the Lake Traverse Reservation in South Dakota, also discussed the "subsequent jurisdictional history" of the area in question but the Court's reliance on those factors is minimal because the subsequent jurisdictional history was "not wholly clear." 420 U.S. at 442. In its most recent opinion on these issues, holding that the Cheyenne River Reservation had not been disestablished, the Court noted that the use of subsequent demographic information may sometimes be appropriate but that the practice is "unorthodox and potentially unreliable." See Solem v. Bartlett, 104 S. Ct. 1161, 1167 n.13 (1984).

44. 463 U.S. 110 (1983).

45. 460 U.S. 605 (1983).

46. The United States attorney who tried the original adjudication represented both the tribe and its major competitor for water, the Truckee-Carson Irrigation District. The necessity of allocating more water to the tribe in order to protect the fishery in Pyramid Lake was presented to the attorney several times, but he never raised the issue with the trial judge. These factual issues involving a conflict between the tribe and the irrigation district were related at length in the lower court opinion, United States v. Truckee-Carson Irrigation Dist., 649 F.2d 1286, 1291–94, 1309–11 (9th Cir. 1981). The Supreme Court dismissed the issue without extensive analysis

of the facts, stating that it is "the nature of a democratic government" to be "charged with more than one responsibility." Nevada v. United States, 463 U.S. 110, 138 n.15 (1983). The *Nevada* Court's view of this dual responsibility is also discussed in the text accompanying notes 164–66, Ch. 3, infra.

47. 460 U.S. 605, 620 (1983) (citations and footnote omitted).

48. 450 U.S. 544 (1981).

49. The Court alluded to established jurisdictional patterns to support its conclusion that hunting and fishing by nonmembers on non-Indian lands within reservation boundaries is not directly related to internal tribal self-government:

> Any argument that Resolution No. 74–05 is necessary to Crow tribal self-government is refuted by the findings of the District Court that the State of Montana has traditionally exercised 'near exclusive' jurisdiction over hunting and fishing on fee lands within the reservation, and that the parties to this case had accommodated themselves to the state regulation. The Court of Appeals left these findings unaltered and indeed implicitly reaffirmed them, adding that the record reveals no attempts by the Tribe at the time of the Crow Allotment Act to forbid non-Indian hunting and fishing on reservation lands.

Id. at 564 n.13 (citations omitted).

50. 435 U.S. 191 (1978).

51. See generally Collins, Implied Limitations on the Jurisdiction of Indian Tribes, 54 Wash. L. Rev. 479, 492–99 (1979). Two narrow decisions also conceivably may have been affected by tribal nonuser. South Carolina v. Catawba Indian Tribe, 106 S. Ct. 2039 (1986), ruled that the 1959 Catawba Act applied the state's statute of limitations to the tribe's old land claim, in spite of a legislative history that seemed to support preservation of the claim. United States v. Mottaz, 106 S. Ct. 2224 (1986), held that a suit against the United States to void a sale of an allotment was barred by the 12-year statute of limitations in the Quiet Title Act, 28 U.S.C. § 2409a (1982). Perhaps more important, however, *Mottaz* suggested that Indians can contest many old allotment sales by proceeding against nonfederal defendants under 25 U.S.C. § 345 (1982). 106 S. Ct. at 2231 n. 9.

52. In Arizona v. California I, the Special Master decreed water rights to 905,596 acre-feet of Lower Basin Colorado River water for the Chemehuevi, Cocopah, Fort Yuma, Fort Mojave, and Colorado River Indian Reservations. 367 U.S. 340 (1964) (decree). The potential diversions to satisfy these rights are to be charged against the state within which each reservation is located. Arizona v. California, 373 U.S. 546, 601 (1963). Thus, reserved water rights must be assimilated into a water system presently structured on priority dates subsequent to Indian reserved rights. Reserved rights of the Navajo Tribe have not been adjudicated, but the potential

award is staggering. See Back & Taylor, Navajo Water Rights: Pulling the Plug on the Colorado River? 20 Nat. Res. J. 71 (1980). See generally New Courses for the Colorado River: Major Issues for the Next Century (G. Weatherford & F. L. Brown Eds., 1986).

53. As a result of the Indian fishing decisions, the State of Washington has imposed moratoriums on licensing of new vessels and has instituted a buy-back program allowing government purchase of vessels. Wilkinson & Conner, supra note 31, at 100–01.

54. Interview with Ken Moore, President, Arizona Division, Peabody Coal Co., Tsaile, Arizona (June 22, 1984).

55. The declaration of policy in the Indian Financing Act of 1974 is an express congressional recognition of tribal self-government as being the best device with which to combat poverty in Indian country:

[Financing support will be provided to tribes so that] the Indians will fully exercise responsibility for the utilization and management of their own resources and . . . will enjoy a standard of living from their own productive efforts comparable to that enjoyed by non-Indians in neighboring communities.

25 U.S.C. § 1451 (1982). See also Indian Self-Determination and Education Assistance Act of 1974, 25 U.S.C. §§ 450, 450a (1982). On contemporary economic development in Indian country, see Williams, Small Steps on the Long Road to Self-Sufficiency for Indian Nations: The Indian Tribal Governmental Tax Status Act of 1982, 22 Harv. J. on Legis. 235 (1985).

56. See generally F. Prucha, American Indian Policy in the Formative Years: The Indian Trade and Intercourse Acts, 1790–1834 (1962); note 34, supra.

57. Prucha, supra note 56, at 1–3. The Nonintercourse Act was also intended to protect tribes against "improvidently disposing of their lands and becoming homeless public charges." United States v. Candelaria, 271 U.S. 432, 441 (1926). See generally Clinton & Hotopp, Judicial Enforcement of the Federal Restraints on Alienation of Indian Land: The Origins of the Eastern Land Claims, 31 Me. L. Rev. 17, 85–86 (1979).

58. See Pueblo Lands Act of 1924, ch. 331, 43 Stat. 636, discussed in Mountain States Tel. & Tel. Co. v. Pueblo of Santa Ana, 105 S. Ct. 2587 (1985); Alaska Native Claims Settlement Act of 1971, Pub. L. No. 92–203, 85 Stat. 688 (codified as amended at 43 U.S.C. §§ 1601–28 (1982)), discussed in Ch. 1, note 13, supra; Maine Indian Claims Settlement Act of 1980, 25 U.S.C. §§ 1721–35 (1982); discussed in Ch. 1, note 13, supra; and County of Oneida v. Oneida Indian Nation, 105 S. Ct. 1245, 1261 (1985).

59. See, e.g., Utah Power & Light Co. v. United States, 243 U.S. 389, 409 (1917).

60. 455 U.S. 130 (1982), discussed in the text at note 32, supra.

61. 455 U.S. at 148.

62. See United States v. Sioux Nation of Indians, 448 U.S. 371, 437 (1980) (Rehnquist, J., dissenting) ("[t]hat there was tragedy, deception, barbarity, and virtually every other vice known to man in the 300-year history of the expansion of the original 13 Colonies into a Nation which now embraces more than three million square miles and 50 States cannot be denied. But in a Court opinion, as a historical and not a legal matter, both settler and Indian are entitled to the benefit of the Biblical adjuration: 'Judge not, that ye be not judged' ").

63. Mescalero Apache Tribe v. New Mexico, 630 F.2d 724, 730 (10th Cir. 1980), vacated and remanded, 450 U.S. 1036 (1981), original opinion reinstated, 677 F.2d 55 (1982), aff'd, 462 U.S. 324 (1983).

64. See generally F. Cohen, supra note 9, at 221–25, 282–86: Brecher, Federal Regulatory Statutes and Indian Self-Determination: Some Problems and Some Proposed Legislative Solutions, 19 Ariz. L. Rev. 285 (1977); Comment, The Applicability of the Federal Pollution Acts to Indian Reservations: A Case for Tribal Self-Government, 48 U. Colo. L. Rev. 63 (1977).

65. See, e.g., Surface Mining Control and Reclamation Act, 30 U.S.C. § 1300 (1982); State and Local Fiscal Assistance Act, 31 U.S.C. § 6701(a)(5)(B) (1982); Clean Water Act, 33 U.S.C. § 1362(4) (1982); Safe Drinking Water Act, 42 U.S.C. § 300f (10) (1982).

66. County of Oneida v. Oneida Indian Nation, 105 S. Ct. 1245, 1258 (1985).

67. See Wilkinson & Volkman, Judicial Review of Indian Treaty Abrogation, 63 Calif. L. Rev. 601, 623–34 (1975).

68. 391 U.S. 404 (1968), discussed in text accompanying note 71, infra.

69. See, e.g., notes 73–79, infra.

70. Washington v. Washington State Commercial Passenger Fishing Vessel Ass'n, 443 U.S. 658 (1979).

71. 443 U.S. at 690.

72. The statute, 25 U.S.C. § 899 (1970) (repealed 1973), is quoted in the text.

Menominee Tribe apparently was a case that the Court badly wanted to hear. An earlier state court decision, State v. Sanapaw, 21 Wis. 2d 377, 124 N.W.2d 41 (1963), had held that the Termination Act had abrogated Menominee hunting and fishing rights by subjecting them to state game laws. 21 Wis. 2d at 388, 124 N.W.2d at 46–47. The tribe then filed in the Court of Claims for a taking of its treaty hunting and fishing rights. The tribe "lost" in the Court of Claims when the court ruled that the tribe was not entitled to compensation because the rights had not been abrogated. Menominee Tribe of Indians v. United States, 388 F.2d 998 (Ct. Cl. 1967).

In the Supreme Court, the tribe (which wanted to continue to hunt and fish), as petitioner, and the United States (which wanted to avoid a judgment against it for a taking in this claims case), as respondent, both urged that tribal rights survived the Menominee Termination Act. 391 U.S. at 407. The fact that the State of Wisconsin appeared in an amicus capacity and argued for the contrary result does not stop one from wondering exactly where the case or controversy was. One can also wonder about principles of appellate procedure that allowed a petitioner to seek to have a lower court ruling *affirmed*, as the Menominee Tribe did in this instance.

73. See, e.g., Merrion v. Jicarilla Apache Tribe, 455 U.S. 130, 150–52 (1982) (neither Act of 1927 regulating oil and gas leasing on Indian reservations nor Natural Gas Policy Act of 1978 impliedly divested tribe's taxing power); United States v. John, 437 U.S. 634, 641 (1978) (recognition of Oklahoma Choctaws in Treaty of Dancing Rabbit Creek of 1831 did not preclude United States from dealing specially with Mississippi Band of Choctaws); McClanahan v. Arizona State Tax Comm'n, 411 U.S. 164, 176–77 (1973) (Buck Act construed so as not to permit application of state income tax to individual Indians).

74. 417 U.S. 535 (1974).

75. See DeFunis v. Odegaard, 416 U.S. 312 (1974) (dismissing affirmative action case on the basis of mootness because the plaintiff was about to graduate from law school) (5–4 decision). See generally the symposia on the *DeFunis* case in 60 Va. L. Rev. 917 (1974) and 75 Colum. L. Rev. 483 (1975).

76. 436 U.S. 49 (1978).

77. 436 U.S. at 59. The act expressly extends habeas corpus relief against tribes in criminal actions. 25 U.S.C. § 1303 (1982).

78. The Court did not squarely rule on issues under § 1343(4). 436 U.S. at 53 n.4.

79. 426 U.S. 373 (1976).

80. On Public Law 280, see Ch. 1, note 18, supra; note 28, supra.

81. County of Oneida v. Oneida Indian Nation, 105 S. Ct. 1245, 1258–59 (1985), discussed at notes 39, 40, supra.

82. 105 S. Ct. 2399 (1985).

83. 420 U.S 425 (1975).

84. Arizona v. San Carlos Apache Tribe, 463 U.S. 545 (1983); Colorado River Water Conservation Dist. v. United States, 424 U.S. 800 (1976).

85. 43 U.S.C. § 666 (1982).

86. 106 S. Ct. 2216 (1986).

87. 450 U.S. 544 (1981). In a separate discussion, the Court in *Montana* also held that the Crow Tribe could not exercise jurisdiction over non-Indian hunters and fishers on the Bighorn River and its banks. See notes 48, 49, supra.

88. Colorado River Water Conservation Dist. v. United States, 424 U.S. 800, 811–12 & nn.18–19 (1976). State court jurisdiction under the McCarran Amendment is concurrent, not exclusive, and there are circum-

stances under which it may be appropriate for a federal court to retain jurisdiction. Arizona v. San Carlos Apache Tribe, 463 U.S 545, 569 (1983).

89. E.g., Pollard v. Hagan, 44 U.S. (3 How.) 212, 222–23, 228–29 (1845); Martin v. Waddell, 41 U.S. (16 Pet.) 367, 409–11 (1842). See generally Engdahl, State and Federal Power over Federal Property, 18 Ariz. L. Rev. 283, 293–96 (1976).

90. See, e.g., Solem v. Bartlett, 104 S. Ct. 1161 (1984) (no disestablishment); United States v. Adair, 723 F.2d 1394 (9th Cir. 1983) (federal jurisdiction appropriate in water rights litigation), cert. denied, 104 S. Ct. 3536 (1984); Confederated Salish & Kootenai Tribes v. Namen, 665 F.2d 951 (9th Cir.) (tribal ownership of bed to navigable watercourse), cert. denied, 459 U.S. 977 (1982); Yankton Sioux Tribe of Indians v. Nelson, 521 F. Supp. 463 (D.S.D. 1981) (same), vacated, 683 F.2d 1160 (1982), reinstated, 566 F. Supp. 1507 (D.S.D. 1983).

91. 417 U.S. 535 (1974), discussed in text accompanying notes 74, 75, supra.

92. 436 U.S 49 (1978), discussed in text accompanying notes 77, 78, supra.

93. 426 U.S. 373 (1976), discussed in text accompanying notes 79–81, supra.

94. See, e.g., Squire v. Capoeman, 351 U.S. 1, 6 (1955); Smith v. Davis, 323 U.S. 111, 117 (1944); Tucker v. Ferguson, 89 U.S. (22 Wall.) 527, 573 (1874).

95. Wilkinson & Volkman, Judicial Review of Indian Treaty Abrogation, 63 Calif. L. Rev. 601 (1975).

96. United States v. Dion, 106 S. Ct. 2216, 2220 (1986).

97. The Court has repeatedly stated that express language of abrogation is normally required. See, e.g., County of Oneida v. Oneida Indian Nation, 105 S. Ct. 1245, 1258 (1985) ("'Absent explicit statutory language,' . . . this Court accordingly has refused to find that Congress has abrogated Indian treaty rights"); Montana v. Blackfeet Tribe, 105 S. Ct. 2399, 2403–04 (1985) ("[T]he States may tax Indians only when Congress has manifested clearly its consent to such taxation. . . . [The 1938 act] contains no explicit consent to state taxation"); Washington v. Washington State Commercial Passenger Fishing Vessel Ass'n, 443 U.S. 658, 690 (1979) ("Absent explicit statutory language, we have been extremely reluctant to find congressional abrogation of treaty rights"); Santa Clara Pueblo v. Martinez, 436 U.S. 49, 59 (1978) ("Nothing on the face of Title I of the [Indian Civil Rights Act of 1968] purports to subject tribes to the jurisdiction of the federal courts in civil actions for injunctive or declaratory relief. . . . In the absence here of any unequivocal expression of contrary legislative intent, we conclude that suits against the tribe under the ICRA are barred by its sovereign immunity from suit"); Bryan v. Itasca County, 426 U.S. 373, 389–90 (1976) ("Congress

knew well how to express its intent directly when that intent was to subject reservation Indians to the full sweep of state laws and state taxation. . . . [I]f Congress in enacting Pub. L. 280 had intended to confer upon the States general civil regulatory powers, including taxation, over reservation Indians, it would have expressly said so"); Mattz v. Arnett, 412 U.S. 481, 504 (1973) ("More significantly, throughout the period from 1871–1892 numerous bills were introduced which *expressly* provided for the termination of the reservation and did so in unequivocal terms. Congress was fully aware of the means by which termination could be effected. But clear termination language was not employed in the 1892 Act. This being so, we are not inclined to infer an intent to terminate the reservation" [emphasis by the Court]). See also United States v. Dion, 106 S. Ct. 2216, 2220 (1986), quoted in the text at 52.

98. United States v. Crittenden, 600 F.2d 478, 480 (5th Cir.), vacated sub. nom. United States v. Kimbell Foods, Inc., 440 U.S. 715 (1979).

CHAPTER 3. THE ELEVATION OF TRIBALISM

1. J. Brierly, The Law of Nations 142 (4th ed. 1949); J. Maritain, Man and the State 28 (1951).

2. The word *sovereign* derives from the old French *soverain*, and Latin *super*, and literally means supreme. Although discussions of the place, function, and justification of the supreme power in a state can be found in antiquity, see, e.g., Aristotle, Politics, bk. III, ch. 6, 136–38, bk. IV, ch. 8, 184–86 (B. Jowett trans. 1943), the concept of sovereignty was not integrated into jurisprudence and political science until after the Middle Ages. On the history and evolution of sovereignty theories, see generally H. Cohen, Recent Theories of Sovereignty (1937); C. Merriam, History of the Theories of Sovereignty Since Rousseau (1900) [hereinafter cited as C. Merriam]; 2 R. Pound, Jurisprudence 284–87, 308 (1959) [hereinafter R. Pound].

Bodin formulated his absolutist formulation of sovereignty to provide a foundation for the French monarchy at a time when France was embroiled in bitter and divisive conflicts between the church and state. See C. Merriam, supra, at 11–17. Bodin's solution, that all political societies ought to be united under a determinate rule of law, is an essentially legalistic assumption that underlies all modern states. See generally R. Pound, supra, at 287–308. Significantly, even though Bodin's theory of sovereignty is considered to be absolutist, vesting undivided and unlimited power in the Crown, Bodin still held that the sovereign was accountable to divine law and natural law. Id. at 309; C. Merriam, supra, at 15–16. For other absolutist philosophers, see, e.g., J. Austin, Lecture IV, Lectures on Jurisprudence: The Philosophy of Positive Law (5th ed. London 1885) (arguing that in every government there is a clear place where absolute power must reside); T. Hobbes, Leviathan (1651) (arguing that rulers were both politically and morally absolute with indivisible, unlimited, and illimitable powers). An early and notable alternative to the absolutist concept of sovereignty was elaborated by Hugo Grotius. See H. Grotius, The Rights of War and Peace bk. I, ch. 3 (A. Campbell trans. 1901); C. Merriam, supra, at 23–24.

3. In other words, the Constitution undermined conventional concepts of sovereignty because it provided for powers to be exercised both by the states and the federal government and by different branches within the federal government. See R. Pound, supra note 2, at 308–23; Quarles, The Nature and Limitations of Sovereignty, 24 Geo. L.J. 69–75 (1935) [hereinafter cited as Quarles].

4. 3 T. Jefferson, Works of Thomas Jefferson 469 (1776) (Ford ed. 1904). Jefferson continued:

> It seems to me, therefore, that we only perplex ourselves when we attempt to explain the relations existing between the general government and the several state governments, according to those ideas of sovereignty which prevail under systems essentially different from our own.

Id.

5. Legal sovereignty refers to the "immediate practical source of precepts and sanctions. It considers whence as a matter of fact the precepts applied by the courts get their immediate force and authority. It asks whence they derive their sanction." R. Pound, supra note 2, at 289. Political sovereignty refers to the "ultimate practical source of sanctions and of the authority of legal precepts. It considers whence, as a matter of fact, governmental powers ultimately proceed." Id. at 289–90. See also J. Tucker, The Constitution of the United States 57–60 (1899). On the idea that neither the states nor the federal government possess absolute power, see, e.g., J. Tucker, supra, at 60–65; Fowler, A Theory of Sovereignty under the Federal Constitution, 21 Am. L. Rev. 399 (1887); Quarles, supra note 3, at 69–71; Willis, The Doctrine of Sovereignty under the United States Constitution, 15 Va. L. Rev. 437, 460–62, 475 (1929). On the accountability of nations to the international community, see, e.g., Garner, Recent Developments in International Law 812 (1925); 1 L. Oppenheim, International Law 117 (5th ed. 1935); 1 G. Schwarzenberger, International Law 121 (3rd ed. 1957); 1 Shotwell, The Great Decision 202 (1944). For arguments that the concept of sovereignty should be discarded, see, e.g., Kennan, Diplomacy and Logic, 3 Federalist News 2 (1956) ("Actually, I think, no one could be more sadly conscious than is the professional diplomatist of the primitiveness, the anarchism, the intrinsic absurdity of the modern concept of sovereignty"); Wagner, The Federal States and Their Judiciary 21 n.4 (1959) ("The concept of sovereignty . . . is completely discarded by [many] modern legal scholars"); Willis, supra, at 437, 451 (1929) ("If sovereignty is defined

as . . . 'absolute, omnipotent, uncontrollable' . . . there is no such thing as sovereignty").

6. Sovereignty presupposes the existence of what would be called a state or nation in jurisprudence and international law. See, e.g., E. Clark, Practical Jurisprudence 165 (1883); 1 L. Oppenheim, International Law § 64 (5th ed. 1937). See generally R. Pound, supra note 2, at 307–27. Theorists commonly point to three essential features or elements that have defined a state or nation for legal theory: defined territorial limits, continuity of organization, and organization of internal administration of justice. See, e.g., W. Hall, A Treatise on International Law 17–19 (8th ed. 1924); 1 L. Oppenheim, supra, § 64 (5th ed. 1937). In federal Indian law, the tribe is the analogue to state. See Weatherhead, What is an "Indian Tribe"? The Question of Tribal Existence, 8 Am. Ind. L. Rev. 1 (1980); F. Cohen, Handbook of Federal Indian Law 3–7 (1982 ed.) [hereinafter cited as F. Cohen] (definition of *tribe*). On the use of the narrow meaning of *sovereignty* today, see, e.g., Willis, supra note 5, at 475. ("[T]he doctrine of sovereignty in the United States is that doctrine which defines sovereignty . . . in the narrow sense of the power to delimit personal liberty by social control or to protect personal liberty against social control"); R. Pound, supra note 2, at 317 ("As a legal conception, sovereignty seems to mean the aggregate of powers possessed by the ruler or the ruling organs of a society").

7. See, e.g., Bean, The Limits of Indian Tribal Sovereignty: The Cornucopia of Inherent Powers, 49 N.D.L. Rev. 303 (1973); Martone, Of Power and Purpose, 54 Notre Dame Law. 829 (1979); Martone, American Indian Tribal Self-Government in the Federal System: Inherent Right or Congressional License?, 51 Notre Dame Law. 600 (1976); McCoy, The Doctrine of Tribal Sovereignty: Accommodating Tribal, State, and Federal Interests, 13 Harv. C.R-C.L. L. Rev. 357 (1978); Mettler, A Unified Theory of Indian Tribal Sovereignty, 30 Hastings L.J. 89 (1978); Werhan, The Sovereignty of Indian Tribes: A Reaffirmation and Strengthening in the 1970s, 54 Notre Dame Law. 5 (1978); Comment, The Indian Battle for Self-Determination, 58 Calif. L. Rev. 445 (1970).

8. 21 U.S. (8 Wheat.) 543 (1823).

9. The land transfers to private individuals at issue in Johnson v. McIntosh occurred before the formation of the Union, but the restrictions on alienation of Indian land were codified in the Nonintercourse Acts. See Ch. 2, note 34, supra.

10. 30 U.S. (5 Pet.) 1 (1831).

11. 31 U.S. (6 Pet.) 515 (1832).

12. 109 U.S. 556 (1883).

13. 163 U.S. 376 (1896).

14. The Major Crimes Act, 18 U.S.C. § 1153 (1982), first enacted in 1885, grants to federal courts jurisdiction over murder and other designated major offenses occurring in Indian country.

15. 163 U.S. at 384. Winters v. United States, 207 U.S. 564 (1908) (establishment of reservation reserves water rights sufficient to fulfill the purposes of the reservation), and Winans v. United States, 198 U.S. 371 (1905) (treaty right to "fish at all usual and accustomed places" reserves an easement of way across privately owned land to reach fishing grounds), were also both based on the premise that tribal rights preexisted the Constitution and survived it, treatymaking, and statehood unless expressly limited by Congress.

16. Act of June 28, 1898, ch. 517, 30 Stat. 495.

17. See, e.g., Choctaw Nation v. United States, 119 U.S. 1 (1886); Holden v. Joy, 84 U.S. (17 Wall.) 211 (1872); Mackey v. Coxe, 59 U.S. (18 How.) 100 (1855); Parks v. Ross, 52 U.S. (11 How.) 362 (1850). Lower courts were occasionally supportive of inherent tribal sovereignty. E.g., Ex parte Tiger, 2 Indian Terr. 41, 44–45, 47 S.W. 304, 305–06 (1898); McCurtain v. Grady, 1 Indian Terr. 107, 129, 38 S.W. 65, 72 (1896).

18. 309 U.S. 506 (1940).

19. 118 U.S. 375 (1886).

20. See note 14, supra.

21. 118 U.S. at 379. This reasoning in *Kagama* is analyzed in Chambers, Judicial Enforcement of the Federal Trust Responsibility to Indians, 27 Stan. L. Rev. 1213, 1224–27 (1975).

22. 135 U.S. 641 (1890).

23. 180 U.S. 261 (1901).

24. F. Cohen, Handbook of Federal Indian Law 122 (1942) [hereinafter cited as F. Cohen, 1942 edition].

25. Johnson v. McIntosh, 21 U.S. (8 Wheat.) 543, 574 (1823), quoted in text at note 8, supra.

26. See F. Cohen, 1942 edition, supra note 24, at 122–23 (emphasis in original).

27. Since 1958, the 1942 edition of F. Cohen's Handbook of Federal Indian Law has been cited in more than one hundred opinions issued by federal and state courts, including Merrion v. Jicarilla Apache Tribe, 445 U.S. 130, 139 n.6 (1982); Southern Pacific Transp. Co. v. Watt, 700 F.2nd 550, 555 n.2 (9th. Cir. 1983); Mashpee Tribe v. Watt, 542 F. Supp. 797, 804 (D. Mass. 1982); Boyer v. Shoshone-Bannock Indian Tribes, 92 Idaho 257, 260, 441 P.2d 167, 170 (1968).

28. For a bibliography of Cohen's work, see A Jurisprudential Symposium in Memory of Felix S. Cohen, 9 Rutgers L. Rev. 351 (1954).

29. On his stature as a legal realist, see, e.g., A. Bickel, The Least Dangerous Branch: The Supreme Court at the Bar of Politics 79–81 (1962).

30. After leaving the Department of the Interior in 1948, Cohen entered private practice, where he briefed and argued several major cases on behalf of Indians before his death in 1953. See F. Cohen, supra note 6, at viii.

31. 358 U.S. 217 (1959), discussed in text accompanying notes 1–6, Introduction, supra.

32. Warren Trading Post v. Arizona State Tax Comm'n, 380 U.S. 685, 690 (1965) (striking down a state gross proceeds tax on licensed trader on the basis of federal statutes regulating trading with Indians but referring to the Navajo Treaty and later congressional action as leaving the tribe "largely free to run the reservation and its affairs without state control"); Kennerly v. District Court 400 U.S. 423, 426–27 (1971) (disallowing state jurisdiction over contract claim and refusing to recognize tribal action transferring jurisdiction to state because Public Law 280 was the only method of transferring tribal jurisdiction to the state, but finding that "'the question has always been whether the state action infringed on the right of reservation Indians to make their own laws and be ruled by them'").

33. 411 U.S. 164 (1973). The other twentieth-century case analyzing sovereignty per se was United States v. United States Fidelity & Guaranty Co., 309 U.S. 506 (1940), discussed in text accompanying note 18, supra.

34. E.g., 411 U.S. at 168 ("'[T]he policy of leaving Indians free from state jurisdiction and control is deeply rooted in the Nation's history,'" quoting from Rice v. Olson, 324 U.S. 786, 789 (1945)); id. at 174–75 ("[I]t cannot be doubted that the reservation of certain lands for the exclusive use and occupancy of the Navajos and the exclusion of the non-Navajos from the prescribed area was meant to establish the lands as within the exclusive sovereignty of the Navajos under general federal supervision"); id. at 179 (state jurisdiction permitted only "up to the point where tribal self-government would be affected"); id. at 179–80 "[S]ince [the plaintiff's] income is derived wholly from reservation sources, her activity is totally within the sphere which the relevant treaty and statutes leave for the Federal Government and for the Indians themselves"). The Court also quoted extensively from *Worcester* to the effect that Indian tribes are "distinct political communities" having exclusive authority within their boundaries, id. at 168–69, and three times took the trouble to limit earlier language in Organized Village of Kake v. Egan, 369 U.S. 60 (1962), to the effect that state law generally applied in Indian country unless an express federal law is to the contrary. 411 U.S. at 172 n.8, 176 n.15, & 180 n.20.

McClanahan's protection of an individual Indian, as opposed to a tribe, was of considerable importance. In Williams v. Lee, 358 U.S. 217 (1959), the Court had suggested that, absent any federal statute, the test for determining the validity of an assertion of state jurisdiction was whether it "infringed on the right of reservation Indians to make their own laws and be ruled by them." Id. at 220. Since the tax in *McClanahan* was on an individual Indian, this "infringement" test might seem to allow state jurisdiction. The Court distinguished the *Williams* test at some length, 411 U.S. at 179–81 and, among other things, made the point that tribes "are, after all, composed of individual Indians and the legislation confers individual rights," id. at 181, thereby giving a broad reading to the interests of tribal self-government.

35. Id. at 172 (citations and footnotes omitted).

36. For a reading of *McClanahan* as denigrating tribal sovereignty, see, e.g., Martone, American Indian Tribal Self-Government in the Federal System: Inherent Right or Congressional License?, 51 Notre Dame Law. 600, 630–31 (1976). ("The result [of *McClanahan*] is that federal preemption, not tribal sovereignty, insulates tribal Indians from state jurisdiction.") Earlier cases such as Warren Trading Post v. Arizona State Tax Comm'n, 380 U.S. 685 (1965), and Kennerly v. District Court, 400 U.S. 423 (1971) had used preemption reasoning, but preemption had never been expressly employed in an Indian law case before *McClanahan*. See F. Cohen, supra note 6, at 271 n.7.

37. 419 U.S. 544 (1975).

38. In addition to the area of liquor regulation, 18 U.S.C. § 1161 (1982), tribes have been delegated limited authority over wildlife management under 18 U.S.C. § 1165 (1982), which makes it a federal offense to hunt or fish on tribal lands "without lawful authority or permission." Tribal authority over liquor regulation is shared with the states. See Rice v. Rehner, 463 U.S. 713 (1983).

39. 435 U.S. 191 (1978).

40. Earlier opinions had held that tribes lack authority to transfer land without federal permission, supra notes 8–9, and that tribes lack authority to align with foreign nations, supra note 10.

41. 435 U.S. at 209 (emphasis by the Court). The reliance upon Justice Johnson's views, see Fletcher v. Peck, 10 U.S. (6 Cranch) 87, 147 (1810) (Johnson, J. concurring), is puzzling. In Cherokee Nation v. Georgia, 30 U.S. (5 Pet.) 1 (1831), for example, Justice Johnson concurred with the dismissal of the Cherokee Nation's suit but did so on the ground that the Cherokee Nation was not a state, a position fundamentally contrary to a majority of the Court in *Cherokee Nation* and the later opinion in Worcester v. Georgia, 31 U.S. (6 Pet.) 515 (1832).

42. 435 U.S. 313 (1978).

43. Id. at 319–32. By explicitly holding that Indian tribes are "not . . . an arm of the federal government" and that they possess their own inherent sovereignty, the Court thus rejected the earlier suggestion in United States v. Kagama, 118 U.S. 375 (1886), to the effect that there are only two lines of sovereignty—federal and state—in our constitutional system. *Kagama* is quoted in the text accompanying note 21, supra.

44. 163 U.S. 376 (1895). *Wheeler* was also the first case since Johnson v. McIntosh, 21 U.S. (8 Wheat.) 543, 574 (1823), to use the term *sovereignty* in an unqualified manner.

45. *Wheeler* involved tribal criminal jurisdiction over a tribal member, an issue as to which there was no serious doubt. The scope of tribal powers is discussed in chapter 4, infra.

46. National Farmers Union Ins. Cos. v. Crow Tribe of Indians, 105 S. Ct. 2447 (1985); Kerr-McGee Corp. v. Navajo Tribe, 105 S. Ct. 1900 (1985); New Mexico v. Mescalero Apache Tribe, 462 U.S. 324 (1983); Merrion v. Jicarilla Apache Tribe, 455 U.S. 130 (1982); Montana v. United States, 450 U.S. 544 (1981); Washington v. Confederated Tribes of the Colville Indian Reservation, 447 U.S. 134 (1980). See chapter 4, infra.

47. E.g., Merrion v. Jicarilla Apache Tribe, 455 U.S. 130, 141 (1982); Washington v. Confederated Tribes of the Colville Indian Reservation, 447, U.S. 134, 152 (1980).

48. See, e.g., Santa Clara Pueblo v. Martinez, 436 U.S. 49, 58 (1978); Puyallup Tribe, Inc. v. Department of Game, 433 U.S. 165, 172–73 (1977).

49. In Merrion v. Jicarilla Apache Tribe, 455 U.S. 130 (1982), Justice Stevens's dissent, in which he was joined by Chief Justice Burger and Justice Rehnquist, argued that tribal power over non-Indians traces not to inherent sovereignty but to tribal powers as proprietors, the right to exclude. Id. at 160, 173 (Stevens, J., dissenting). The majority opinion squarely rejected that argument and held that tribal power over non-Indians traces to sovereignty, not to proprietorial authority. Id. at 144–48. Tribal assertions over non-Indians on non-Indian land within Indian country are permissible if the tribal regulation is tied to a legitimate tribal interest. See Montana v. United States, 450 U.S. 544, 565–66 (1981), and chapter 4, infra.

50. Santa Clara Pueblo v. Martinez, 436 U.S. 49, 56 (1978); Talton v. Mayes, 163 U.S. 376, 384 (1896).

51. E.g., United States v. John, 437 U.S. 634, 651–54 (1978), and pp. 75–78, infra.

52. E.g., Santa Clara Pueblo v. Martinez, 436 U.S. 49, 66–70 (1978).

53. Kerr-McGee Corp. v. Navajo Tribe, 105 S. Ct. 1900 (1985).

54. National Farmers Union Ins. Cos. v. Crow Tribe of Indians, 105 S. Ct. 2447, 2454 (1985), quoted in text in Ch. 4 at note 148, infra.

55. E.g., Washington v. Washington State Commercial Passenger Fishing Vessel Ass'n, 443 U.S. 658, 675–79 (1979); Winters v. United States, 207 U.S. 564, 576–77 (1908).

56. Merrion v. Jicarilla Apache Tribe, 455 U.S. 130 (1982), is a leading example of this approach. To explain the Jicarilla Apache Tribe's power to raise revenue for essential services, the Court drew a direct analogy to the United States:

[I]t derives from the tribe's general authority, as sovereign, to control economic activity within its jurisdiction, and to defray the cost of providing governmental services by requiring contributions from persons or enterprises engaged in economic activities within that jurisdiction. See, e.g., Gibbons v. Ogden, 9 Wheat. 1, 199 (1824).

Id. at 137. In supporting the power of a sovereign to contract for royalties with an entity, and then later to tax the same entity on the transaction, the Court analogized tribes to state and local governments. Id. at 147–48. See also, e.g., Three Affiliated Tribes of the Fort Berthold Reservation v. Wold Engineering, 54 U.S.L.W. 4654, 4658 (1986) (comparing "perceived inequity" of tribal sovereign immunity with "perceived inequity" of federal and state sovereign immunity).

57. This discussion does not refer to the internal exercise of powers by a tribe; there are major differences under the laws of the various tribes concerning such matters as enrollment, constitutional rights, distribution of tribal property interests, distribution of tribal proceeds, requirements for holding office, and many other issues. Rather, the question posed here is whether there is a commonality among tribes, as a matter of federal law, in regard to external relations with states and the federal government.

58. Treaty making with Indian tribes was discontinued by the United States in 1871, with existing treaties remaining fully in effect. 25 U.S.C. § 71 (1982). See Ch. 1, note 3, supra. The various forms of recognition are discussed in text accompanying Ch. 1, notes 2–5, supra.

59. See, e.g., Tulee v. Washington, 315 U.S. 681 (1942) (reserved fishing rights); United States v. Winans, 198 U.S. 371 (1905) (reserved fishing rights). Winters v. United States, 207 U.S. 564 (1908) (reserved water rights) involved a bilateral agreement, not a treaty. Nevertheless, as this section shows, litigants continued to argue well into the modern era for a distinction between treaties and other forms of recognition.

60. 420 U.S. 194 (1975).

61. The Colville Indian Reservation was initially established by an 1872 executive order. The original reservation was then reduced in size by the 1891 agreement and statutes implementing it, but the remaining land now had the sanction of Congress, not just of the executive. These developments are recounted at 428 U.S. 197–98. See also Seymour v. Superintendent, 368 U.S. 351, 354 (1962). No treaty was ever negotiated by the United States with the Confederated Tribes of the Colville Indian Reservation.

62. State v. Antoine, 82 Wash. 2d 440, 444–45, 511 P.2d 1351, 1354–55 (1973), quoted by the Court in *Antoine* at 420 U.S. 194, 200–01.

63. 420 U.S. 194, 203–04 (emphasis in original) (citations omitted).

64. See, e.g., Perrin v. United States, 232 U.S. 478 (1914) (cession agreement prohibiting sale of liquor on ceded lands overrides state liquor laws); Choate v. Trapp, 224 U.S. 665 (1912) (agreement exempting allotments from taxation precludes state from assessing property tax); Winters

v. United States, 207 U.S. 564 (1908) (water rights reserved by agreement establishing reservation exempt from state water appropriation laws).

65. See Ch. 1, notes 87–92, supra.

66. The president's authority as commander-in-chief of the military, U.S. Const., art. II, § 2, had relevance early in the Republic. Indian affairs were initially under the aegis of the War Department. Act of Aug. 7, 1789, ch. 7, § 1, 1 Stat. 49. The Indian office remained there until 1849, when the Department of the Interior was created and authority over Indian affairs was transferred to it. Act of March 3, 1849, ch. 108, § 5, 9 Stat. 395 (codified, as amended, at 43 U.S.C. § 1457 (1982)). The practice of creating Indian reservations by executive order did not begin until 1855, Ch. 1, note 5, supra, so that any justification for basing the validity of such reservations upon the president's authority as commander-in-chief was greatly attenuated.

67. 236 U.S. 459 (1915).

68. Id. at 468–69. See generally Getches, Managing the Public Lands: The Authority of the Executive to Withdraw Lands, 22 Nat. Resources J. 279, 287 n.46, 290–92 (1982), and the authorities cited there.

69. In the events leading up to *Midwest Oil*, the director of the Geological Survey reported that, at the rate at which oil lands in California were being patented by private parties, it would "'be impossible for the people of the United States to continue ownership of oil lands for more than a few months. After that the Government will be obliged to repurchase the very oil that it has practically given away.' " 236 U.S. at 466–67. Notice was given to potential developers because federal withdrawals of land are recorded in the land offices of the Bureau of Land Management.

70. The kind of reservation established in *Midwest Oil* was in fact quite narrow, since it affected only the extraction of minerals. For example, state wildlife and water law are both in effect on the public lands except to the extent that they are specifically preempted by federal law. California v. United States, 438 U.S. 645 (1978) (water); Kleppe v. New Mexico 426 U.S. 529, 542–43 (1976) (wildlife). The establishment of an Indian reservation, on the other hand, amounts to a comprehensive exclusion of most state wildlife and water laws. See generally F. Cohen, supra note 6, chs. 5, 5B, 8 & 10. For a comparison of state jurisdiction on public lands and Indian lands, see Wilkinson, Cross-jurisdictional Conflicts: State Authority on Federal and Indian Lands, 2 UCLA J. Envtl. Law & Policy 135 (1982).

71. One can argue that western water users should have been put on notice by the decision in Winters v. United States, 207 U.S. 564 (1908), which recognized extensive Indian reserved water rights. In fact, however, until recently potential water users have traditionally looked to the state recording systems (which do not include Indian reserved rights) when making their determinations as to the amount of water available for appropriation in light of the appropriations already on record. On the appropriation of

water under state administrative systems, see generally 1 W. Hutchins, Water Rights Laws in the Nineteen Western States 226–436 (1971).

72. 373 U.S. 546 (1963).

73. See Donnelly v. United States, 228 U.S. 243 (1913), holding that the Hoopa Valley Reservation in California, set aside by executive order, was Indian country for the purpose of criminal prosecutions: "[I]n our judgment, nothing can more appropriately be deemed 'Indian Country,' . . . than a tract of land that, being a part of the public domain, is lawfully set apart as an Indian reservation." Id. at 269. In 1948, the definition of *Indian country* was codified, and Indian country expressly includes "all land within the limits of any Indian reservation under the jurisdiction of the United States Government." 18 U.S.C. § 1151(a) (1982). The intent was to codify *Donnelly* and other cases that had earlier defined *Indian country*. See 18 U.S.C. § 1151 Historical and Revision Notes (1982).

74. The main stem of the Colorado River is approximately 1,300 miles long and drains lands in parts of seven of the eleven western states. "The system is the only significant source of surface water in an area bounded by the Rocky Mountains on the east and the Sierras on the west and encompassing one-twelfth of the continental United States, excluding Alaska." See Meyers, The Colorado River, 19 Stan. L. Rev. 1 (1966), where the Arizona v. California litigation is recounted in detail. Among many other events indicating the level of tensions over who controls the river, in 1934 the governor of Arizona sent state troops to halt construction of a federal dam that had one foot on Arizona soil. Id. at 40. Five Indian reservations—the Colorado River Yuma, Fort Mohave, Cocopah, and the Chemehuevi Reservations—received an allocation of more than 900,000 acre-feet. California received 4.4 million acre-feet, Arizona 2.8 million acre-feet, and Nevada 300,000 acre-feet. See Arizona v. California, 376 U.S. 340 (1964) (decree). See generally P. Fradkin, A River No More: The Colorado River (1981).

75. 207 U.S. 564 (1908).

76. Arizona v. California I, 373 U.S. 546, 598 (footnote omitted). All of the tribes in the litigation are small tribes, U.S. Dep't of Commerce, Federal and State Indian Reservations 41, 43, 94, 107, 108 (1975), the largest being the Colorado River Reservation, with a population of 2,072 in 1972. Id. at 43. As of 1957 the largest amount of land ever irrigated on the Fort Mohave Indian Reservation, was twenty-three acres; the population at that time was one family. See C. Meyers & A. D. Tarlock, Water Resource Management 209 (2d ed. 1980).

77. 316 U.S. 317 (1942). See also Confederated Band of Ute Indians v. United States, 330 U.S. 169 (1947). In 1927, Congress prohibited any changes in the boundaries of executive order reservations except by act of Congress, 25 U.S.C. § 398d (1982), and one writer has concluded that this

statute amounts to recognition of executive order reservations so that any taking must be accompanied by compensation. Note, Tribal Property Interests in Executive-Order Reservations: A Compensable Indian Right, 69 Yale L.J. 627 (1960).

Even though the United States is not constitutionally required to compensate when executive order land is taken, legislation providing for claims by tribes has included takings of executive order reservations so that the distinctions between congressionally sanctioned reservations and executive order reservations in this respect "may be of chiefly historical significance." F. Cohen, supra note 6, at 496–97. But see Newton, At the Whim of the Sovereign: Aboriginal Title Reconsidered, 31 Hastings L.J. 1215, 1257–59 (1980).

78. The Court in Arizona v. California I expressly followed *Winters* and held that enough water was reserved to irrigate all "practicably irrigable acreage on the reservations," 373 U.S. at 600, but the United States requested a priority date as of the time that the reservations were established, not earlier, and the Court ruled accordingly. 373 U.S. at 600. It may be, however, that executive orders reserving aboriginal Indian land are entitled to an aboriginal priority date. See, F. Cohen, supra note 6, at 591 n.100.

79. See 25 U.S.C. 398c (1982), a 1927 law allowing state taxation of mineral production on executive order reservations. Leases of minerals executed pursuant to other legislation do not allow state taxation. See Montana v. Blackfeet Tribe of Indians, 105 S. Ct. 2399 (1985); Merrion v. Jicarilla Apache Tribe, 455 U.S. 130, 151 n.17 (1982).

80. 455 U.S. 130 (1982).

81. See Ch. 1, note 76, supra.

82. The provisions on tribal powers are contained in 25 U.S.C. § 476 (1982):

> Any Indian tribe, or tribes residing on the same reservation, shall have the right to organize for its common welfare, and may adopt an appropriate constitution and bylaws. . . .
>
> In addition to all powers vested in any tribe or tribal council by existing law, the constitution adopted by said tribe shall also vest in such tribe or its tribal council the following rights and powers: To employ legal counsel, the choice of counsel and fixing of fees to be subject to the approval of the Secretary of the Interior; to prevent the sale, disposition, lease, or encumbrance of tribal lands, interests in lands, or other tribal assets without the consent of the tribe; and to negotiate with the Federal, State, and local Governments.

These powers are all within the ambit of reserved tribal authority, see pp. 57–63, supra, with the exception of the provision allowing tribes with IRA constitutions to prevent the transfer of tribal property. There has been no definitive construction of the provision. See Hynes v. Grimes Packing Co., 337 U.S. 86, 107 (1949).

83. 105 S. Ct. 1900 (1985).

84. Id. at 1903. The Court seems to have acknowledged the minimal impact of the IRA in its few passing references to the act. See, e.g., Oliphant v. Suquamish Indian Tribe, 435 U.S. 191, 195 n.6 (1978) ("Respondents do contend that Congress has 'confirmed' the power of Indian tribes to try and to punish non-Indians through the Indian Reorganization Act of 1934 and the Indian Civil Rights Act of 1968 [citations omitted]. Neither Act, however, addresses, let alone 'confirms,' tribal criminal jurisdiction over non-Indians. The Indian Reorganization Act merely gives each Indian Tribe the right 'to organize for its common welfare' and to 'adopt an appropriate constitution and bylaws.' With certain specific additions not relevant here, the tribal council is to have such powers as are vested 'by existing law' "); Mescalero Apache Tribe v. Jones, 411 U.S. 145, 151–53 (1973) (discussion of general purposes of Indian Reorganization Act). Several opinions during the modern era have involved tribes chartered under the Indian Reorganization Act, but in each instance the Court has not limited its analysis to tribal powers under the IRA, relying instead upon notions of inherent sovereignty applicable to all tribes. See e.g., Merrion v. Jicarilla Apache Tribe, 455 U.S. 130, 134, 137 (1982); Oliphant v. Suquamish Indian Tribe, 435 U.S. 191, 208–11 (1978); Fisher v. District Court, 424 U.S. 382, 387–88, 390 (1976). In at least one opinion, the Court held that an IRA tribe (Makah) and two non-IRA tribes (Lummi and Colville) had identical powers. Washington v. Confederated Tribes of the Colville Indian Reservation, 447 U.S. 134, 143 n.11, 152 (1980).

85. 31 U.S. (6 Pet.) 515 (1832), discussed in note 11, supra. Only the Cherokee treaty was at issue in *Worcester* but Marshall traced federal policy and tribal powers in regard to tribes generally, making it clear that the opinion was setting out broad rules applicable to all or most Indian tribes.

86. Most modern statutes have dealt uniformly with all tribes recognized by the United States, regardless of the form of the recognition. E.g., Indian Self-Determination and Education Assistance Act of 1975, 25 U.S.C. § 450b(b) (1982) ("*Indian tribe* means any Indian tribe, band, nation, or other organized group or community . . . which is recognized as eligible for the special programs and services provided by the United States to Indians because of their status as Indians"); Indian Financing Act of 1974, 25 U.S.C. § 1452(c) (1982) ("Tribe means any Indian tribe, band, group, pueblo, or community . . . which is recognized by the Federal Government as eligible for services from the Bureau of Indian Affairs"); Indian Child Welfare Act of 1978, 25 U.S.C. § 1903(8) (1982) ("Indian tribe means any Indian tribe, band, nation, or other organized group or community of Indians recognized as eligible for the services provided to Indians by the Secretary because of their status as Indians"). Similarly, distinctions have not been made on the basis of the form of recognition during the appropriations process. E.g., Note, Tribal Property Interests in Executive-Order Reservations: A Compensable Indian Right, 69 Yale L.J. 627, 638–39 (1960).

87. 207 U.S. 564 (1908).

88. Most aboriginal Indian societies were oral cultures maintained and ordered by clearly understood rules developed by consensus and enforced by peer pressure or, in extreme cases, by penalties including compensation and corporal punishment. See F. Cohen, supra note 6, at 229–30; D. Getches, D. Rosenfelt, & C. Wilkinson, Federal Indian Law, Cases and Materials 300–01 (1979). With few exceptions, see, e.g., R. Strickland, Fire and the Spirits: Cherokee Law From Clan to Court (1975), tribal governments began to develop written legal codes and formal judicial systems only recently. See generally W. Hagan, Indian Police and Judges: Experiments in Acculturation and Control (1966); McCoy, The Doctrine of Tribal Sovereignty: Accommodating Tribal, State, and Federal Interests, 13 Harv. C.R.-C.L. L. Rev. 357 (1978).

89. See National Farmers Union Ins. Cos. v. Crow Tribe of Indians, 105 S. Ct. 2447 (1985); United States v. Wheeler, 435 U.S. 313 (1978); Fisher v. District Court, 424 U.S. 382 (1976); Kennerly v. District Court, 400 U.S. 423 (1971); Williams v. Lee, 358 U.S. 217 (1959).

90. F. Cohen, supra note 6, at 431–32.

91. Early cases include Buster v. Wright, 135 F. 947 (1905) (upholding a tribal tax on non-Indians conducting business in tribal territory), appeal dismissed, 203 U.S. 599 (1906); Morris v. Hitchcock, 194 U.S. 384 (1904) (upholding a tribal permit tax on livestock owned by non-Indians in Indian country); Maxey v. Wright, 3 Indian Terr. 243, 54 S.W. 807 (1900) (upholding a tribal occupation tax on non-Indians practicing law in tribal territory), aff'd mem., 105 F. 1003 (1901). The issue was discussed in the 1942 edition of the Cohen treatise. F. Cohen, 1942 edition, supra note 24, at 142–43, 266–67. Two cases involving tribal taxation arose during the 1950s. Barta v. Oglala Sioux Tribe of Pine Ridge Reservation, 259 F.2d 553 (8th Cir. 1958) (upholding tribal tax on non-Indian lessees of tribal trust lands), cert. denied, 358 U.S. 932 (1959); Iron Crow v. Oglala Sioux Tribe of Pine Ridge Reservation, 231 F.2d 89 (8th Cir. 1956) (upholding tribal tax on non-Indian lessees of allotted land held by individual Indians within the reservation boundaries), both discussed in text accompanying Ch. 1, notes 108, 109, supra.

92. Kerr-McGee Corp. v. Navajo Tribe, 105 S. Ct. 1900 (1985) (coal severance tax); Merrion v. Jicarilla Apache Tribe, 455 U.S. 130 (1982) (oil and gas severance tax); Washington v. Confederated Tribes of the Colville Indian Reservation, 447 U.S. 134 (1980) (cigarette taxes).

93. The prior appropriation doctrine was in force from the beginning in the Rocky Mountain states (Montana, Idaho, Wyoming, Utah, Colorado, Arizona, New Mexico, and Nevada). Since then, the six states along the 100th meridian (North Dakota, South Dakota, Nebraska, Kansas, Oklahoma, and Texas), the three mainland states on the Pacific Coast (Washington, Oregon, and California), and Alaska have substantially adopted the

prior appropriation doctrine. See generally W. Hutchins, Water Rights Laws in the Nineteen Western States (1971) [hereinafter cited as W. Hutchins].

94. See Winters v. United States, 207 U.S. 564 (1908). For the first detailed scholarship on the factual background of the Winters case, see Hundley, The "Winters" Decision and Indian Water Rights: A Mystery Reexamined, 13 W. Hist. Q. 17 (1982). On the question of whether reservations in some instances carry aboriginal priority dates rather than the date of the reservation, see United States v. Adair, 723 F.2d 1394 (9th Cir. 1983), cert. denied, 104 S. Ct. 3536 (1984); F. Cohen, supra note 6, at 590–91.

95. 373 U.S. 546, 595–601 (1963). Arizona v. California, 460 U.S. 605 (1983) (Arizona v. California II), is discussed in text accompanying Ch. 2, notes 45–47, supra. On the exclusion of Indian lands from the reclamation program, see National Water Comm'n, Water Policies for the Future— Final Report to the President and to the Congress of the United States 474–75 (1973). The intervening case is United States v. Powers, 305 U.S. 527 (1939).

96. See, e.g., Ranquist, The Winters Doctrine and How It Grew: Federal Reservation of Rights to the Use of Water, 1975 B.Y.U. L. Rev. 639, 656. In most states operating under the prior appropriation doctrine, qualifying municipalities are permitted to establish a water right with a priority date of the year in which the filing was made but with the quantity to be determined generally by the future needs of the municipality. 1 W. Hutchins, supra note 93 at 245–50. The restrictions on such municipal appropriations, however, are considerably greater than is the case with the tribes' right to priority for future uses. See, e.g., City & County of Denver v. Northern Colorado Water Conservancy Dist., 130 Colo. 375, 276 P.2d 992 (1954). The reservation of water for future tribal needs had been suggested in Winters, 207 U.S. at 576. See also Conrad Inv. Co. v. United States, 161 F. 829, 831–32 (9th Cir. 1908).

97. The Court approved Special Master Rifkind's findings on these issues. 373 U.S. at 600. The evidence before Special Master Rifkind referred to modern technology on several occasions. See Reporter's Transcript, proceedings before Special Master S. Rifkind 14,120–23 (Jan. 6, 1960)—Arizona v. California, 373 U.S. 546 (1963) (use of modern pump-lifts). When the case was reopened in the 1970s, Special Master Tuttle concluded that Special Master Rifkind had relied on a standard of modern technology. "My reading of the transcript reveals that the evidence of 'practicable irrigability' was determined by then-current standards. I am similarly convinced that my determinations of practicable irrigability should be based on present standards. . . . Given that these issues are to be litigated presently, the most sensible method of determining feasibility is by using present standards."

E. Tuttle, Report of the Special Master 98 (Feb. 22, 1982)—Arizona v. California, 460 U.S. 605 (1983) (citations omitted). Special Master Tuttle used the modern technology standard on several occasions. See, e.g., id. at 130 (finding sandy soil farmable despite its low-moisture capacity). The Department of the Interior has enacted regulations to set procedures for determining the extent of practicable irrigable acreage on reservation lands; the regulations are premised upon the use of sophisticated hydrologic equipment. 43 C.F.R. § 417.5 (1985).

98. See Escondido Mutual Water Co. v. La Jolla Band of Mission Indians, 104 S. Ct. 2105 (1984) (Indian reserved water rights not protected reservations within meaning of Federal Power Act, 16 U.S.C. § 797(e) (1982)); Nevada v. United States, 436 U.S. 110 (1983) (refusal to allow reopening of decree unfavorable to tribe); Arizona v. San Carlos Apache Tribe, 463 U.S. 545 (1983) (construing McCarran Amendment of 1953, 43 U.S.C. § 666a (1982); general stream adjudications to be heard in state courts); Arizona v. California II, 460 U.S. 605 (1983) (refusal to reopen Supreme Court decree issued pursuant to Court's original jurisdiction); Colorado River Water Conservation Dist. v. United States, 424 U.S. 800 (1976) (general stream adjudications to be heard in state court).

99. Arizona v. California II, 460 U.S. 605, 625 (1983).

100. Arizona v. San Carlos Apache Tribe, 463 U.S. 545, 571 (1983).

101. For a thorough and fascinating review of the elaborate fishing technologies of Northwest Coast Indians, see H. Stewart, Indian Fishing: Early Methods on the Northwest Coast (1977). After describing in detail the seemingly endless variety of hooks, nets, traps, weirs, spears, and harpoons crafted by the coast cultures as the culmination of thousands of years of living "so completely in tune with the ways of the sea and river and all that was in it," id. at 21, Stewart repeatedly marvels at the efficiency and productivity of the technology as well as the skill and adroitness of the fishermen. See also, e.g., E. Röstlund, Freshwater Fish and Fishing in Native North America (1952); Wilkinson & Conner, The Law of the Pacific Salmon Fishery: Conservation and Allocation of a Transboundary Common Property Resource, 32 Kan. L. Rev. 17, at 28–29 (1983). On the use of gillnets in aboriginal times, see, e.g., United States v. Washington, 384 F. Supp. 312, 352 (W.D. Wash. 1974), aff'd, 520 F.2d 676 (9th Cir. 1975), cert. denied, 423 U.S. 1086 (1976); H. Stewart, supra, at 80–81, 86. See also E. Röstlund, supra, at 86 ("The distribution of fish nets on the Pacific slope was irregularly spotty both in types of nets employed and in the prevalence of their use. Certain highly specialized forms of the dip-net family characterized the fishery in some localities but not in others; large towed nets, hauled seines, and set gillnets are reported, but they were not universally used"). Modern gillnets are described in Puyallup Tribe v. Department of Game, 391 U.S. 392, 396 n.8, 400 nn.12, 13 (1967).

102. See generally American Friends Service Committee, Uncommon Controversy—Fishing Rights of the Muckleshoot, Puyallup, and Nisqually Indians 82–86, 118–20 (1970); A. Netboy, The Columbia River Salmon and Steelhead Trout—Their Fight for Survival 124 (1980).

103. State v. Gurnoe, 53 Wis. 2d 390, 412, 192 N.W.2d 892, 902 (1972).

104. United States v. Washington, 384 F. Supp. 312, 407 (W.D. Wash. 1974), aff'd., 520 F.2d 676 (9th Cir. 1975), cert. denied, 423 U.S. 1086 (1976).

105. 443 U.S. 658 (1979).

106. Puyallup Tribe v. Department of Game, 391 U.S. 392 (1968); Department of Game v. Puyallup Tribe, 414 U.S. 44 (1973); Puyallup Tribe, Inc. v. Department of Game, 433 U.S. 165 (1977); Mattz v. Arnett, 412 U.S. 481 (1973).

107. On the pressures on the Pacific salmon and steelhead resource, see generally Wilkinson & Conner, supra note 101.

108. 31 U.S. (6 Pet.) 515, 558 (1832), quoted in text accompanying note 11, supra.

109. See, e.g., Merrion v. Jicarilla Apache Tribe, 455 U.S. 130, 137 (1982), and text accompanying notes 42–46, supra.

110. Williams v. Lee, 358 U.S. 217, 220 (1959).

111. Merrion v. Jicarilla Apache Tribe, 455 U.S. 130, 137 (1982). The organic powers of tribes can also be described as follows: The power to determine form of tribal government, the power to determine membership, the power to legislate, the power to administer justice, and the power to exclude persons from tribal territory. See F. Cohen, supra note 6, at 246–52.

112. Thus all cultural systems include strategies for maintaining the biological functioning of the group, socializing new members, producing and distributing goods and services, maintaining social and political order, and providing a meaningful world view. J. Bennett & M. Tumin, Social Life, Structure and Function 45–59 (1974). Individuals in society do not adapt directly to their physical environment but rather through their culture: "The cultural environment . . . includes means for their individual survival and guides their adaptation along established channels." R. LeVine, Culture, Behavior, and Personality 4 (1973). See generally L. Spindler, Culture Change and Modernization 3–9 (1977) [hereinafter cited as L. Spindler].

113. See, e.g., Vogt, On the Concept of Structure and Process in Cultural Anthropology, 62 Am. Anthro. 18–33 (1962). Before the massive intrusion of Western civilization, most theories of culture tended to emphasize its stable and unchanging qualities. Cultural adaptation in societies was viewed as a semipermanent state rather than a continuous process.

Even after disruption, it was thought that cultural systems always tended toward equilibrium. See R. Keesing & F. Keesing, New Perspectives in Cultural Anthropology 375–402 (1971). Modern theories have recognized that cultures, far from being static, are constantly changing. See, e.g., Murdock, How Culture Changes, in Man, Culture, and Society 319 (H. Shapiro ed. 1971) [hereinafter cited as Murdock]. Murdock argues that it is erroneous to assume that the elements of any culture are in a state of near integration or equilibrium. In fact, such equilibrium is never achieved or even approached:

> The adjustment of other elements of culture to an innovation, and of it to them, requires time—often years or even generations. In the meantime, other innovations have appeared and set into motion new processes of integration. At any given time, therefore, a culture exhibits numerous instances of uncompleted integrative processes as well as examples of others which have been carried through to relatively satisfactory completion.

Id. at 332.

114. Murdock explains that changes in coping strategies, and hence in culture, normally have their origin in some significant alteration in the life conditions of a society:

> The net effect of the various processes of cultural change is to adapt the collective habits of human societies progressively over time to the changing conditions of existence.... [Thus h]owever halting or harsh it may appear to participants, cultural change is always adaptive and usually progressive. It is also inevitable, and will endure as long as the earth can support human life.

Id. Innovations are inventions or discoveries by an individual within a culture. While an innovation is usually a combination of existing ideas and a new idea, it can be an entirely new practice, tool, or principle. Innovations result in cultural change when they are accepted by a majority of a society's members. See, e.g., L. Spindler, supra note 112, at 13–16. See generally H. Barnett, Innovation: The Basis of Cultural Change (1953). On cultural borrowing, see L. Spindler, supra note 112, at 17–23; B. Malinowski, The Dynamics of Culture Change (1945); R. Linton, The Study of Man (1936). Linton claims that more than 90 percent of any culture's content, from foods to artifacts to social inventions, is borrowed. Id. at 325–27. Thus, for example, colonial Americans borrowed the use of plants domesticated by the American Indians—plants that today furnish almost half of the world's plant food supply. H. Driver, Indians of North America 555 (2d ed. 1969).

115. See, e.g., Redfield, Linton & Herskovitz, Memorandum for the Study of Acculturation, 38 Am. Anthro. 149 (1936). Changes that occur as a result of direct and prolonged contact between societies is referred to as

acculturation. This element of contact distinguishes the process of acculturation from diffusion; ideas and items can be diffused without two cultures being in contact. See L. Spindler, supra note 112, at 17. While force is not always a necessary element of the acculturation process, it is often inevitable where a technologically superior society dominates one that is technologically inferior. L. Spindler, supra note 112, at 48.

116. Cultural aggression is manifest in the West's export of "technology, science, comfort and hardware" as well as its condescension toward, and suppression of, non-Western cultures. See R. Keesing & F. Keesing, supra note 113, at 352–65. See generally G. Foster, Traditional Cultures and the Impact of Technological Change (1962). On the importance of ethnocentrism in the world views of traditional societies, see L. Spindler, supra note 112, at 38. A society's world view is likely to be one of the most stable and persistent features of its culture; if it is "disturbed voluntarily or by force," the "most serious stress and disorganization" will result. R. Keesing & F. Keesing, supra note 113, at 353. On the struggle of non-Western societies to adapt, see, e.g., Redfield, Linton & Herskovitz, supra note 115, at 149. Indeed, the study of cultural change has in large part become a study of the adaptive strategies of non-Western societies to the impact of Anglo-European culture. See L. Spindler, supra note 112, at 31–51.

117. E. Hoebel, The Law of Primitive Man 275 (1967).

118. On assimilationist motives and the allotment policy of the late nineteenth century, see, e.g., D. Otis, The Dawes Act and the Allotment of Indian Lands 8–32 (2d ed. 1973); F. Prucha, American Indian Policy in Crisis 227–64 (1976); Ch. 1, notes 67–71, supra. Congress set out its policy during the termination era as follows:

> [I]t is the policy of Congress, as rapidly as possible, to make the Indians within the territorial limits of the United States subject to the same laws and entitled to the same privileges and responsibilities as are applicable to other citizens of the United States, to end their status as wards of the United States, and to grant them all of the rights and prerogatives pertaining to American citizenship.

H.R. Con. Res. 108, 83rd Cong., 1st sess., 67 Stat. B132 (1953). See generally Wilkinson & Biggs, The Evolution of the Termination Policy, 5 Am. Ind. L. Rev. 139 (1977). The American Indian Policy Review Commission recommended that congressional policy in Indian affairs proceed on six basic premises, the first of which was that Indian tribes should be treated as permanent, governmental institutions in the United States. Final Report, American Indian Policy Review Comm'n, 95th Cong., 1st sess. 6–9 (Comm. Print 1977).

119. United States v. Sandoval, 231 U.S. 28, 46 (1913); The Kansas Indians, 72 U.S. (5 Wall.) 737, 755–57 (1866). See also pp. 78–86, infra.

120. 391 U.S. 404 (1968).

121. The treaty did not expressly refer to hunting and fishing rights, but it did provide that Menominee lands were to be held "as Indian lands are held." See Treaty of Wolf River with the Menominee, May 12, 1854, art. 2, 10 Stat. 1064, 1065. The Court's holding that the Menominee Termination Act, 25 U.S.C. §§ 891–902 (1970) (repealed 1973), did not abrogate the tribes' treaty hunting and fishing rights is discussed at Ch. 2, note 72, supra.

122. Menominee Tribe of Indians v. United States, 388 F.2d 998, 1000–01 (Ct. Cl. 1967).

123. Wisconsin's argument is made at Reply Brief and Appendix of the State of Wisconsin, Amicus Curiae on Re-argument at 2–5, Menominee Tribe of Indians v. United States, 391 U.S. 404 (1968). On the Court's interest in the issue, see, e.g., Supplemental Brief for the Menominee Tribe at 16–19, Menominee Tribe of Indians v. United States, 391 U.S. 404 (1968).

124. See F. Cohen, supra note 6, at 451–52 (hunting and fishing rights as tribal rights). The Court of Claims held that the tribe was not entitled to compensation for a taking because the rights had never been abrogated, and the Supreme Court affirmed. See Ch. 2, note 72, supra.

125. 391 U.S at 409 n.10.

126. Kimball v. Callahan, 590 F.2d 768, 775–76 (9th Cir.), cert. denied, 444 U.S. 826 (1979), cited in Oregon Dept. of Fish & Wildlife v. Klamath Indian Tribe, 105 S. Ct. 3420, 3426 n.12, 3428 n.18 (1985) (description of tribal government's activities after termination and statement that "we agree . . . that [tribal treaty hunting and fishing rights] may survive the termination of an Indian reservation"). See also Joint Tribal Council of the Passamaquoddy Tribe v. Morton, 528 F.2d 370, 377–78 (1st Cir. 1975) (federal recognition of a tribe for some, but not all, purposes).

127. 437 U.S. 634 (1978).

128. See generally A. Debo, The Rise and Fall of the Choctaw Republic (1967).

129. 437 U.S. at 653. On the power of Congress to alter ethnological definitions of tribes and bands, see F. Cohen, supra note 6, at 5–7.

130. This is an aspect of an Indian tribe's right to change in order to meet new societal conditions. See notes 112–16, supra.

131. See Menominee Restoration Act of 1973, 25 U.S.C. §§ 903–903f (1982). See also, e.g., Siletz Indian Tribe Restoration Act of 1977, 25 U.S.C. §§ 711–711f (1982); Grand Ronde Restoration Act of 1983, 25 U.S.C. §§ 713–713g (Supp. 1983); Paiute Indian Tribe of Utah Restoration Act of 1980, 25 U.S.C. §§ 762–68 (1982).

132. See Eastern Band of Cherokee Indians v. North Carolina Wildlife Resources Comm'n, 588 F.2d 75 (4th Cir. 1978), cert. dismissed, 446 U.S.

960 (1980); Seminole Tribe of Florida v. Butterworth, 658 F.2d 310 (5th Cir. 1981), cert. denied, 102 S. Ct. 1717 (1982); Cow Creek Band of Umpqua Tribe of Indians Recognition Act of 1983, 25 U.S.C. §§ 712–712d (Supp. 1985); Texas Band of Kickapoo Act of 1983, 25 U.S.C. §§ 1300b–11 to 1300b–16 (1983).

133. See generally F. Cohen, supra note 6, at 62–74, 108–17; F. Prucha, American Indian Policy in the Formative Years (1970); F. Prucha, American Indian Policy in Crisis 290–91 (1976) (government contracts with religious schools to educate Indian children); L. Schmeckebier, The Office of Indian Affairs 212 (1927).

134. Worcester v. Georgia, 31 U.S. (6 Pet.) 515, 559 (1832).

135. 118 U.S. 375 (1886), quoted in text accompanying Ch. 1, note 90, supra.

136. 187 U.S. 553 (1903).

137. See Johnson v. McIntosh, 21 U.S. (8 Wheat.) 543, 573–74, 591–92 (1823) (doctrine of discovery); Cherokee Nation v. Georgia, 30 U.S. (5 Pet.) 1, 17–18 (1831) (tribes as domestic dependent nations; any attempt to treat with them would be an act of hostility); Lone Wolf v. Hitchcock, 187 U.S. 553, 568 (1903) (transfer of tribal lands into allotments; treaty abrogation).

138. 417 U.S. 535 (1974), discussed in Ch. 2, notes 74, 75, supra. Earlier opinions include Pueblo of Santa Rosa v. Fall, 273 U.S. 315 (1927); United States v. Sandoval, 231 U.S. 28 (1913); Choate v. Trapp, 224 U.S. 665 (1912).

139. 430 U.S. 73 (1977).

140. 448 U.S. 371 (1980).

141. The 1868 treaty provided that there could be no cession of reservation land "unless executed and signed by at least three fourths of all the adult male Indians, occupying or interested in the same." Treaty of Fort Laramie with the Sioux, April 29, 1868, art. XIII, 15 Stat. 635, 639. Negotiations were held with Sioux leaders concerning cession of the Black Hills, but the agreement was signed by only 10 percent of the adult male Sioux population. 448 U.S. at 382. Congress ratified the agreement in spite of the requirement of the 1868 treaty. Act of Feb. 28, 1877, ch. 72, 19 Stat. 254.

142. The first opinion is Sioux Tribe of Indians v. United States, 97 Ct. Cl. 613, 601 F.2d 1157, cert. denied, 318 U.S. 789 (1942). In the second decision, United States v. Sioux Nation, 207 Ct. Cl. 234, 518 F.2d 1298, cert. denied, 423 U.S 1016 (1975), the Court of Claims held that the taking claim was barred by the res judicata effect of the 1942 decision. Nevertheless, the tribe had been awarded damages by the Indian Claims Commission, and the Court of Claims allowed the damage award to stand because the government had appealed the decision only on the question of whether

an unconstitutional taking had occurred. While the Sioux were entitled to the value of the land at the time of the taking, without interest, under the "unfair and dishonorable dealings" provision of the Indian Claims Commission Act of 1946, 25 U.S.C. §§ 70–70v (1976)(expired 1978), only a finding of an unconstitutional taking would allow the Sioux to recover interest on the damages award. The value of the land was $17.1 million; interest since the taking amounted to nearly $90 million. United States v. Sioux Nation of Indians, 448 U.S. 371, 387, 390 (1980); Sioux Nation of Indians v. United States, 601 F.2d 1157, 1159, 1172 (Ct. Cl. 1979).

143. "[T]he 1877 Act effected a taking of tribal property, property which had been set aside for the exclusive occupation of the Sioux by the Fort Laramie Treaty of 1868. That taking implied an obligation on the part of the government to make just compensation to the Sioux Nation, and that obligation, including an award of interest, must now, at last, be paid." 448 U.S. at 424.

144. The Court approved and quoted the test employed in Three Affiliated Tribes of the Fort Berthold Reservation v. United States, 182 Ct. Cl. 543, 553, 390 F.2d 686, 691 (1968):

> It is obvious that Congress cannot simultaneously (1) act as trustee for the benefit of the Indians, exercising its plenary powers over the Indians and their property, as it thinks is in their best interests, and (2) exercise its sovereign power of eminent domain, taking the Indians' property within the meaning of the Fifth Amendment to the Constitution. In any given situation in which Congress has acted with regard to Indian people, it must have acted either in one capacity or the other. Congress can own two hats, but it cannot wear them both at the same time.
>
> Some guideline must be established so that a court can identify in which capacity Congress is acting. The following guideline would best give recognition to the basic distinction between the two types of congressional action: Where Congress makes a good faith effort to give the Indians the full value of the land and thus merely transmutes the property from land to money, there is no taking. This is a mere substitution of assets or change of form and is a traditional function of a trustee.

448 U.S. at 408–09 (citation omitted).

145. The *Sioux Nation* Court described the *Lone Wolf* presumption as "conclusive," noting that it was based on the premise that federal–tribal relations are a "political matter, not amenable to judicial review." 448 U.S. at 413.

146. Id. at 413–14. For a comprehensive analysis of Congress's extensive power in this field, see Newton, Federal Power Over Indians: Its Sources, Scope, and Limitations, 132 U. Pa. L. Rev. 195 (1984). See also

Comment, Federal Plenary Power in Indian Affairs After Weeks and Sioux Nation, 131 U. Pa. L. Rev. 235 (1982).

147. The Sioux Nation continues to seek judicial and legislative avenues for obtaining a return of the Black Hills, rather than the money damages approved by the Supreme Court. See, e.g., Oglallala Sioux v. United States, 650 F.2d 140 (8th Cir. 1981), cert. denied, 445 U.S. 907 (1982) (holding that the Indian Claims Commission Act of 1946, Ch. 1, note 91, supra, provides an exclusive remedy for the wrongful taking of Indian lands).

148. In 1979, in response to equitable arguments by the Sioux Nation, Congress took the unusual step of allowing the Court of Claims to review the taking of the Black Hills in spite of the 1942 case that had established a res judicata bar. See note 142, supra; 448 U.S. at 389. The thrust of Justice Rehnquist's dissenting opinion in Sioux Nation was that Congress impermissibly intruded on the judicial power by allowing a final judgment to be revised. 448 U.S. 424–37 (Rehnquist, J. dissenting).

149. On changes in sovereign immunity, see the several avenues of judicial relief, many of them created by statute, against the United States and its officials as discussed in 14 C. Wright, A. Miller & E. Cooper, Federal Practice and Procedure, §§ 3654–59 (2d ed. 1985). On the political question doctrine, see generally Henkin, Is There A "Political Question" Doctrine?, 85 Yale L.J. 597 (1976). Executive and legislative flexibility in foreign relations is discussed in Clark v. Allen, 331 U.S. 503, 514 (1947). On the use of international law principles in Indian law, see, e.g., Red Fox v. Red Fox, 23 Or. App. 393, 399–400, 542 P.2d 918, 921–22 (1975) (analogizing comity extended by state courts to tribal courts to the comity extended by states to decrees of another nation).

150. In Choate v. Trapp, 224 U.S. 665 (1912), the Court struck down a shortening of the nontaxable period for certain allotments on the ground that just compensation was required by the Fifth Amendment. Like Sioux Nation, however, Choate recognized that Congress can accomplish the taking by awarding just compensation.

151. One of the first legislative successes of the modern era was achieved by Alaska Native leaders in the form of the Alaska Native Claims Settlement Act of 1971, Pub. L. No. 92–203, 85 Stat. 688, codified at 43 U.S.C. §§ 1601–28 (1982). See Ch. 1, note 13, supra. At about the same time, other tribes were engaged in lobbying activity that resulted in the return of tribal lands. See, e.g., Act of December 15, 1970, Pub. L. No. 91–550, 84 Stat. 1437 (restoration of Blue Lake and 48,000 acres of land to Taos Pueblo of New Mexico); Act of September 21, 1972, Pub. L. No. 92–427, 86 Stat. 719 (return of McQuinn Strip, comprising approximately 61,000 acres, to the Warm Springs Tribe of Oregon). Tribes in the eastern United States have been successful in settling land claims court cases by means of legislation. See e.g., Maine Indian Claims Settlement Act of 1980,

Pub. L. No. 96–420, 94 Stat. 1785 (codified at 25 U.S.C. §§ 1721–35 (1982));
Rhode Island Indian Claims Settlement Act, Pub. L. No. 95–395, 92 Stat.
813 (codified at 25 U.S.C. §§ 1701–12 (1982)). In addition to these and
many other actions involving individual tribes, see, e.g., F. Cohen, supra
note 6, at 196–200, Indian tribes and organizations have conceptualized,
and obtained the passage of, the major omnibus bills of the last decade.
See Indian Self-Determination and Education Assistance Act of 1975, Pub.
L. No. 93–638, 88 Stat. 2203 (codified at 25 U.S.C. §§ 450–450n, 455–458e
(1982)); Indian Child Welfare Act of 1968, Pub. L. No. 95–608, 92 Stat.
3069 (codified at 25 U.S.C. §§ 1901–63 (1982)); Indian Land Consolidation
Act of 1982, Pub. L. No. 97–459, 96 Stat. 2517 (codified at 25 U.S.C. §§
2201–2210 (1982); Indian Financing Act of 1974, Pub. L. No. 93–262, 88
Stat. 77 (codified at scattered sections of 25 U.S.C.); Indian Tribal Governmental Tax Status Act of 1982, Pub. L. No. 97–473, 96 Stat. 2607
(codified in scattered sections of 26 and 29 U.S.C. (1982)); American Indian
Religious Freedom Act of 1978, Pub. L. No. 95–341, 92 Stat. 469 (codified
in part at 42 U.S.C. § 1996 (1982)).

152. In 1971, Forrest Gerard, a Blackfeet Indian, was appointed as
counsel to the Indian Affairs Subcommittee of the Senate Committee on
Interior and Insular Affairs; in the same year Franklin Ducheneaux, a Standing Rock Sioux, was appointed counsel to the Indian Affairs Subcommittee
for the House Committee on Interior and Insular Affairs. Gerard served
until 1976 and Ducheneaux continues as special counsel for Indian affairs
to the House Interior Committee. Gerard and Ducheneaux moved cau-
tiously—indeed, they have received their share of criticism from Indians—
but both of them were knowledgeable, skilled staff members who brought
an Indian point of view to their influential positions. They were key elements
in the explosion of Indian-supported legislation since 1970. See generally
note 151, supra.

The Senate subcommittee has been succeeded by a permanent Committee on Indian Affairs, see Ch. 1, note 91, supra, and the tradition of
appointing Indians or Indian advocates to most committee staff positions
has continued. Many western senators and members of Congress now have
staff members specializing in Indian affairs; often those positions are held
by Indians. Increasingly, committee staffs outside of the committees and
subcommittees dealing specifically with Indian issues include persons with
expertise in Indian legislation.

153. National organizations such as the National Congress of American
Indians (the largest Indian organization) and the National Tribal Chairmen's
Association regularly testify on legislation affecting Indians. Regional ent-
ities, such as the All-Indian Pueblo Council (in the Southwest) and the
Northwest Affiliated Indian Tribes (in the Pacific Northwest), have orga-
nized along geographical lines. Several of the larger tribes have paid lob-

byists in Washington. The political efforts of these organizations are complemented by several professional support groups, including the Association on American Indian Affairs, the Native American Rights Fund, the American Indian Law Center, the American Indian Lawyer Training Program, Americans for Indian Opportunity, the National Indian Education Association, the Council of Energy Resource Tribes, the Indian Law Resource Center, and others; these organizations identify, analyze, and advocate issues affecting Indians in Congress.

154. Some Indian testimony on the 1968 act, Ch. 1, note 24, supra, was generally supportive, but there was considerable opposition, especially among the Pueblos of New Mexico. See generally Burnett, An Historical Analysis of the 1968 "Indian Civil Rights" Act, 9 Harv. J. on Legis. 557 (1972). Although much of the act received opposition from Indians, amendments to the 1968 act relatively late in the legislative process were actively sought by the tribes; this is particularly true with regard to Title IV of the act, which limited the impact of Public Law 280 by requiring an affected tribe's consent before a state could assert criminal or civil jurisdiction over Indian country. See Pub. L. No. 90–284, Titles II–IV, 82 Stat. 73, 77–79. These amendments to Public Law 280 are discussed in F. Cohen, supra note 6, at 362–72.

Of course, in the legislation passed since 1968, e.g., supra note 151, compromises often have been made from the original proposals submitted by the tribes; but no Indian statute, as finally written, has received substantial Indian opposition since 1968.

155. See, e.g., Brest, The Conscientious Legislator's Guide to Constitutional Interpretation, 27 Stan. L. Rev. 585 (1975); Hearings Before the Senate Committee on Commerce on S. 1732, 88th Cong., 1st Sess., parts 1 & 2 (1963), reprinted in G. Gunther, Constitutional Law: Cases and Materials 159–62 (11th ed. 1985).

156. See, e.g., S. 954, 99th Cong., 1st Sess., 131 Cong. Rec. 54,401–02 (daily ed. Apr. 18, 1985) (authorizing state regulation of steelhead trout fishing by Indians on and off reservations); S. 2084, 97th Cong., 2d Sess., 128 Cong. Rec. 1229–30 (1982) (extinguishing all land and natural resources claims arising prior to January 1, 1912); H.R. 9951, 95th Cong., 1st Sess., 123 Cong. Rec. 37,033 (1977) (abolishing aboriginal water rights and establishing a reservation's priority for water according to the date of the federal reserving document).

157. See, e.g., 5 U.S.C. §§ 701–76 (1982). Morton v. Ruiz, 415 U.S. 199 (1973); Tooahnippah v. Hickel, 397 U.S. 598 (1970). See generally Chambers, Judicial Enforcement of the Federal Trust Responsibility to Indians, 27 Stan. L. Rev. 1213 (1975).

158. 415 U.S. 199 (1973).

159. One leading scholar of administrative law has identified five prop-

ositions in Morton v. Ruiz that exceed the standards normally imposed upon administrative agencies. Davis, Administrative Law Surprises in the Ruiz Case, 75 Colum. L. Rev. 823 (1975).

160. United States v. Mitchell, 445 U.S. 535 (1980).

161. United States v. Mitchell, 463 U.S. 206 (1983).

162. 463 U.S. 110 (1983), discussed in Ch. 2, notes 44–46, supra.

163. The physical facts are set out in the Supreme Court opinion. 463 U.S. at 114–16 & n.7. On the conflicts of interest, see Ch. 2, note 46, supra.

164. See text accompanying Ch. 2, note 46, supra. During the same term the Supreme Court also handed down Arizona v. California II, 460 U.S. 605 (1983), which similarly emphasized the importance of the finality of adjudications in western water law. See id. at 620, quoted in text accompanying Ch. 2, note 47, supra.

165. The Court stated as follows:

> These cases, we believe, point the way to the correct resolution of the instant cases. The United States undoubtedly owes a strong fiduciary duty to its Indian wards. See Seminole Nation v. United States, 316 U.S. 286, 296–297, 62 S. Ct. 1049, 1054, 86 L. Ed. 1480 (1942); Shoshone Tribe v. United States, 299 U.S. 476, 497–498, 57 S. Ct. 244, 251–252, 81 L. Ed. 360 (1937). It may be that where only a relationship between the Government and the tribe is involved, the law respecting obligations between a trustee and a beneficiary in private litigation will in many, if not all, respects, adequately describe the duty of the United States. But where Congress has imposed upon the United States, in addition to its duty to represent Indian tribes, a duty to obtain water rights for reclamation projects, and has even authorized the inclusion of reservation lands within a project, the analogy of a faithless private fiduciary cannot be controlling for purposes of evaluating the authority of the United States to represent different interests.

Nevada v. United States, 463 U.S. at 142.

166. See, e.g., United States v. Mitchell, 463 U.S. 206 (1983); Seminole Nation v. United States, 316 U.S. 286 (1924); Navajo Tribe of Indians v. United States, 364 F.2d 320, 322–23 (Ct. Cl. 1966).

167. In numerous situations Indian interests are pitted directly against conflicting resource uses. The leading study is Chambers, Discharge of the Federal Trust Responsibility to Enforce Legal Claims of Indian Tribes: Case Studies of Bureaucratic Conflict of Interest, Subcom. on Administrative Practice and Procedure, Senate Comm. on the Judiciary, 91st Cong., 2d Sess., A Study of Administrative Conflicts of Interest in the Protection of Indian Natural Resources 4–11 (Comm. Print 1971).

168. See Pyramid Lake Paiute Tribe of Indians v. Morton, 354 F.

Supp. 252 (D.D.C. 1973), where the court ruled that "[t]he burden rested on the Secretary to justify any diversion of water from the Tribe with precision. It was not his function to attempt an accommodation." Id. at 256.

169. At the time of the 1973 decision, the United States had taken the position in an original action pending in the United States Supreme Court that the tribe did possess reserved water rights pursuant to the Executive Order of 1874 establishing the reservation. 354 F. Supp. at 254–55. Therefore, the 1973 opinion assumed, *arguendo*, that the rights existed. Nevada v. United States, 463 U.S. 110 (1983), held that the tribe was barred by res judicata from asserting the rights.

170. The role of the trust obligation as a premise for the canons of construction is discussed in F. Cohen, supra note 6 at 221–25.

171. Morton v. Mancari, 417 U.S. 535, 554–55 (1974) ("The [special BIA hiring] preference, as applied, is granted to Indians not as a discrete racial group, but, rather, as members of quasi-sovereign tribal entities whose lives and activities are governed by the BIA in a unique fashion. . . . As long as the special treatment can be tied rationally to the fulfillment of Congress' unique obligation toward the Indians, such legislative judgments will not be disturbed").

172. See, e.g., Fisher v. District Court, 424 U.S. 382, 391 (1976) (upholding exclusive jurisdiction of tribal courts and stating that such exclusive jurisdiction "is justified because it is intended to benefit the [Indians] by furthering the congressional policy of Indian self-government").

CHAPTER 4 TERRITORIAL JURISPRUDENCE

1. See Ch. 1, supra.

2. Among the eleven western states, statehood came early in California (1850), Oregon (1859), and Nevada (1864). Then came Colorado (1876), Montana and Washington (both 1889), Idaho and Wyoming (both 1890), Utah (1896), and Arizona and New Mexico (both 1912). See P. Gates, History of Public Land Law Development, app. C (1968).

3. 104 U.S. 621 (1882).

4. The terms of the Indian Country Crimes Act, 18 U.S.C. § 1152 (1982), which were in force at the time of *McBratney*, provide generally for exclusive federal jurisdiction over crimes in the Indian country. The statute sets out three exceptions, but none of them applies to an an alleged murder by a non-Indian of another non-Indian. See F. Cohen, Handbook of Federal Indian Law 264–66 (1982 ed.) [hereinafter cited as F. Cohen]. The *McBratney* opinion suggested that state jurisdiction was required for crimes involving only non-Indians because Colorado had entered the Union "upon an equal footing with the original States in all respects whatever." 104 U.S. at 624. Later cases, however, have made it clear that the equal

footing doctrine does not operate to extend state jurisdiction into Indian country. See, e.g., United States v. Winans, 198 U.S. 371, 382–84 (1905), discussed in Ch. 1, note 93, supra. Because of the dubious reasoning in *McBratney*, litigants have often requested that it be reconsidered, although such requests have been unsuccessful. In New York ex rel. Ray v. Martin, 326 U.S. 496 (1946), the Court offered the modern policy justification for the *McBratney* rule:

> The entire emphasis in treaties and Congressional enactments dealing with Indian affairs has always been focused upon the treatment of the Indians themselves and their property. Generally no emphasis has been placed on whether state or United States courts should try white offenders for conduct which happened to take place upon an Indian reservation, but which did not directly affect the Indians.

Id. at 501.

5. See pp. 106–11 infra.

6. F. Prucha, American Indian Policy in the Formative Years 13 (1970). On this era, and the Royal Proclamation generally, see id. at 13–25.

7. See, e.g., Act of July 22, 1790, ch. 33, § 3, 1 Stat. 137. See also Mohegan Tribe v. Connecticut, 638 F.2d 612 (2d Cir. 1980), cert. denied, 452 U.S. 968 (1981); F. Cohen, supra note 4, at 29 n.31.

8. Act of June 30, 1834, ch. 161, § 1, 4 Stat. 729. Section 29 of the 1834 act provided that the Trade and Intercourse Act of 1802 would remain in effect for tribes east of the Mississippi. Id. at 734.

9. United States v. John, 437 U.S. 634, 649 n.18 (1978). See also F. Cohen, supra note 4, at 31 & n.37.

10. See, e.g., United States v. Ramsey, 271 U.S. 467, 470–72 (1926) (definition of Indian country includes restricted allotment); United States v. Pelican, 232 U.S. 442, 448–51 (1914) (definition of Indian country includes a single trust allotment); Donnelly v. United States, 228 U.S. 243, 268–69, 255–59 (1913) (Indian country includes lands set aside for Indian tribes pursuant to executive order; Indian country can be established within the boundaries of a state); United States v. McGowan, 302 U.S. 535, 537–39 (1938) (Indian country includes land purchased by federal government after statehood and transferred into trust for Indians); United States v. Sandoval, 231 U.S. 28, 48 (1913) (lands held by Pueblo Indians in New Mexico are Indian country even though lands not formally held in trust).

11. Bates v. Clark, 95 U.S. 204, 207, 209 (1877).

12. See generally Clinton, Criminal Jurisdiction Over Indian Lands: A Journey Through a Jurisdictional Maze, 18 Ariz. L. Rev. 503, 507–13 (1976), discussing the statute and the codification of existing case law.

13. 420 U.S. 425, 427 n.2 (1975).

14. 448 U.S. 136, 142–45 (1980) ("The Court has repeatedly emphasized that there is a significant geographical component to tribal sovereignty, a component which remains highly relevant to the pre-emption inquiry; though the reservation boundary is not absolute, it remains an important factor to weigh in determining whether state authority has exceeded the permissible limits").

15. 458 U.S. 832, 837–38 (1982).

16. 411 U.S. 164 (1973), discussed in Ch. 3, notes 33–36, supra.

17. 411 U.S. 145 (1973).

18. On personal law, which follows a person wherever located, see 1 J. Beale, A Treatise on the Conflict of Laws 52 (1935); 1 E. Rabel, The Conflict of Laws 109–93 (2d ed. 1985); A. Ehrenzweig, A Treatise on the Conflict of Laws 372–75 (1962). In some instances special principles of Indian law apply outside of Indian country. See note 24, infra.

19. 411 U.S. at 148–49. An exception is the sovereign immunity of tribes, an issue not raised in *Mescalero Apache* since suit was instituted by the tribe. Tribes possess sovereign immunity, and the immunity exists in regard to transactions and activities outside of Indian country. See, e.g., Puyallup Tribe, Inc. v. Department of Game, 433 U.S. 165, 170–72 (1977).

20. Seymour v. Superintendent, 368 U.S. 351, 358 (1962).

21. See note 114, infra.

22. 448 U.S. 136 (1980).

23. 448 U.S. at 142, quoting Williams v. Lee, 358 U.S. 217, 220 (1959). For later decisions using the test, see, e.g., Three Affiliated Tribes of the Fort Berthold Reservation v. Wold Engineering, 104 S. Ct. 2267, 2274 (1984); New Mexico v. Mescalero Apache Tribe, 462 U.S. 324, 332–33 (1983); Ramah Navajo School Bd. v. Bureau of Revenue, 458 U.S. 832, 837 (1982); Central Machinery Co. v. Arizona State Tax Comm'n 448 U.S. 160, 165–66 (1980).

24. In both historical and modern circumstances Congress has exercised its broad power over Indian affairs outside of Indian country. The special laws prohibiting sales of liquor to Indians were in force outside of Indian country, United States v. 43 Gallons of Whiskey, 93 U.S. 188 (1876), although the applicable code provision, 18 U.S.C. § 1154 (1982), is now confined to Indian country by the operation of 18 U.S.C. § 1161 (1982). Some tribes possess off-reservation fishing and hunting rights. See e.g., Washington v. Washington State Commercial Passenger Fishing Vessel Ass'n, 443 U.S. 658 (1979). Several federal programs providing services to individual Indians in health, education, and housing extend to nonreservation Indians. See generally F. Cohen, supra note 4, at 673–738.

25. See, e.g., White Mountain Apache Tribe v. Bracker, 448 U.S. 136, 143 (1980).

26. See text accompanying Ch. 1, notes 44–64, supra.

27. See pp. 106–11, infra.

28. White Mountain Apache Tribe v. Bracker, 448 U.S. 136 (1980), and each case involving state jurisdiction in Indian country decided thereafter, supra note 23, with the exception of Three Affiliated Tribes of the Fort Berthold Reservation v. Wold Engineering, 104 S. Ct. 2267 (1984), has relied upon subject matter preemption rather than geographical preemption.

29. On the vague language of treaties and treaty substitutes and the role of common law case development, see text accompanying Ch. 1, notes 26–31, supra.

30. 411 U.S. 164, 172 (1973).

31. White Mountain Apache Tribe v. Bracker, 448 U.S. 136, 143 (1980).

32. See, e.g., Three Affiliated Tribes of the Fort Berthold Reservation v. Wold Engineering, 54 U.S.L.W. 4654, 4656 (1986); White Mountain Apache Tribe v. Bracker, 448 U.S. 136, 144 (1980); Fisher v. District Court, 424 U.S. 382, 388–89 (1976); and McClanahan v. Arizona State Tax Comm'n, 411 U.S. 164, 174–75 (1973), where the Court noted that the "treaty nowhere explicitly states that the Navajos were to be free from state law or exempt from state taxes," but construed the treaty as intending "to establish the lands as within the exclusive sovereignty of the Navajos under general federal supervision."

33. See, e.g., Montana v. Blackfeet Tribe of Indians, 105 S. Ct. 2399, 2403–04 (1985); Three Affiliated Tribes of the Fort Berthold Reservation v. Wold Engineering, 104 S. Ct. 2267, 2271 (1984) (recognizing "the general principle that Indian territories were beyond the legislative and judicial jurisdiction of state governments"); White Mountain Apache Tribe v. Bracker, 448 U.S. 136, 144 (1980); Bryan v. Itasca County, 426 U.S. 373, 392 (1976). See generally D. Getches, D. Rosenfelt, & C. Wilkinson, Federal Indian Law, Cases and Materials 295–99 (1979).

34. See Pacific Gas & Electric Co. v. State Energy Comm'n, 461 U.S. 190, 206, 216 (1983); Note, The Preemption Doctrine: Shifting Perspective on Federalism and The Burger Court, 75 Colum. L. Rev. 623, 653 (1975).

35. See, e.g., Montana v. Blackfeet Tribe of Indians, 105 S. Ct. 2399, 2403 (1985) (trust relationship); New Mexico v. Mescalero Apache Tribe, 462 U.S. 324, 332 (1983) (tribal self-government policy); Ramah Navajo School Bd. v. Bureau of Revenue, 458 U.S. 832, 837–38 (1982) (tribal self-government policy); Central Machinery Co. v. Arizona State Tax Comm'n, 448 U.S. 160, 163 (1980) (long and extensive federal activity); White Mountain Apache Tribe v. Bracker, 448 U.S. 136, 142 (1980) (long and extensive federal activity). There is, of course, a small number of other fields where the federal interest is very strong, thus presumptively leaving little room for the operation of state law. See, e.g., Hines v. Davidowitz, 312 U.S. 52 (1941) (immigration law).

36. Mescalero Apache Tribe v. Jones, 411 U.S. 145, 148–49 (1973), discussed and quoted in text accompanying notes 16–19, supra.

37. 31 U.S. (6 Pet.) 515 (1832).

38. Williams v. Lee, 358 U.S. 217, 219 (1959); McClanahan v. Arizona State Tax Comm'n, 411 U.S. 164, 171 (1973); White Mountain Apache Tribe v. Bracker, 448 U.S. 136, 141 n.9 (1980). On the citation of *Worcester* by modern courts, see text accompanying Ch. 3, note 112, supra.

39. For authorities arguing in favor of constitutional limits to state jurisdiction in Indian country under the Indian Commerce Clause, see Clinton, Isolated in Their Own Country: A Defense of Federal Protection of Indian Autonomy and Self-Government, 33 Stan. L. Rev. 979 (1981); Clinton, Book Review, 47 U. Chi. L. Rev. 846 (1980); Walters, Review Essay: Preemption, Tribal Sovereignty, and Worcester v. Georgia, 62 Or. L. Rev. 127 (1983). The solicitor general has made similar arguments, but the Court has refused to adopt the approach. See Ramah Navajo School Bd. v. Bureau of Revenue, 458 U.S. 832, 845–46 (1982); Merrion v. Jicarilla Apache Tribe, 455 U.S. 130, 153–54 (1982).

40. "[T]he Acts of the legislature of Georgia seize on the whole Cherokee country, parcel it out among the neighbouring counties of the state, extend her code over the whole country, abolish its institutions and its laws, and annihilate its political existence." 31 U.S. (6 Pet.) at 542.

41. "The Indian nations had always been considered as distinct, independent political communities, retaining their original natural rights." Id. at 559. See United States v. Wheeler, 435 U.S. 313, 322–23 (1978) ("Before the coming of the Europeans, the tribes were self-governing sovereign political communities. . . . Indian tribes still possess those aspects of sovereignty not withdrawn by treaty or statute, or by implication as a necessary result of their dependent status").

42. "[A] weaker power does not surrender its independence—its right to self-government, by associating with a stronger, and taking its protection." 31 U.S. (6 Pet.) at 561. See Merrion v. Jicarilla Apache Tribe, 455 U.S. 130, 159 (1982), quoting the cited language from Worcester.

43. The Court referred to, among other things, "the pre-existing rights of [the country's] ancient possessors." 31 U.S. (6 Pet.) at 543. See Washington v. Washington State Commercial Passenger Fishing Vessel Ass'n, 443 U.S. 658 (1979) (recognizing tribal reserved fishing rights).

44. The *Worcester* opinion recognized the unequal bargaining power possessed by the United States in regard to language:

> The words 'treaty' and 'nation' are words of our own language, selected in our diplomatic and legislative proceedings, by ourselves, having each a definite and well understood meaning. We have applied them to Indians, as we have applied them to the other nations of the earth.

31 U.S. (6 Pet.) at 559–60. The modern cases analyzing the canons of construction in Indian law are discussed in Ch. 2, supra.

45. Citing *Worcester* the Court has recognized "the general principle that Indian territories were beyond the legislative and judicial jurisdiction of state governments." Three Affiliated Tribes of the Fort Berthold Reservation v. Wold Engineering, 104 S. Ct. 2267, 2271 (1984).

46. Williams v. Lee, 358 U.S. 217, 219 (1959). See also, e.g., Three Affiliated Tribes of the Fort Berthold Reservation v. Wold Engineering, 104 S. Ct. 2267, 2271 (1984); Merrion v. Jicarilla Apache Tribe, 455 U.S. 130, 159 (1982); White Mountain Apache Tribe v. Bracker, 448 U.S. 136, 141–42 (1980). See generally F. Cohen, supra note 4, at 259–70.

47. The early provisions are discussed in F. Prucha, American Indian Policy in the Formative Years 45–50 (1962). The modern traders statutes are codified at 25 U.S.C. §§ 261–64 (1982).

48. 380 U.S. 685 (1965).

49. 448 U.S. 160 (1980).

50. Id. at 165. The trial court opinion, written by then-Maricopa County Superior Court Judge Sandra Day O'Connor, tracked the reasoning used by the Supreme Court. See Central Machinery Co. v. Arizona State Tax Comm'n, No. C 297070 (Maricopa County Superior Court, Aug. 31, 1976).

51. Corporate executives frequently express concern about the lack of predictability in regard to business dealings in Indian country. This is based in part upon unresolved legal issues and in part upon a perceived instability of some tribal governments. See, e.g., Bathke, Common Industry Concerns Regarding Business on Indian Reservations (Institute for Resource Management, 1984).

52. There is no subject matter preemption of state taxing authority when sales are made to non-Indians; the traders statutes extend federal controls only when goods are "sold to the Indians." 25 U.S.C. § 261 (1982). There is no bar due to geographical preemption because the tribal interest in a sale by a non-Indian to a non-Indian is considered by the Court to be minimal. Cf. Washington v. Confederated Tribes of the Colville Indian Reservation, 447 U.S. 134, 154–58 (1980) (upholding requirement that tribes collect state sales tax on sales of cigarettes to non-Indians).

53. See United States v. Mazurie, 419 U.S. 544, 557 (1975), construing 18 U.S.C. § 1161 (1982).

54. 463 U.S. 713 (1983).

55. The issue of state taxation of liquor sales in Indian country was raised in the Ninth Circuit in companion cases to Rice v. Rehner, but those cases were remanded by the Ninth Circuit to the District Court for further consideration. Id. at 716 n.5. The Supreme Court taxation decisions discussed in this chapter, including prominently Montana v. Blackfeet Tribe of Indians, 105 S. Ct. 2399 (1985), have been rigorous in requiring an express congressional statement before state taxation of Indians will be allowed.

The liquor statutes, which refer to "the laws of the state" but do not mention taxation, would seem to fall short of that requirement. On the other hand, Rice v. Rehner has broad language about the reach of state law under the liquor statutes. The Court emphasized the important state interest in liquor traffic, 463 U.S. at 724, and the lack of an important tribal interest due to the early and extensive federal control over the liquor traffic in Indian country. Id. at 722. Thus the Ninth Circuit recently has upheld state taxation and regulation of tribal liquor enterprises. Squaxin Island Tribe v. Washington, 781 F.2d 715 (9th Cir. 1986). The application of Rice v. Rehner to tribes could have at least one especially untoward result: if all sellers of liquor in Indian country are subject to all state laws, even tribes might have to obtain state liquor licenses, often an expensive proposition—in some states, including New Mexico, the market transfer price of liquor licenses often exceeds $100,000.

56. "The State has an unquestionable interest in the liquor traffic that occurs within its borders, and this interest is independent of the authority conferred on the States by the Twenty-first Amendment. Crowley v. Christensen, 137 U.S. 86, 91 (1890)." 463 U.S. at 724. The statute quoted in the text is 18 U.S.C. § 1161 (1982).

57. See Ramah Navajo School Bd. v. Bureau of Revenue, 458 U.S. 832 (1982), finding subject matter preemption based upon the fact that "Congress has enacted numerous statutes empowering the BIA to provide for Indian education both on and off the reservation." Id. at 839–40 (citing authority).

58. The *Ramah Navajo* Court relied in significant part upon the Indian Self-Determination and Education Assistance Act of 1975, 25 U.S.C. §§ 450–450n (1982), in finding subject matter preemption in the field of education. 458 U.S. at 840–41. The self-determination act applies also to Indian health programs administered by the secretary of health and human services. See, e.g., 25 U.S.C. § 450g (1982) (contracts by secretary of health and human services with tribal organizations). Construction of other tribal buildings would seem to be within the self-determination act of 1975, Ch. 1, note 19, supra, which included a finding that Indian people should have "an effective voice in the planning and implementation of programs for the benefit of Indians which are responsive to the true needs of Indian communities," 25 U.S.C. § 450(a) (1982), and declared that "[t]he Congress hereby recognizes the obligation of the United States to respond to the strong expression of the Indian people for self-determination by assuring maximum Indian participation in the direction of educational as well as other Federal services to Indian communities so as to render such services more responsive to the needs and desires of those communities." 25 U.S.C. § 450a(a) (1982). The general congressional policy, expressed in the 1975 act, of promoting self-determination by tribes has been highlighted in sev-

eral decisions. See, e.g., New Mexico v. Mescalero Apache Tribe, 462 U.S. 324, 334–35 & n. 17 (1983); Ramah Navajo School Bd. v. Bureau of Revenue, 458 U.S. 832, 840–41 (1982); Merrion v. Jicarilla Apache Tribe, 455 U.S. 130, 137–41 (1982).

59. 448 U.S 136 (1980).

60. The quoted phrase was first used in the context of cigarette sales in Washington v. Confederated Tribes of the Colville Indian Reservation, 447 U.S. 134, 155 (1980). In White Mountain Apache Tribe v. Bracker, 448 U.S. 136 (1980), the Court stated:

> Finally, the imposition of state taxes would adversely affect the Tribe's ability to comply with the sustained-yield management policies imposed by federal law. Substantial expenditures are paid out by the Federal Government, the Tribe, and its contractors in order to undertake a wide variety of measures to ensure the continued productivity of the forest. These measures include reforestation, fire control, wildlife promotion, road improvement, safety inspections, and general policing of the forest. The expenditures are largely paid for out of tribal revenues, which are in turn derived almost exclusively from the sale of timber.

448 U.S. at 149–50.

61. 462 U.S. 324 (1983).

62. The contours of the law on this issue, which implicates tens of millions of dollars annually, now seem set. Tribes can tax mineral extraction on tribal lands. Merrion v. Jicarilla Apache Tribe, 455 U.S. 130 (1982). States cannot tax tribes. Montana v. Blackfeet Tribe of Indians, 105 S. Ct. 2399 (1985). As to state taxation of non-Indian companies, the federal statutory and administrative regulatory activity in the area of leasing of Indian minerals, see, e.g., Indian Mineral Leasing Act of 1938, 25 U.S.C. §§ 396a–396g (1982), is at least as extensive as federal statutory and administrative regulation of timber and wildlife, where state taxation has been expressly struck down. New Mexico v. Mescalero Apache Tribe, 462 U.S. 324 (1983); White Mountain Apache Tribe v. Bracker, 448 U.S. 136 (1980). In *Mescalero Apache*, the Court barred the state from stacking its wildlife license fees on top of tribal license fees and showed that it was well aware of the effects of allowing the stacking:

> It is important to emphasize that concurrent jurisdiction would effectively nullify the Tribe's authority to control hunting and fishing on the reservation. Concurrent jurisdiction would empower New Mexico wholly to supplant tribal regulations. . . . The Tribe would thus exercise its authority over the reservation only at the sufferance of the State. The Tribal authority to regulate hunting and fishing by non-members, which has been repeatedly confirmed by federal treaties and laws . . .

would have a rather hollow ring if tribal authority amounted to no more than this.

462 U.S. at 338. Thus the lower court cases to date have held that states cannot stack their mineral severance taxes upon tribal taxes if the imposition of the state taxes would substantially affect the tribe's ability to offer government services. Crow Tribe of Indians v. Montana, 650 F.2d 1104, 1109, amended, 665 F.2d 1390 (9th Cir. 1981), cert. denied, 459 U.S. 916 (1982).

63. Ramah Navajo School Bd. v. Bureau of Revenue, 458 U.S. 832, 856–57 (1982) ("Thus, the Court accords an Indian Tribe, whose sovereignty 'exists only at the sufferance of Congress and is subject to complete defeasance,' greater immunity from state taxes than is enjoyed by the sovereignty of the United States on whom it is dependent" (citation and note omitted)) (Rehnquist, J., dissenting).

64. Compare McClanahan v. Arizona State Tax Comm'n, 411 U.S. 164 (1973) (reservation Indian not subject to state personal income tax) with United States v. County of Fresno, 429 U.S. 452 (1977) (employee of United States Forest Service subject to county possessory interest tax on federal housing located in National Forest). *County of Fresno* did not arise in a federal enclave, the classification of federal lands where insulation from state law is the most extensive, see Wilkinson, The Field of Public Land Law: Some Connecting Threads and Future Directions, 1 Public Land L. Rev. 1, 17–19 (1980), but even in federal enclaves federal employees and other persons are required to pay income taxes pursuant to the Buck Act, 4 U.S.C. §§ 104–10 (1982). See generally Evans v. Cornman, 398 U.S. 419, 424 (1970).

65. Existing waivers of tribal sovereign immunity are extremely limited. See Santa Clara Pueblo v. Martinez, 436 U.S. 49, (1978), discussed in text accompanying notes 134, 135, infra. Much broader waivers of federal sovereign immunity exist under statutes such as the Contract Disputes Act of 1978, Nov. 1, 1978, Pub. L. No. 95–563, 92 Stat. 2383 (codified as amended in scattered sections of 28 and 41 U.S.C. (1982)) and the Federal Tort Claims Act of 1946, ch. 753, Title IV, 60 Stat. 812, 842, (codified as amended in scattered sections of 28 U.S.C. (1982)). Suit against the United States is also allowed under the Administrative Procedure Act, 5 U.S.C. §§ 701–06 (1982), for which there is no parallel as to Indian tribes. See Santa Clara Pueblo v. Martinez, supra.

66. Compare Commonwealth Edison Co. v. Montana, 453 U.S. 609 (1981) (upholding the imposition of Montana's 30 percent severance tax on extraction of minerals by private companies from public lands) with the authorities cited in note 62, supra (denying the authority of states to tax extraction of minerals by private companies from Indian lands when state taxation would interfere with tribe's ability to offer governmental services).

67. Compare Baldwin v. Montana Fish & Game Comm'n, 436 U.S. 371 (1978) (upholding Montana state hunting license fees for non-Indians on public lands) with New Mexico v. Mescalero Apache Tribe, 462 U.S. 324 (1983) and Washington v. Washington State Commercial Passenger Fishing Vessel Ass'n, 443 U.S. 658 (1979) (both denying state licensing and regulatory authority over Indian lands and Indian fishing rights).

68. Compare United States v. New Mexico, 438 U.S. 696 (1978) (denying most federal reserved rights on national forest lands) with Arizona v. California, 373 U.S. 546 (1963) (upholding Indian reserved rights sufficient to irrigate the practicably irrigable portions of the reserved lands).

69. Compare Engdahl, State and Federal Power over Federal Property, 18 Ariz. L. Rev. 283, 379–82 (1976) (extensive state judicial jurisdiction over causes of action arising on federal lands) with F. Cohen, supra note 4, at 348–77 (limited state judicial jurisdiction in Indian country absent express federal delegation).

70. See, e.g., National Farmers Union Ins. Cos. v. Crow Tribe of Indians, 105 S. Ct. 2447 (1985); Three Affiliated Tribes of the Fort Berthold Reservation v. Wold Engineering, 104 S. Ct. 2267 (1984); Fisher v. District Court, 424 U.S. 382 (1976); Williams v. Lee, 358 U.S. 217 (1959).

71. See, e.g., Washington v. Confederated Tribes of the Colville Indian Reservation, 447 U.S. 134, 152–54 (1980); Bryan v. Itasca County, 426 U.S. 373, 392–93 (1976); McClanahan v. Arizona State Tax Comm'n, 411 U.S. 164, 179–81 (1973).

72. Washington v. Confederated Tribes of the Colville Indian Reservation, 447 U.S. 134, 154–57 (1980).

73. See notes 47–68, supra.

74. See Tee-Hit-Ton Indians v. United States, 348 U.S. 272, 279 (1955). See generally Newton, At the Whim of the Sovereign: Aboriginal Title Reconsidered, 31 Hastings L.J. 1215 (1980). Chief Justice Marshall described the European nations, and later the United States, as holding "ultimate dominion" in the land. Johnson v. McIntosh, 21 U.S. (8 Wheat.) 543, 574 (1823).

75. See text accompanying Ch. 2, notes 33–40, supra.

76. See generally Cohen, Original Indian Title, 32 Minn. L. Rev. 28, 34–43 (1947).

77. See Ch. 3, supra.

78. Perhaps the richest source of material on traditional tribal governments is a series of government-commissioned studies. See U.S. Bur. of Am. Ethnology Ann. Reps. (1879–80 to 1930–31). See generally H. Driver, Indians of North America 287–308 (2d rev. ed. 1969). Driver cites additional sources on individual tribes. Id. at 308. See also, e.g., W. Washburn, The Indian in America, 42–51 (1975); D. McNickle, They Came Here First 52–65 (rev. ed. 1975); K. Llewellyn & E. Hoebel, The Cheyenne Way (1941).

On the Iroquois, see, e.g., L. Morgan, League of the Ho-De'-No-Sau-Nee or Iroquois (1954); Russell, The Influence of the Indian Confederations on the Union of the American Colonies, 22 J. Am. Hist. 53 (1928). Less formal governmental organization was particularly prevalent in California and along the Northwest Coast. H. Driver, supra, at 292–98.

79. See text accompanying Ch. 1, notes 37–64, supra.

80. See text accompanying Ch. 1, notes 65–74, supra.

81. Of course, in the original thirteen states and in several of the early admitted states, statehood often preceded the creation of reservations. The pattern tended to be the opposite in the West, where statehood often came long after acquisitions of land from France, England, Mexico, and Russia. On the dates of statehood for western states, see, note 2, supra. In any event, it seems clear that the United States intended first to encourage settlement of the West; territorial status, and then statehood, was to follow the settlers. See generally P. Gates, History of Public Land Law Development 75–86 (1968). In some cases, the matter of statehood was explicitly referred to in the treaties. When the Five Civilized Tribes were removed from the Southeast to what is now Oklahoma, some of them negotiated provisions (which were later abrogated) providing that their western reservations would never be included within the territorial limits or jurisdiction of any state. See, e.g., Treaty of New Echota with the Cherokee Nation, Dec. 29, 1835, art. 5, 7 Stat. 478, 481; Treaty with the Creeks, Mar. 24, 1832, art. 14, 7 Stat. 366, 368. See also Treaty of Lewiston with the Seneca & Shawnee Indians, July 20, 1831, art. 11, 7 Stat. 351, 353. Other treaties, especially those in the Pacific Northwest, made provision for off-reservation fishing rights "in common with all citizens of the Territory." See Washington v. Washington State Commercial Passenger Fishing Vessel Ass'n, 443 U.S. 658 (1979).

82. See text accompanying Ch. 1, notes 37–64, supra.

83. See generally Executive Orders Relating to Indian Reservations 1855–1922 (1975).

84. For most purposes the courts and Congress have treated the treaties identically with bilateral agreements, executive orders, and unilateral statutes. See Ch. 3, supra. See also text accompanying Ch. 1, notes 2–5, supra.

85. See Ch. 1, notes 26–28, supra.

86. See text accompanying Ch. 3, notes 85, 86, supra.

87. The Court commonly makes generic references to the powers of state and local governments. For examples in Indian law, see Merrion v. Jicarilla Apache Tribe, 455 U.S. 130, 147–48 (1982) (comparing tribes with states and cities); United States v. Wheeler, 435 U.S. 49 (1978) (comparing state and local governments, territories, and tribes for the purpose of the "separate sovereign" rule under the Double Jeopardy Clause).

88. Indian law is based in major part on federal treaties and statutes

and on tribal inherent sovereignty, but the field is also heavily influenced
by constitutional law. This applies to the tribes' aboriginal land title, Ch.
2, note 34, supra; the tribes' inherent sovereignty, Ch. 3, supra; the United
States' broad power over Indian land and internal matters, Ch. 3, supra;
and Congress's authority under the Indian Commerce Clause to preempt
state law, notes 47–68, supra. Some authorities in constitutional law give
Indian issues slightly more than passing mention, L. Tribe, American Constitutional Law 1012–19 (1978), but most of the standard texts ignore the
field in spite of the fact that Indian lands compose approximately 2 1/2
percent of all land in the United States and raise increasingly important
matters of public policy, especially in the American West. See generally
Wilkinson, The Place of Indian Law in Constitutional Law and History
(Newberry Library, 1985).

   89. Andrus v. Utah, 446 U.S 500, 507 (1980). On the nature of the
negotiations leading up to state enabling acts, see generally, P. Gates, supra
note 81, at 319–40.

   90. Washington v. Washington State Commercial Passenger Fishing
Vessel Ass'n, 443 U.S. 658, 675 (1979).

   91. The Court has said that tribal sovereignty "exists only at the sufferance of Congress and is subject to complete defeasance." United States
v. Wheeler, 435 U.S. 313, 323 (1978). Of states, the Court has said that
"the Framers chose to rely on a federal system in which special restraints
on federal power over the States inhered principally in the workings of the
National Government itself, rather than in discrete limitations on the objects
of federal authority. State sovereign interests, then, are more properly
protected by procedural safeguards inherent in the structure of the federal
system than by judicially created limitations on federal power." Garcia v.
San Antonio Metro. Transit Auth., 105 S. Ct. 1005, 1018 (1985).

   92. On the rules of construction requiring explicit congressional action
before courts will hold that tribal powers are abridged, see pp. 46–52,
supra. Somewhat similar formulations often are applied for federal preemption of state authority. See, e.g., Chicago & N.W. Transp. Co. v. Kalo
Brick & Tile Co., 450 U.S. 311, 317 (1981) ("Preemption of the state law
by federal statute [is] not favored in the absence of persuasive reasons—
either that the nature of the regulated subject matter permits no other
conclusion, or that the Congress has unmistakably so ordained," citing
Florida Lime & Avocado Growers, Inc. v. Paul, 373 U.S 132, 142 (1963)).
In the case of Indian law, of course, the tribes and states are often competitors, and the question is which authority—tribal or state—must fall to
a federal law. If the law is to be applied in Indian country, the tribe normally
has the benefit of the express statement requirement. If the application is
outside of Indian country, state power normally is in force unless it is
expressly preempted. See, e.g., notes 70–87, supra.

93. The states do not lack power over any large class of citizens in the manner that Indian tribes lack authority over non-Indians. See Oliphant v. Suquamish Indian Tribe, 435 U.S. 191 (1978); Montana v. United States, 450 U.S. 544 (1981). Further, as this chapter shows, no state is subject to as many laws of any outside, nonfederal government as is a tribe to the laws of the state within which it is located. Tribes are less shackled than states in the sense that they are limited neither by the Bill of Rights nor by the Fourteenth Amendement, but Congress has obviated much of that distinction by passage of the Indian Civil Rights Act of 1968, 25 U.S.C. §§ 1301–03 (1982). See generally Santa Clara Pueblo v. Martinez, 436 U.S. 49 (1978).

94. U.S. Const. art. VI, cl. 2 ("all Treaties made... shall be the supreme Law of the Land"); id., art. I, § 2, cl. 3 (allocation of seats in the House of Representatives and levying of direct federal taxes); id., amend. XIV, § 2 (revision of apportionment formula for House of Representatives to eliminate the slave fraction); id., art. I, § 8, cl. 3 (Indian Commerce Clause). These clauses are discussed in F. Cohen, supra note 4, at 207–08, 388–89.

95. Merrion v. Jicarilla Apache Tribe, 455 U.S. 130, 148 (1982).

96. In McCulloch v. Maryland, 17 U.S. (4 Wheat.) 316 (1819), Chief Justice Marshall expounded on the dynamic nature of the Constitution in a statement that has since become one of the most frequently quoted passages in constitutional law:

> [The] constitution [is] intended to endure for ages to come, and, consequently, to be adapted to the various crises of human affairs.... It would have been an unwise attempt to provide, by immutable rules, for exigencies which, if foreseen at all, must have been seen dimly, and which can be best provided for as they occur.

Id. at 415.
The idea that the Constitution is a living and evolving document has been commonly advanced by various jurists and legal scholars. See, e.g., B. Cardozo, The Growth of the Law 4 (1924) ("Law must be stable, and yet it cannot stand still. Here is the great anomaly confronting us at every turn. Rest and motion, unrelieved and unchecked, are equally destructive. The law, like human kind, if life is to continue, must find some path of compromise"); A. Miller, Social Change and Fundamental Law 4, 11 (1979) ("[I]t is accurate to say that the American Constitution is Darwinian rather than Newtonian, that it follows the laws of life rather than of mechanics. ... Change is not only the law of life; it is the life of the law"); W. Wilson, Constitutional Government in the United States 56–57 (1908) ("[G]overnment is not a machine, but a living thing. It falls, not under the theory of the universe, but under the theory of organic life. It is accountable

to Darwin, not to Newton. It is modified by its environment, necessitated by its tasks, shaped to its functions by the sheer pressure of life. . . . Living political constitutions must be Darwinian in structure and in practice"); Rehnquist, 54 Tex. L. Rev. 693, 694 (1976) ("The framers of the Constitution wisely spoke in general language and left to succeeding generations the task of applying that language to the unceasingly changing environment in which they would live").

97. In describing the approach of interpretivists, Dean Ely points out that they, too, allow some growth beyond the literal words of the Constitution: to them, it is appropriate "to identify the *sorts of evils* against which the provision was directed and to move against their contemporary counterparts. Obviously this will be difficult, but it will remain interpretivism— a determination of 'the present scope and meaning of a decision that the nation, at an earlier time, articulated and enacted into the Constitutional text.' " J. Ely, Democracy and Distrust: A Theory of Judicial Review 13 (1980) (emphasis in original). Thus proponents of interpretive review argue that the Court should "stick close to the text and the history, and their fair implications." Bork, Neutral Principles and Some First Amendment Problems, 47 Ind. L.J. 1, (1971). See also Linde, Judges, Critics, and the Realist Tradition, 82 Yale L.J. 227, 254 (1972) (describing the Court's task as "controlling the living meaning of the past political decision").

98. See Ch. 2, supra (insulation against time; canons of construction); Ch. 3, supra (right to change).

99. See note 33, supra (presumption against state jurisdiction); text accompanying Ch. 3, notes 45, 55, supra (tribal reserved rights).

100. 411 U.S 164 (1973).

101. Treaty of Fort Sumner with Navajo Tribe, June 1, 1868, 15 Stat. 667. The treaty provided that the reservation would be set aside "for the use and occupation of the Navajo tribe of Indians" and that "no persons except those herein so authorized to do . . . shall ever be permitted to pass over, settle upon, or reside in, the territory described in this article." Id., art. 2, 15 Stat. at 668. In *McClanahan*, the Court stated that "[t]he treaty nowhere explicitly states that the Navajos were to be free from state law or exempt from state taxes. But the document is not to be read as an ordinary contract agreed upon by parties dealing at arm's length with equal bargaining positions." 411 U.S. at 174.

102. 411 U.S. at 175. See also Washington v. Confederated Tribes of the Colville Indian Reservation, 447 U.S. 134 (1980); Bryan v. Itasca County, 426 U.S 373 (1976). Although *Colville* struck down state taxes levied on sales of cigarettes to Indians, the Court held that the tax must be collected for sales made to non-Indians. 447 U.S. at 154–60.

103. 358 U.S. 217 (1959).

104. 400 U.S. 423 (1971).

105. 424 U.S. 382 (1976).

106. 104 S. Ct. 2267 (1984). The Court seems to have reached the result in *Wold* as a matter of fairness to Indians, but I have doubts about the wisdom of the rule. See note 112, infra.

107. On subject matter preemption, see White Mountain Apache Tribe v. Bracker, 448 U.S. 136, 144–49 (1980) (federal regulation of tribal timber and roads preempts the imposition of state motor carrier license and fuel use tax on non-Indian contractor). See generally text accompanying notes 47–69, supra. On geographical preemption, see Williams v. Lee, 358 U.S. 217, 220 (1959) (state interferes with Indians' rights to "make their own laws and be ruled by them" when state court hears action brought by non-Indian against Indian for acts arising on reservation); Three Affiliated Tribes of the Fort Berthold Reservation v. Wold Engineering, 104 S. Ct. 2267, 2274–75 (1984) (tribal self-government is not impeded when a state court hears an action brought by an Indian tribe against a non-Indian for acts arising on reservation). See generally text accompanying, notes 70–87, supra. On tribal civil jurisdiction, see, e.g., National Farmers Union Ins. Cos. v. Crow Tribe of Indians, 105 S. Ct. 2447, 2454 (1985) (extent of tribal court's jurisdiction to be decided, in the first instance, by the tribal court). See generally p. 106, supra. On natural resources cases, see, e.g., Arizona v. California, 373 U.S 546, 595–601 (1963). (sufficient water reserved to satisfy the future as well as the present needs of the Indian reservations, i.e., sufficient water to irrigate all the practicably irrigable acreage); Washington v. Washington State Commercial Passenger Fishing Vessel Ass'n, 443 U.S. 658, 686 (1979) (reservation of up to 50 percent of harvestable runs of anadromous fish, or enough to provide the Indians with a livelihood, i.e., a moderate living). On validity of federal legislation, see United States v. Sioux Nation, 448 U.S. 371, 415 (1980) (question of whether a specific statute is subject to the constitutional command of the Just Compensation Clause depends upon "whether a particular measure was appropriate for protecting and advancing the tribe's interest"); Morton v. Mancari, 417 U.S. 535, 555 (1974) (legislation concerning Indians will be upheld "as long as the special treatment can be tied rationally to the fulfillment of Congress' unique obligation toward the Indians"). See generally Ch. 3, supra (the higher sovereign).

In a few instances the Court has cross-cited among these doctrines within Indian law. For example, in Montana v. United States, 450 U.S. 544, 566 n.15 (1981), the Court briefly noted, in analyzing tribal interests necessary to support an exercise of jurisdiction over non-Indians, that "[a]s a corollary, this Court has held that Indian tribes retain rights to river waters necessary to make their reservations livable," citing Arizona v. California, 373 U.S. 546, 599 (1963). See also National Farmers Union Ins. Cos. v. Crow Tribe of Indians, 105 S. Ct. 2447, 2454 n.20 (1985).

108. See, e.g., United States v. Sioux Nation, 448 U.S. 371 (1980) (statute removing Black Hills from Sioux Reservation), and Morton v. Mancari, 417 U.S. 535 (1974) (statute granting Indian preference for government employment).

109. Tribal proprietary reserved rights are found in, for example, Arizona v. California, 373 U.S. 546 (1963) (water rights); Washington v. Washington State Commercial Passenger Fishing Vessel Ass'n, 443 U.S. 658 (1979) (fishing rights), both discussed in text accompanying Ch. 3, notes 93–107, supra. For governmental authority see, e.g., Merrion v. Jicarilla Apache Tribe, 455 U.S. 130 (1982) (taxation of mineral extraction by non-Indian companies), discussed in text accompanying Ch. 2, notes 32, 60, 61, supra. The quotation on the federal policy of tribal self-sufficiency is from White Mountain Apache Tribe v. Bracker, 448 U.S. 136, 143 (1980) (footnote omitted).

On disallowing state taxes due to the economic burden on the tribe, see, e.g., Ramah Navajo School Bd. v. Bureau of Revenue, 458 U.S. 832, 844 n.8 (1982); White Mountain Apache Tribe v. Bracker, 448 U.S. 136, 151 (1980). Although the Court normally determines whether the economic burden will ultimately rest on the tribe, the opinions have allowed state taxes based on the legal incidence test in those instances where there is no subject matter preemption and where the goods sold were not the result of some value generated on the reservation. See Washington v. Confederated Tribes of the Colville Indian Reservation, 447 U.S 134, 150–51 (1980), discussed in note 60, supra.

110. Merrion v. Jicarilla Apache Tribe, 455 U.S. 130, 137 (1982).

111. Id. at 138 n.5, quoting from Merrion v. Jicarilla Apache Tribe, 617 F.2d 537, 550 (1980) (McKay, J. concuring).

112. On the rule of exclusive tribal jurisdiction in civil cases, see, e.g., Williams v. Lee, 358 U.S. 217 (1959), discussed in text accompanying introduction, note 2, supra. On tribal criminal jurisdiction over Indians, see, e.g., United States v. Wheeler, 435 U.S 313 (1978). With tribal authority over most reservation civil and criminal wrongs solidified by the cases and statutes of the modern era, tribal lawmaking has burgeoned. Tribes have revised their constitutions or adopted entirely new ones. See generally University of Washington Law Library, Compilation of Indian Tribal Constitutions (1983). Tribal codes have become more extensive. See Navajo Tribal Code (1984) (three volumes). Tribal judges are rendering increasing numbers of written opinions. See generally American Lawyer Training Program, Indian Law Reporter (1977–86).

Because tribes have the power and duty to build communities, the decision in Three Affiliated Tribes of the Fort Berthold Reservation v. Wold Engineering, 104 S. Ct. 2267 (1984), may have been misguided. The rule of exclusive tribal jurisdiction for suits brought by non-Indians against Indians for reservation transactions, which *Wold* reaffirmed, id. at 2274–75, has the salutary effect of giving tribes an incentive to evaluate and improve their tribal institutions: since tribal courts are the only forum available for many reservation transactions, there is every reason to upgrade the quality of tribal justice systems. *Wold,* which allowed the tribe to institute suit in state court against a non-Indian corporation over a reservation transaction, seems to have been based on notions of fairness, i.e., that it would be wrong to deny a tribe equal access to state courts and that no tribal interests could possibly be infringed if the tribal council itself made the decision to resort to state court. In fact, the tribal interest in the adjudication of reservation wrongs was infringed, even if by the tribal council. Tribal interests might well have been furthered in the long run by a holding that state courts lack subject matter jurisdiction when Indians sue non-Indians for acts arising in Indian country (just as subject matter jurisdiction is absent in the reverse situation) thus giving even greater legitimacy (and immediacy) to the tribal forum.

113. 435 U.S. 191 (1978). For the quotation in the text, see id. at 210.

114. National Farmers Union Ins. Cos. v. Crow Tribe of Indians, 105 S. Ct. 2447, 2453–54 (1985); Montana v. United States, 450 U.S. 544, 565–66 (1981).

115. Washington v. Washington State Commercial Passenger Fishing Vessel Ass'n, 443 U.S. 658, 686 (1979). Water rights also seem to come within the rule because the Court in *Passenger Fishing Vessel* relied upon Arizona v. California, 373 U.S. 546 (1963), in announcing the "moderate living" standard. The entire "moderate living" passage in *Passenger Fishing Vessel* reads as follows:

> It bears repeating however, that the 50% figure imposes a maximum but not a minimum allocation. As in Arizona v. California and its predecessor cases, the central principle here must be that Indian treaty rights to a natural resource that once was thoroughly and exclusively exploited by the Indians secures so much as, but not more than, is necessary to provide the Indians with a livelihood—that is to say, a moderate living. Accordingly, while the maximum possible allocation to the Indians is fixed at 50%, the minimum is not; the latter will, upon proper submissions to the District Court, be modified in response to changing circumstances. If, for example, a tribe should dwindle to just a few members, or if it should find other sources of support, that lead it to abandon its fisheries, a 45% or 50% allocation of an entire run that passes through its customary fishing grounds would be manifestly inappropriate because the livelihood of the tribe under those circumstances could not reasonably require an allotment of a large number of fish.

443 U.S. at 686–87.

116. See text accompanying Ch. 1, notes 1–31, supra.

117. Washington v. Confederated Tribes of the Colville Indian Reservation, 447 U.S. 134, 155–57 (1980). This is a special limit for Indian tribes and is not applicable to state and local governments, who can, and do, market tax exemptions. See, e.g., Review & Outlook: New England Revival, Wall Street Journal, Sept. 22, 1980, at 24, col. 1 ("[a] bold and skillful high tech lobby persuaded the liberal, 80% Democratic [Massachusetts] legislature to slash the capital gains tax by 60%"); "It Pays to Shop Around—Taxing Matters," Forbes, p. 70 (Oct. 25, 1982) ("Last year Delaware created legislation making it profitable for banks to relocate there. The tax rate starts at 8.7% but drops to 2.7% once income passes $30 million. The result? Twelve banks, including Citicorp and Chase Manhattan, have opened facilities in Delaware since the legislation passed"); Regions: States Paid Dearly, Gained Little in Competition to Lure Industry, Wall Street Journal, July 1, 1980, at 25, col. 1 ("States offer a cornucopia of tax credits, exemptions, rollbacks, reductions and deferrals. Many also tout industrial-revenue bonds and municipally owned industrial parks. Lately, New York has led the sweepstakes with 27 inducement programs").

The rule in Indian cases prohibiting tribes from marketing their tax exemptions, which plainly is a substantial limit on tribal revenue raising, seems to have been born mainly of the Court's concern with the impact on nearby, off-reservation businesses. 443 U.S. at 155. Perhaps a more restrictive rule for tribes than for states is justified on a policy basis by the locations of reservations: they are in-holdings within the states, and the possibility of economic disruption is in fact greater simply because numerically many more conflicts between the differing tax systems would occur at reservation boundaries than at state boundaries.

118. See White Mountain Apache Tribe v. Bracker, 448 U.S. 136 (1980) (timber); Merrion v. Jicarilla Apache Tribe, 455 U.S 130 (1982) (minerals); New Mexico v. Mescalero Apache Tribe, 462 U.S. 324 (1983) (wildlife).

119. See F. Cohen, supra note 4, at 180–206 (self-determination policy); Ch. 3, supra (tribal right to change); notes 96–98, supra (evolution of treaties and treaty substitutes).

120. See Ch. 2, supra (protection against modern statutes).

121. For a discussion of legitimate state interests within Indian country, see Wilkinson, Cross-Jurisdictional Conflicts: An Analysis of Legitimate State Interests on Federal and Indian Lands, 2 UCLA J. Envtl. L. & Pol'y 145, 156–62 (1982).

122. The opinions are not entirely consistent on this point. In Washington v. Confederated Tribes of the Colville Indian Reservation, 447 U.S. 134 (1980), the Court analyzed only tribal and federal interests. In White Mountain Apache Tribe v. Bracker, 448 U.S 136 (1980), the Court stated that state jurisdiction over non-Indians in Indian country involves "a particularized inquiry into the nature of the state, federal, and tribal interests at stake." Id. at 145.

123. See, e.g., National Farmers Union Ins. Cos. v. Crow Tribe of Indians, 105 S. Ct. 2447 (1985); Three Affiliated Tribes of the Fort Berthold Reservation v. Wold Engineering, 104 S. Ct. 2267 (1984); Rice v. Rehner, 463 U.S. 713 (1983); New Mexico v. Mescalero Apache Tribe, 462 U.S. 324 (1983); Ramah Navajo School Bd. v. Bureau of Revenue 458 U.S. 832 (1982); White Mountain Apache Tribe v. Bracker, 448 U.S. 136 (1980).

124. See, e.g., 1 American Indian Policy Review Comm'n, Final Report 611–13 (1977) (dissenting views of Congressman Lloyd Meeds).

125. See United States v. Mazurie, 419 U.S. 544 (1975) where Justice Rehnquist stated for a unanimous Court:

> The fact that the Mazuries could not become members of the tribe, and therefore could not participate in the tribal government, does not alter our conclusion. This claim, that because respondents are non-Indians Congress could not subject them to the authority of the Tribal Council with respect to the sale of liquor, is answered by this Court's opinion in Williams v. Lee, 358 U.S. 217 (1959). In holding that the authority of tribal courts could extend over non-Indians, insofar as concerned their transactions on a reservation with Indians, we stated: "It is immaterial that respondent is not an Indian. He was on the Reservation and the transaction with an Indian took place there. The cases in this Court have consistently guarded the authority of Indian governments over their reservations. Congress recognized this authority in the Navajos in the Treaty of 1868, and has done so ever since. If this power is to be taken away from them, it is for Congress to do it.'

Id. at 557–58 (citation and footnote omitted).

126. In dissenting from the ruling upholding a tribal tax of non-Indian mineral companies, Justice Stevens, joined by Chief Justice Burger and Justice Rehnquist, stated that

> The tribes' authority to enact legislation affecting nonmembers is therefore of a different character than their broad power to control internal tribal affairs. This difference is consistent with the fundamental principle that '[i]n this Nation each sovereign governs only with the consent of the governed.' Nevada v. Hall, 440 U.S. 410, 426 [1979]. Since nonmembers are excluded from participation in tribal government, the powers that may be exercised over them are appropriately limited.

Merrion v. Jicarilla Apache Tribe, 455 U.S. 130, 172–73 (1982) (Stevens, J., dissenting). In an opinion granting a stay, Justice Rehnquist raised similar concerns about tribal court jurisdiction. National Farmers Union Ins. Cos. v. Crow Tribe of Indians, 105 S. Ct. 7 (1985). Although the question of political representation was not explicitly mentioned in the only two modern opinions that have struck down exercises of tribal power over non-Indians, Montana v. United States, 450 U.S. 544 (1981); Oliphant v. Suquamish

Indian Tribe, 435 U.S. 191 (1978), the factor must inevitably have weighed heavily during the Justices' deliberations. See also, e.g., Dry Creek Lodge, Inc. v. Arapahoe & Shoshone Tribes, 623 F.2d 682, 685 (10th Cir. 1980), cert. denied, 449 U.S. 1118 (1981), where the Tenth Circuit allowed suit to proceed in federal court against the tribe in spite of a sovereign immunity defense, saying "[i]t is obvious that the [non-Indians] in this appeal have no remedy witin the tribal machinery nor with the tribal officials in whose election they cannot participate. . . . There must exist a remedy for parties in the position of plaintiffs to have the dispute resolved in an orderly manner."

127. See, e.g., UNC Resources, Inc. v. Benally, 518 F. Supp. 1046 (D. Ariz. 1981); UNC Resources, Inc. v. Benally, 514 F. Supp. 358 (D.N.M. 1981); Dry Creek Lodge, Inc. v. Arapahoe & Shoshone Tribes, 623 F.2d 682 (10th Cir. 1980), cert. denied, 449 U.S. 1118 (1981), discussed in note 126, supra.

128. See generally Ch. 3, supra.

129. See, e.g., Fisher v. District Court, 424 U.S. 382, 390 (1976) ("[t]he exclusive jurisdiction of the Tribal Court does not derive from the race of the plaintiff but rather from the quasi-sovereign status of the Northern Cheyenne Tribe under federal law"); Morton v. Mancari, 417 U.S. 535, 554 (1974) (federal employment preference statute deals with "Indians not as a discrete racial group, but, rather, as members of quasi-sovereign tribal entities"). See generally text accompanying Ch. 3, notes 170–72, supra.

130. See Solem v. Bartlett, 104 S. Ct. 1161, 1164–65 (1984).

131. For examples of opinions employing notions of international law in Indian law, see Ch. 3, notes 82–126, supra.

132. On early European recognition of special tribal status, see, e.g., Cohen, The Spanish Origin of Indian Rights in the Law of the United States, 31 Geo. L.J. 1 (1942); Williams, The Medieval and Renaissance Origins of the Status of the American Indian in Western Legal Thought, 57 S. Cal. L. Rev. 1 (1983). On the long-time recognition of special attributes by the three federal branches, see, e.g., Worcester v. Georgia, 31 U.S. (6 Pet.) 515 (1832); Merrion v. Jicarilla Apache Tribe, 455 U.S. 130, 139–40 (1982); F. Cohen, supra note 4, at 253–55.

133. Throughout most of the nineteenth century tribal affiliation was viewed as being inconsistent with United States citizenship. See, e.g., F. Prucha, American Indian Policy in Crisis 341–52 (1976); 2 F. Prucha, The Great Father 681–86 (1984). Allotted Indians achieved citizenship under the allotment policy of the late nineteeth century, e.g., Act of Feb. 8, 1887, ch. 119, § 6, 24 Stat. 388, 390, and United States citizenship was extended to all native-born Indians in 1924. See 8 U.S.C. § 1401 (b) (1982). Nevertheless, it took decades for Indians to achieve their right to vote in several western states. See, e.g., Harrison v. Laveen, 67 Ariz. 337, 196 P.2d 456

(1948); Allen v. Merrell, 6 Utah 2d 32, 305 P.2d 490 (1956), vacated, 353 U.S. 932 (1957). Several states were also slow to recognize the right of Indians to hold elective office. See, e.g., Shirley v. Superior Court, 109 Ariz. 510, 513 P.2d 939 (1973), cert. denied, 415 U.S 917 (1974). Today, however, the right of Indians to participate in state and local government is well established. See F. Cohen, supra note 4, at 639–53.

134. 436 U.S 49 (1978).

135. On the preconstitutional and extraconstitutional status, see id. at 56 ("[A]s separate sovereigns pre-existing the Constitution, tribes have historically been regarded as unconstrained by those constitutional provisions framed specifically as limitations on federal or state authority"); canons of construction, see id. at 60 ("[A] proper respect both for tribal sovereignty itself and for the plenary authority of Congress in this area cautions that we tread lightly in the absence of clear indications of legislative intent"); tribal sovereign immunity, see id. at 58 ("Indian tribes have long been recognized as possessing the common-law immunity from suit traditionally enjoyed by sovereign powers").

136. Title I of the ICRA is codified at 25 U.S.C. §§ 1301–03 (1982). Other titles of the act contained important provisions, including modifications of Public Law 280, but Title I is commonly referred to as the Indian Civil Rights Act. The provisions of the act as a whole are discussed at F. Cohen, supra note 4, at 202–04.

The free exercise, due process, and equal protection provisions are found at 25 U.S.C. §§ 1302 (1), 1302 (8). Several constitutional limitations on the state and federal governments are not included in the ICRA, including the prohibition against the establishment of religion, the guarantee of a republican form of government, and the prohibition against denials of privileges and immunities. The ICRA expressly provides that the writ of habeas corpus shall be available to test detention by an Indian tribe. 25 U.S.C. § 1303 (1982). No other remedy is expressly set out in the act.

137. See, e.g., Puyallup Tribe, Inc. v. Department of Game, 433 U.S. 165, 170–71 (1977).

138. Federal sovereign immunity does not bar a defendant from countersuing for offsets "arising out of the same transaction or occurrence" when the United States institutes an action. 6 C. Wright & A. Miller, Federal Practice & Procedure 140 (1971).

139. The Department of the Interior, for example, has asserted administrative authority to review tribal codes in several areas important to non-Indians, including water policy. Federal review of an agency decision involving a tribal code might then be reviewable under the Administrative Procedure Act, 5 U.S.C. §§ 701–06 (1982). There is some suggestion in the Santa Clara opinion, however, that the sovereign immunity bar as to tribal action attaches to supervisory action by the Department of the Interior. 436 U.S. at 66 n.22.

140. 105 S. Ct. 2447 (1985).

141. 105 S. Ct. 1900 (1985).

142. See 436 U.S. 72–83 (White, J., dissenting); Burnett, An Historical Analysis of the 1968 "Indian Civil Rights" Act, 9 Harv. J. on Legis. 557 (1972); Comment, The Indian Bill of Rights and the Constitutional Status of Tribal Governments, 82 Harv. L. Rev. 1343 (1969).

143. 436 U.S. at 59–60.

144. Several pre-*Santa Clara* opinions had suggested that the ICRA equal protection and due process guarantees need not always be identical to the constitutional provisions and that modifications should be made to fit the tribal context. See, e.g., McCurdy v. Steele, 506 F.2d 653, 655, 656 (10th Cir. 1974) ("The [ICRA] tracks to some extent the language of the United States Constitution, but this does not necessarily mean that the terms 'due process' or 'equal protection'. . . carry their full constitutional impact"); Groundhog v. Keeler, 442 F.2d 674, 682 (10th Cir. 1971) (ICRA equal protection provision "not as broad as" the Fourteenth Amendment); Conroy v. Frizzell, 429 F. Supp. 918, 925 (D.S.D. 1977) ("this Court has neither the inclination nor the power to review or overturn [the tribal court's] determination by forcing concepts of Anglo-American law upon the Tribe"). But see Crowe v. Eastern Band of Cherokee Indians, Inc., 506 F.2d 1231, 1234 (4th Cir. 1974).

145. Use of tests such as the clearly erroneous and arbitrary and capricious standards, which could be drawn from the Administrative Procedure Act, 5 U.S.C. §§ 701–06 (1982), would be a recognition that the role of the federal district court is to act as a reviewing court, not as a court hearing the case de novo. Thus review of tribal actions would be similar in some respects to review of federal administrative agency action in that a heavy presumption would exist in favor of the decision under review, although review under the ICRA would have the additional requirement that courts respect tribal traditions and reservation conditions. See note 144, supra.

146. The exhaustion of remedies requirement has been uniformly applied when federal review has been invoked under the ICRA. See, e.g., National Farmers Union Ins. Cos. v. Crow Tribe of Indians, 105 S. Ct. 2447 (1985); O'Neal v. Cheyenne River Sioux Tribe, 482 F.2d 1140 (8th Cir. 1973); Jacobson v. Forest County Potawotomi Community, 389 F. Supp. 994 (E.D. Wis. 1974).

147. See B. Schwartz, Administrative Law 499–503 (1976).

148. National Farmers Union Ins. Cos. v. Crow Tribe of Indians, 105 S. Ct. 2447, 2454 (1985).

149. "[C]ourts have certain capacities for dealing with matters of principle that legislatures and executives do not possess. . . . And it is for legislatures, not courts, to impose what are merely solutions of expediency.

Courts must act on true principles, capable of unremitting application." A. Bickel, The Least Dangerous Branch: The Supreme Court at the Bar of Politics 25, 58 (1962).

150. The rationale for solicitous judicial protection of racial minorities is reflected in Justice Stone's oft-cited footnote 4 in United States v. Carolene Products Co., 304 U.S. 144, 152 n.4 (1938), where the Court suggested that special standards of judicial review apply when reviewing possible prejudice against "discrete and insular" minorities. The role of courts in intervening in order to protect minorities is discussed at length in Ely, Toward a Representation-Reinforcing Mode of Judicial Review, 37 Md. L. Rev. 451 (1978). The *Carolene Products* footnote is a major basis of John Hart Ely's important book Democracy and Distrust; A Theory of Judicial Review (1980), in which he argues that much of the Constitution is directed toward access to the political process and that the courts should police the process to protect the rights of minorities.

151. Several writers have applied fundamental rights theories to Indian rights. See R. Barsh & J. Henderson, The Road: Indian Tribes and Political Liberty (1980); Newton, Federal Power Over Indians: Its Sources, Scope, and Limitations, 132 U. Pa. L. Rev. 195 (1984); Clinton, Isolated in Their Own Country: A Defense of Federal Protection of Indian Autonomy and Self-government, 33 Stan. L. Rev. 979 (1981).

152. United States v. Kagama, 118 U.S. 375, 384 (1886). See also Washington v. Washington State Commercial Passenger Fishing Vessel Ass'n, 443 U.S. 658, 696 n.36 (1979).

153. 358 U.S. 217, 223 (1959).

154. Solem v. Bartlett, 104 S. Ct. 1161, 1167 (1984).

155. See, e.g., County of Oneida v. Oneida Indian Nation, 105 S. Ct. 1245, 1261 (1985) ("We agree that this litigation makes abundantly clear the necessity for congressional action"); Merrion v. Jicarilla Apache Tribe, 455 U.S. 130 (1982) ("Finally, Congress is well aware that Indian tribes impose mineral severance taxes such as the one challenged by petitioners. Congress, of course, retains plenary power to limit tribal taxing authority or to alter the current scheme under which the tribes may impose taxes") (citation omitted); Santa Clara Pueblo v. Martinez, 436 U.S 49, 72 (1978) ("Congress retains authority expressly to authorize civil actions for injunctive or other relief to redress violations of [the Indian Civil Rights Act] in the event tribes themselves prove deficient in applying and enforcing its substantive provisions").

156. The Commission on State-Tribal Relations has been created by the joint efforts of the National Conference of State Legislatures and the National Conference of American Indians. Literally hundreds of tribal–state agreements have been negotiated to date. See American Indian Law Center, Handbook of State–Tribal Relations (1983). In Arizona alone, approx-

imately sixty agreements have been negotiated between Arizona and the tribes within the state. Interview with Edd Brown, assistant director of intergovernmental relations, State of Arizona, at Tsalie, Arizona (June 20, 1984). Tribal–state agreements have become especially commonplace in implementing the Indian Child Welfare Act of 1978. See American Indian Lawyer Training Program, Handbook: The Indian Child Welfare Act (1983). On state statutes, see, e.g., 1984 Idaho Sess. Laws ch. 72 (authorizing local governments, state and public agencies to enter agreements with tribes for the concurrent exercise of powers and transfer of real and personal property); 1984 Idaho Sess. Laws ch. 119 (aa) (exempting from state taxes on-reservation sales of tangible personal property by a tribe); 1985 Mont. Laws ch. 38 (authorizing state, county, and municipal agencies to enter agreements with tribes for administrative services, amending Mont. Code Ann. §§ 18–11–101 to 18–11–111 (1983)); 1985 Nev. Stat. ch. 115, § 3 (authorizing tribal police to make arrests outside reservation boundaries when the tribal officer is in "fresh pursuit" of a person who committed a crime on the reservation); 1985 Or. Laws ch. 267 (authorizing local governments and state agencies to cooperate with tribes); 1985 Or. Laws ch. 148 (authorizing motor vehicles owned by tribal governments to be registered in the same manner as state-owned vehicles); 1985 Or. Laws ch. 317 (exempting from state income taxes income earned by member and nonmember Indians living on a reservation).

Index